ROUTLEDGE LIBRARY EDITIONS: PHENOMENOLOGY

Volume 13

MICHOTTE'S EXPERIMENTAL PHENOMENOLOGY OF PERCEPTION

MICHOTTE'S EXPERIMENTAL PHENOMENOLOGY OF PERCEPTION

Edited by
GEORGES THINÈS, ALAN COSTALL AND
GEORGE BUTTERWORTH

Routledge
Taylor & Francis Group
LONDON AND NEW YORK

First published in 1991

This edition first published in 2014
by Routledge

Published 2016 by Routledge

2 Park Square, Milton Park, Abingdon, Oxon, OX14 4RN

Simultaneously published in the USA and Canada
by Routledge
711 Third Avenue, New York, NY 10017

Routledge is an imprint of the Taylor & Francis Group, an informa business

First issued in paperback 2015

British Library Cataloguing in Publication Data
A catalogue record for this book is available from the British Library

ISBN: 978-0-415-70515-8 (hbk)
ISBN: 978-1-138-99582-6 (pbk)

Publisher's Note
The publisher has gone to great lengths to ensure the quality of this reprint but points out that some imperfections in the original copies may be apparent.

Disclaimer
The publisher has made every effort to trace copyright holders and would welcome correspondence from those they have been unable to trace.

Michotte's Experimental Phenomenology of Perception

EDITED BY

GEORGES THINÈS

ALAN COSTALL

GEORGE BUTTERWORTH

LAWRENCE ERLBAUM ASSOCIATES, PUBLISHERS

1991 Hillsdale, New Jersey Hove and London

Lawrence Erlbaum Associates, Inc., Publishers
365 Broadway
Hillsdale, New Jersey 07642

Library of Congress Cataloging-in-Publication Data

Michotte, Albert, 1881–1965.
Michotte's experimental phenomenology of perception / edited and translated by Georges Thinès, Alan Costall, and George Butterworth.
p. cm. – (Resources for ecological psychology)
Includes bibliographical references and indexes.
ISBN 0-89859-606-8
1. Perception. 2. Michotte, Albert, 1881–1965.
3. Phenomenological psychology. I. Thinès, Georges 1923–
II. Costall, Alan. III. Butterworth, George. IV. Title.
V. Series.
BF311.M498 1990
153.7–dc20 90-14024
CIP

Printed in the United States of America
10 9 8 7 6 5 4 3 2 1

Contents

RESOURCES for ECOLOGICAL PSYCHOLOGY

Edited by
Robert E. Shaw, William M. Mace, and Michael Turvey

This series of volumes is dedicated to furthering the development of psychology as a branch of ecological science. In its broadest sense, ecology is a multidisciplinary approach to the study of living systems, their environments, and the reciprocity that has evolved between the two. Traditionally, ecological science emphasizes the study of the biological bases of *energy* transactions between animals and their physical environments across cellular, organismic, and population scales. Ecological psychology complements this traditional focus by emphasizing the study of *information* transactions between living systems and their environments, especially as they pertain to perceiving situations of significance to planning and execution of purposes activated in an environment.

The late James J. Gibson used the term *ecological psychology* to emphasize this animal-environment mutuality for the study of problems of perception. He believed that analyzing the environment to be perceived was just as much a part of the psychologist's task as analyzing animals themselves, and hence that the "physical" concepts applied to the environment and the "biological" and "psychological" concepts applied to organisms would have to be tailored to one another in a larger system of mutual constraint. His early interest in the applied problems of landing airplanes and driving automobiles led him to pioneer the study of the perceptual guidance of action.

The work of Nicolai Bernstein in biomechanics and physiology presents a complementary approach to problems of the coordination and control of movement. His work suggests that action, too, cannot be studied without reference to the environment, and that physical and biological concepts must be developed together. The coupling of Gibson's ideas with those of Bernstein forms a natural basis for looking at the traditional psychological topics of perceiving, acting, and knowing as activities of ecosystems rather than isolated animals.

The purpose of this series is to form a useful collection, a resource, for people who wish to learn about ecological psychology and for those who wish to contribute to its development. The series will include original research, collected papers, reports of conferences and symopsia, theoretical monographs, technical handbooks, and works from the many disciplines relevant to ecological psychology.

Series Dedication

To James J. Gibson, whose pioneering work in ecological psychology has opened new vistas in psychology and related sciences, we respectfully dedicate this series.

Preface

Toward the end of a long and productive career, the Belgian psychologist, Albert Michotte, embarked upon a fresh phase of research, his experimental phenomenology of perception. Only a small portion of this important research has been published in English translation; therefore, the purpose of our book is to present a selection of the most significant and representative papers. Michotte's work has a clear and lively style, illustrated by many telling examples, and, in our view, can be left very much to speak for itself. We have, however, provided introductions to the various themes and more general accounts of his career and work in order to provide historical context and some indication of links with current research.

It would be no exaggeration to say that James Gibson was astounded by the close similarity between Michotte's later work and his own. As he explained in his autobiography:

> There are other psychologists who have thought about perception almost as I do, but not quite. The one with whom in recent years I have been in strikingly near agreement is Albert Michotte, of Louvain – in everything but the notion of external information and external meaning. . . . It is a notable lesson in the convergence of experimental science that such a man as he and such a one as I, from totally different backgrounds, should have found ourselves agreeing so thoroughly and so delightedly – he, a student of Cardinal Mercier and I of the materialist Holt; he, a believer and phenomenologist and I a skeptic and behaviorist; he, a member of the

> conservative Belgian nobility, a prince of the Catholic Church, and I a Midwestern Sunday-school radical with an underlying suspicion of popery. We got the same results. This is what counts. It makes one believe in the possibility of getting at the truth. (Gibson, 1967, p. 142–143)*

Michotte, like Gibson, challenged the view, prevalent in the theory of vision since Medieval times, that perception is ultimately dependent upon the intervention of intellect, and both argued that meaning can be perceived in a non-mediated way. Their shared interest in the problem of meaning derived from a common concern, the relegation, in the ontology of modern science, of meaning and value to the status of the 'unreal' and purely subjective. This issue is fundamental to the very idea of a scientific psychology.

Michotte's work, however, has further relevance for modern psychology. Needless to say, Michotte's ideas have been very influential in the recent research on perceptual development, and his work on social perception has continued to be very influential in social psychology. Yet there are other areas of his work that are equally important but seldom cited. For example, there is a remarkable set of articles by Michotte on pictorial representation (including film) that is virtually unknown to contemporary researchers in this field. In short, Michotte, who was unquestionably a significant figure in the history of psychology, has plenty to contribute to current debates.

Our own interest in Michotte is long-standing. Georges Thinès was Michotte's last assistant at Louvain. Alan Costall was introduced as an undergraduate to Michotte's work by Tim Miles (who, with Elaine Miles, prepared the English translation of Michotte's text on the perception of causality). George Butterworth first encountered Michotte's writings on perception and cognition, and phenomenal permanance, during his doctoral research on the development of the concept of object permanence.

We have benefited from the help of many people. We thank most of all Bill Mace, not simply for his remarkable patience but for his real care and relentless encouragement. The son of Albert Michotte, Baron Fritz Michotte de Bruxelles, has been very kind in providing us with many letters that his father received from fellow psychologists. Tim and Elaine Miles generously contributed a translation of Michotte's work on amodal completion. Françoise Carré and Patrick Stevenson of the Language Centre at Southhampton University were most helpful in their advice on difficult points of translation. We are also very grateful to the following people for their assistance: Derek Boyle, Paolo Bozzi, Nicola Bruno, Walter Gerbino, Ed Reed, Ann Richards, and Paul Whittle.

---

*Gibson, J. J. (1967) Autobiography. In E. G. Boring & G. Lindzey (Eds.), *A history of psychology in autobiography, Vol. V.* (pp. 127–143). New York: Appleton-Century-Crofts.

We acknowledge with thanks the following copyright holders for permission to translate and reproduce the articles contained in this volume:

The Elsevier Science Publishers BV who hold copyright on A. Michotte, (1950), A propos de la permanence phénoménale: Faits et théories. *Acta Psychologica, 7,* 298–322. Also for Michotte, (1955), Perception et cognition. *Acta Psychologica, 11,* 70–91.

L'Académie Royal des Sciences, des Lettres et des Beaux Arts de Belgique who hold copyright on Michotte, A. (1960). Le réel et l'irréel dans l'image. *Bulletin de la Classe des Lettres de l'Académie Royal de Belgique,* 5e Série, *46,* 330–344.

Les Presses Universitaires de France who hold copyright on A. Michotte & G. Thinès, (1963). La causalité perceptive. *Journal de Psychologie Normale et Pathologique, 60,* 9–36.

Prof. Joseph Nuttin and Louvain University Press who hold copyright on A. Michotte, G. Thinès, & G. Crabbé, (1964). *Les compléments amodaux des structures perceptives.* (Studia Psychologica.) Louvain: Publications Universitaires.

L'Académie Royale des Sciences, des Lettres et des Beaux Arts de Belgique for: A. Michotte, (1948). L'énigme psychologique de la perspective dans le dessin linéaire. *Bulletin des Lettres de l'Académie Royale de Belgique.* 5e Série, *34,* 268–288.

American Psychological Association who placed the following article in the public domain: A. Michotte, (1929). Quelques aspects de la psychologie de la perception negligés dans les récherches expériméntales. In *IXth International Congress of Psychology, held at Yale University, New Haven, Connecticut, 1929: Proceedings and Papers.* Princeton, NJ: Psychological Review Company, pp. 307–308.

Professor F. Rositi for permission to publish: A. Michotte, (1948). Le caractère de "réalité" des projections cinématographiques. *Revue Internationale de Filmologie, 1,* 249–261.

Baron Michotte van den Berck for permission to publish: A. Michotte, (1950). La préfiguration dans les données sensorielles de notre conception spontanée du monde physique. *Proceedings and papers of the XIIth International Congress of Psychology.* Edinburgh: Oliver and Boyd. Pp. 20–22.

Professor T. Husén for permission to publish: A. Michotte, (1951). La perception de la fonction "outil." In *Essays in Psychology, Dedicated to David Katz.* Uppsala: Almqvist & Wiksells, 193–213.

The Belgian Psychological Society for permission to publish: A. Michotte, (1954). Autobiographie. *Psychologica Belgica, 1,* 190–217.

Alan Costall

RESOURCES FOR ECOLOGICAL PSYCHOLOGY

A Series of Volumes Edited by:
Robert E. Shaw, William M. Mace, and Michael T. Turvey

REED/JONES • *Reasons for Realism: Selected Essays of James J. Gibson*

WARREN/SHAW • *Persistence and Change*

KUGLER/TURVEY • *Information, Natural Law, and the Self-Assembly of Rhythmic Movement*

McCABE/BALZANO • *Event Cognition: An Ecological Perspective*

LOMBARDO • *The Reciprocity of Perceiver and Environment: The Evolution of James J. Gibson's Ecological Psychology*

ALLEY • *Social and Applied Aspects of Perceiving Faces*

WARREN/WERTHEIM • *Perception & Control of Self-Motion*

THINÈS/COSTALL/BUTTERWORTH • *Michotte's Experimental Phenomenology of Perception*

1
General Introduction

GENERAL INTRODUCTION
Alan Costall

Albert Michotte is regarded as a classic figure in the history of psychology. For English speaking psychologists, however, his reputation is based almost exclusively on his research on the perception of causality.

Michotte was well into his 60s when his work on causality was first published in 1946 (an English translation of the second edition appeared in 1963). Yet this research marked just the beginning of what Michotte came to regard as the culmination of his life's work, his experimental phenomenology of perception. In fact, Michotte remained an active researcher until shortly before his death in 1965, publishing many papers on further aspects of causality and the perception of "functional relations," and also on phenomenal permanence and reality. Although a few of these later papers are referred to by American and British researchers, very little of Michotte's work has been translated. Apart from *The Perception of Causality* (Michotte, 1963), only two further works by Michotte have been published in English. The first is Michotte's own contribution to *The History of Psychology in Autobiography* (Michotte, 1952), and the other is his paper "The Emotions Regarded as Functional Connections" (Michotte, 1950). Neither of these papers is easily obtainable through university libraries.

The present text provides translations of almost all of Michotte's papers published after 1946. Our purpose is to draw the English reader's attention to his writings on phenomenal permanence and reality, as well as to developments of his better known work on causality. This book, therefore, complements *The perception of causality* (Michotte, 1963) to make available in translation the full scope of Michotte's experimental phenomenology of perception.

Michotte's writings in this final phase of his research centered upon four main themes: phenomenal causality, phenomenal permanence, phenomenal reality, and the relation between perception and thought. We have organized the book according to these themes, and each section begins with an introduction to each specific theme. The purpose of this initial section is to relate Michotte's work to its intellectual and historical context. As part of this general introduction, we include Michotte's own account of his scientific career, in which he identifies three distinct phases of his research: initial studies associated with the research on "imageless thought" by the Würzburg psychologists; a second phase, dating from the end of World War I, influenced by behaviorism and the growing criticism of introspectionism; and the final phase, his experimental phenomenology.

In this introductory section, we expand and underscore Michotte's own account of the background to the final phase of his research and then attempt to characterize Michotte's approach to theory and research in his experimental phenomenology. Certainly, Michotte is a significant figure in the history of psychology not solely for his experimental phenomenology. He had achieved an international reputation very early in his career, and, as Fauville (1947, p. 14) has noted, his work almost coincides with the history of psychology. However, we aim to do more than merely offer an account of Michotte as an historical figure. Michotte's work is directly relevant to current debates and developments in psychology Many of the assumptions *challenged* by Michotte even in his earliest work have regained a dominant hold on psychological theory. These include the "intellectualist" interpretation of perception (e.g., the treatment of perception as a process of logical inference or hypothesis-making); the commitment to a view of the individual as a mere spectator, and the consequent neglect of human activity and artifacts; and the assumption that meaning is purely "subjective" and derivative—a mental projection upon a neutral and colorless world.

THE BACKGROUND TO MICHOTTE'S EXPERIMENTAL PHENOMENOLOGY

Alan Costall

Michotte and the Würzburg School of "Imageless Thought"

Psychologists seem to be faced with the unfortunate choice of being either vague or irrelevant. Michotte was certainly aware of this dilemma, for it was one he sought to resolve throughout his long career. A fundamental key to his work is the attempt to promote psychology both as an exact science and also as one relevant to human concerns. In effect, Michotte was trying to reconcile two conflicting traditions within the history of psychology, those of natural and moral science.

Michotte encountered the tension between the natural and moral sciences while still a student at the Catholic University of Louvain, between 1897 and 1905, for he not only received a thorough training in natural science but also studied philosophy with the man who was later to become Cardinal Mercier. According to Michotte, Mercier's influence was crucial in his later intellectual and "human" development (Michotte, 1952; for further biographical details, see Nuttin, 1947, 1966).

Mercier was the first president of the newly established Institut Supérieur de Philosophie at Louvain, a center devoted to the attempt to base Catholic theology on the philosophy of St. Thomas Aquinas and to bridge the gulf between philosophy and natural science (Kenny, 1980). In 1891, Mercier had already organized a course in experimental psychology and a laboratory, to which Michotte was appointed after he graduated in 1905.

In accord with a recent papal doctrine (the encyclical of Pope Leo XIII of 1879), Mercier viewed Thomism as an important counter to Cartesianism, and his many writings on psychology were directed against positivism, materialism, and idealism (Strasser, 1951; Misiak & Staudt, 1954, pp. 34–65). Mercier himself saw psychology as foundational not only for the other sciences but for philosophy itself, and viewed Wundt's psychology with great enthusiasm as having direct implications for philosophy. Michotte did not share Mercier's high opinion of Wundt, and, on the many occasions when he referred to the relations between philosophy and psychology, he took care to warn of the dangers of psychologism, and denied any *direct* relation, at least, between the two disciplines (e.g., Michotte, 1947, 1951). Nevertheless, some important Thomist themes emerge in much of Michotte's research, such as the problems of intentionality and embodiment and the emphasis on perception as the source, if not the limit, of all of our knowledge (Gilson, 1924; Kenny, 1984; and Pieper, 1963).

Between 1905 and 1906, Michotte spent some time at Wundt's laboratory but, as he makes clear in his autobiography, he found Wundt's system ultimately unsatisfying (Michotte, 1952). Thanks to the recent, important corrections to the standard accounts of Wundt's psychology (e.g., Blumenthal, 1979, 1985; Danziger, 1979; Mischel, 1970), the reasons for Michotte's disenchantment are now quite clear. Although Wundt is credited as the founder of experimental psychology, he was quite emphatic that its method could only be applied to a highly restricted domain, the study of sensations and feelings, since only these phenomena, he believed, were subject to direct experimental manipulation. However, Wundt did not ignore the problems of meaning and value but he argued that these could only be investigated by the methods of cultural and historical analysis. In contrast, Michotte, as he himself stressed, was not only by nature an experimenter but was also resolved to tackle the problems of what he called "the higher mental processes" by the methods of natural science.

While Michotte was on the rebound, as it were, from Wundt's psychology, he very soon met up with Külpe and went to work at his laboratory at Würzburg in 1907 and 1908. Külpe had come to rely almost exclusively on introspection and had extended the method to the study of higher mental processes. Indeed, introspectionism is very much an invention of the present century. As Woodworth has explained, "so far from experimental psychology having begun as a purely introspective enterprise and needing young upstarts to force it into objective channels, it made its beginning with nonintrospective studies of reaction time, psychophysics, and memory" (Woodworth, 1924, p. 258). In fact, Wundt subjected the studies of the Würzburg school to merciless criticism, describing their research as "sham experiments which have the appearance of being systematic only because they take place in a psychological laboratory" (Wundt, 1907, cited in Humphrey, 1951, pp. 107, 114). Despite these unpromising testimonials, Michotte's early work adopted Külpe's method of systematic introspection, and Michotte's early studies were identified as very much part of the Würzburg school of "imageless thought" (e.g. Aveling, 1931; Pillsbury, 1947).

Külpe had reacted strongly against his earlier commitment to positivism in favor of realism (Ogden, 1951). Külpe, along with Husserl who had strongly influenced him, was a dominant figure in the general reaction against positivism within continental psychology and philosophy in the early part of this century (Leichtman, 1979; Waterhouse, 1981). The specific targets of the Würzburg researchers were phenomenalism and sensationalism. They had extended the introspective method to show that the phenomenalists held too narrow a concept of experience—that there was more to the content of experience than mere sensations and images (Humphrey, 1951; Lindenfeld, 1978). Incidentally, it is curious how close the aims of the Würzburg school were to Thomism in this respect. To quote a brief section from *A Sketch of Medieval Philosophy,* by D.J.B. Hawkins (cited in Freemantle, 1955, p. 149):

> St. Thomas was completely Aristotelian in finding the whole material of thought in sense-experience. Thomism is, therefore, a philosophy of experience, but it is not a mere empiricism, which stops short at *sense*-experience, and refuses to see in the development of thought anything but an elaboration of sensations and images.

Michotte's major studies of this period (Michotte & Prüm, 1910; Michotte & Ransy, 1912) are very clearly in accord with this view. Michotte's work on choice, which claimed to identify an awareness of one's own activity beyond mere sensation, drew his attention to the dynamic aspect of mental functioning and to action rather than static content (Nuttin, 1966). Michotte's other main studies at this time, those on logical memory, led him to recognize the integrating function of thought in memory so that (as he later put it):

> [the items become] embedded in a complex relational unit (a Gestalt!) . . . from this moment I was convinced that observational data justified, aside from any metaphysical considerations, the distinction of two levels of psychic activity: on the one hand, the level of sensory experience and of everything related to it (formation of units, associations, emotions, etc.), and, on the other, a higher level, that of thought. (Michotte, 1952, p. 218)

For Michotte, however, this higher level of thought did not involve the introduction of further mental elements but rather special functions of symbolism and integration, which serve to organize and abstract from sensory experience. This view persisted and remained central in his later phenomenology, where he argued that such perceptual categories as causality, permanence, and reality serve to "prefigure" our intellectual concepts.

Michotte's Reaction to Behaviorism

So far, I have tried to establish the ideological context within which Michotte was working and that shaped his later phenomenology. Wider developments, both within psychology and also in Catholic philosophy, encouraged Michotte's stance against posivitism, and the related "isms" of sensationalism, atomism, and intellectualism. Indeed, some of the obvious similarities between Michotte and the Gestaltists, as he himself made clear, were not due to any direct influence but rather a consequence of a more general reaction against positivism at the beginning of this century. I have also attempted to show how Michotte had begun, in his early studies based on systematic introspection, to bridge the gulf between natural and moral science by tackling problems associated with the former with methods associated with the latter and hence had brought meaning and value within the domain of experimental science.

Michotte's early researches were well received, and by the second decade of this century he had already established a considerable reputation. The future course of his research seemed clear. However, the First World War intervened, and Louvain was devastated. The personal impact on Michotte was severe: He lost his home and his father died of exposure. He moved with his family to Holland where he continued to perform research but in the quite different field of acoustics.

Even before the War, Michotte had come to have doubts about the direction his research was taking. In a paper published in 1907, he criticized the method of systematic introspection, and, more specifically, the method of retrospection—the technique adopted by the Würzburg researchers themselves (Michotte, 1907; see Danziger, 1980). These doubts about introspectionism only became really pressing, however, once he had returned to Louvain after the war to resume his psychological research.

The period from Michotte's return to psychology until he began his program of experimental phenomenology in 1939 marked not merely a stage of transition but one of deep and prolonged intellectual crisis. How was he to proceed in his attempt to bring the problem of meaning within the scope of natural science now that he could no longer trust his earlier experimental methods?

In 1923, Michotte made his first contacts with the Gestalt psychologists, when he met Köhler and Koffka at the International Congress held at Oxford. The Gestaltists had themselves been highly critical of both analytical introspectionism and Külpe's appeal to further mental elements. They insisted on the need for a full-blown holistic approach (e.g., Koffka, 1924). Michotte was clearly impressed by the convergence of his concerns with those of the Gestaltists, but he was also critical of what he saw as their formalism, their failure to address the problem of the intentionality of perception or, in other words, the problem of meaning.

A special symposium was held at the next International Congress at Groningen in 1926, on the psychology of form. Michotte's contribution was devoted to the problem of the relation between perceptual organization and meaning (Michotte, 1927; for brief commentaries, see Elmgren, 1939; Koffka, 1928; for an excellent account of Gestaltism from the 'French perspective,' see Guillaume, 1937). On the basis of tachistoscopic experiments, Michotte argued that one does not immediately experience the meaning of the perceived form; the "taking on of meaning" involves a separate stage, the intervention of past experience (cf. Köhler, 1930). Clearly, Michotte's view at this time, and for some time after, differed considerably from that central to his later phenomenology, that meaning can also be intrinsic to perception itself. However, even in this early paper, Michotte took care to stress that the "taking on of meaning" involves the embedding of the perceptual structure in a wider context, not a mere addition to the perceptual form. As he put it, "it is not a juxtaposition, the appearance of something joined to the form . . . the relations between them are very intimate because the meaning is obviously connected to the intuitive organization. Furthermore the inverse relation also exists, and meaning can have a considerable influence on the structure of perception" (Michotte, 1927, pp. 169–170).

In this paper, Michotte had explicitly omitted any reference to what he called the "action perspective." In 1929, however, at the International Congress at Yale University, he directly addressed the question of the relation between perception and action. Unfortunately, this paper was never published in full, but a substantial abstract did appear in the proceedings of that conference and is sufficient to indicate how much the paper itself anticipated his later phenomenology (Michotte, 1929). In this paper, he insisted that perception should not be considered the last stage in a process initiated by stimulation, but rather as a phase of action itself. This was the first occasion on which Michotte presented his views on the importance of functional relations in perception and raised the possibility that such meanings are intrinsic to perception itself. As Michotte later explained:

> The thesis which I put forward at the Yale conference was in direct disagreement with all theories of the traditional kind . . . , since I expressed the opinion that certain physical events give an immediate causal impression, and that one can 'see' an object *act* on another object, *produce* in it certain changes, and *modify* it in one way or another. . . . The question that arises is this: when we observe these operations, is our perception limited to the impression of two movements spatially and temporally co-ordinated, such as the advance of the knife and the cutting of the bread? Or rather do we directly perceive the action as such—do we see the knife actually cut the bread? (Michotte, 1963, p. 15)

On the face of it, Michotte's paper of 1929 would seem to open the way for his later phenomenology, with its central emphasis on the spontaneously meaningful character of our everyday world. Why, then, the delay of 10 years before he started his program for an experimental phenomenology of perception? The reason becomes clear on reading a substantial paper published by Michotte in 1936, titled "Psychology and Philosophy" (Michotte, 1936), for it is quite evident in this later paper that Michotte was still struggling to reconcile his driving interest in the problem of meaning with his equally long-standing commitment to experimental science. Indeed, Michotte begins this paper by stressing that by "science" he specifically meant experimental or positive science (Michotte, 1936).

Despite its title, Michotte's paper on philosophy and psychology is essentially methodological, being concerned with psychology's status as a science following the deadlock of Külpe's introspectionism. Behaviorism had been a major influence on Michotte during the middle phase of his work, and not only in a negative way. Its functionalist emphasis conformed well with Michotte's own interests and led him to concentrate his research on motor reactions or, as he put it, the "morphology of movement" (Michotte, 1952, pp. 222–223). Indeed, by this time, Michotte had become convinced that psychology was a science of behavior, though he never described himself as a behaviorist, but rather as a "psychologist of action." As I shall shortly explain, Michotte's reason for making this distinction was that he was equally convinced that the psychologist should be concerned with behavior not as mere movement but as meaningful action (cf. Heider, 1958; Holt, 1915).

The basic point of Michotte's paper was to argue that, although there could never be a science of inner experience, a scientific psychology was nevertheless possible. In relation to perception, Michotte insisted that the reports obtained from observers can provide information about whether they respond similarly or differently to different situations, even if they can tell us nothing about what they actually experienced.

In this paper, Michotte adopts what he calls the "Situation-Response" formula of the behaviorists, but then immediately raises the important question of how we should understand the terms "Situation" and "Response." This is the way Michotte himself put the matter:

> Consider the example of someone taking pity at the sight of a beggar, and giving him some money. Can one really believe that either the situation or response of such a person can be exhaustively defined in purely physical and physiological terms? . . . Clearly there is something which evades such an analysis, and it is exactly this that seems so essential to psychological knowledge – this is the "meaning" or "significance". For anyone

> observing this act of charity, the situation would have the same meaning—the presence of a beggar, despite the fact that they would see it from different vantage points and hence receive different retinal stimulation. Similarly, the act of giving could be performed in limitless ways, using quite different groups of muscles, and yet every observer would experience it as the same act of donation. (Michotte, 1936, p. 221)

Michotte's recurrent point in his 1936 paper is that it is not the situation or response as such, but rather their meaning that really matters for psychology. Thus, as Michotte put it, we must consider human actions in the same terms as we use in everyday life, and he even went so far as to draw an analogy with the language of moralists and novelists.

However, Michotte insisted that the meaning of the situation and the response are derivative, an inference based on past experience. To quote Michotte, it follows that "the meaning is nothing but the end result of a vast synthesis, and stands only as a sign, the only effective indicator, of such a synthesis" (Michotte, 1936, pp. 221–222).

The Move Toward Experimental Phenomenology

Michotte dated the beginning of his Experimental Phenomenology from the year 1939, but what exactly set this final phase of his work apart from his earlier research?

In his autobiography, Michotte defines his Experimental Phenomenology in terms of its *content:* the fundamental problems of causality, permanence, and reality. Yet these topics, in that they concern issues central to positivism, are largely continuous with his early attempts to show that "will" and "our sense of agency" are more than mere fictions. [In fact, one of Michotte's later papers discusses the perceptual basis of 'self-identity' (Michotte, 1953).] Even the emphasis in his experimental phenomenology on the importance of the *meaning* of the situation to the individual was stated very clearly by Michotte in his earlier writings, as in his Yale address of 1929 and also in his criticism of the S-R formula (Michotte, 1936). It is tempting instead, therefore, to identify this final stage of Michotte's research solely in terms of its new technique. But, as I shall argue, what best defines Michotte's experimental phenomenology is its remarkable reconciliation of his theoretical and methodological concerns. For, in this final research, theory and method became thoroughly interwoven as a consequence of Michotte's claim that meaning is directly experienced. In the middle of his career, Michotte had been forced, in effect, to acknowledge Wundt's arguments for the restricted scope of experimental psychology. Wundt had criticized the attempt by the introspectionists to study the higher mental functions for the lack of replicability and the absence of "concomitant variation" of effects in relation to the experimental conditions (Hall, 1924). Michotte, even in his earliest studies using "systematic introspection," was alert to such criticisms, and sought to introduce systematic variation of the conditions or at least to record objective "symptoms" such as reaction times (Michotte 1952; see also Thinès, 1977). However, if perceptual meanings are indeed *derivative* (as he for a long time believed) then, of course, such meanings would hardly be amendable to precise, experimental control. In fact, in the mid-1930s, Michotte came to look to the statistical techniques of mental testing as the most promising field of scientific advance in psychology (Michotte, 1936), although these techniques never came to play an important role in his own research. As Katz (1947) has noted, Michotte's idea of good research was the identification all the relevant variables through exhaustive experimental analysis.

Toward the end of the 1930s, however, Michotte discovered a means by which phenomenal causality could be subjected to psychophysical study (concomitant variation) in just the same way as colour, shape and movement, and with similarly precise results. His new method involved the use of simple schematic displays in which the spatiotemporal conditions of stimulation could be readily manipulated. Under the appropriate conditions, he found that observers reliably reported seeing a causal collision—one object 'pushing' another and making it move. Minor variations in the conditions would either destroy this effect, or else give rise to different kinds of casual effect (such as one object 'carrying' another along, and so on).

Michotte's demonstration that perceived causality can be brought under lawful experimental control does mark an important extension of the scope of experimental psychology. It served not only to address what Michotte saw as a neglected topic in the psychology of perception—the problem of meaning—but also to counter Wundt's denial of the very possibility of an experimental approach to this topic. These new researches were indeed an ingenious development of experimental technique, and are often assessed solely in these terms. Yet, as far as Michotte was concerned, this was not a question of experimentation merely for its own sake. His new technique at last freed him to pursue a long-standing project which had much wider theoretical and indeed personal significance.

According to Michotte, the demonstration of lawful experimental control (concomitant variation) constituted a vivid confirmation of his view that meaning could be *intrinsic* to perception, or "directly lived" (Michotte, 1963, p. 15). The experimental displays, he contended, "abstract" the relevant light patterns available in everyday situations

(Michotte, 1941), so that the experiment itself models the relation between the perceiver and his or her world. Thus the possibility of precise experimental control is, in fact, a reflection of a more general lawful relation—the adaptation of perceiver and world.

So many aspects of Michotte's personal and intellectual life served to give prominence to the question of meaning. As I have argued, his work can be seen as an aspect of the widespread "revolt against positivism" in European thought, and this revolt involved a diversity of new intellectual movements. In Michotte's case, perhaps first in importance was the rise of neo-Thomism in Catholicism. The appeal to Thomist philosophy was explicitly intended to counter the Cartesian (and ultimately Platonist) notion of the body as an obstacle to knowledge rather than the means through which it is obtained. In fact, this challenge within Catholicism to dualism—so fundamental to the scheme of modern science—addressed the theological assumptions from which dualism itself largely derives. On this alternative view, our existence as embodied beings within the world is the natural and necessary condition of all human knowledge (including spiritual knowledge). The body is not a "prison," nor is the world devoid of significance.

Secondly, in his choice of the term "experimental phenomenology," Michotte clearly intended to identify his work with the wider development of phenomenology in psychology and philosophy. Early in his career, he had been introduced by Külpe to the works of the major figures (Michotte, 1952) but, in addition, phenomenology came to figure prominently at the Institut Supérieur in its work of reconstructing Catholic philosophy (Spiegelberg, 1960). The details of Michotte's commitment to this movement are unclear, for, as in the case of Thomism, he wrote very little about his philosophical views. But, in this case too, meaning figured as a fundamental issue. Brentano's principle of the intentionality of consciousness (itself derived from scholastic philosophy) gave meaning this central position; indeed Brentano's students considered the basic task of phenomenology to be to "explicate the sense this world has for us all, prior to any philosophizing" (Husserl, 1929, cited in Lundh, 1983, p. 175). Michotte himself evidently concurred with Stumpf, rather than Husserl, in supposing that such "explication" could involve empirical inquiry instead of *a priori* investigation.

Finally, Michotte's biological orientation also served to alert him to the problem of meaning. For, if he concentrated upon the structure or 'morphology' of perception, thought, motivation or action, then it was always with a view to *function*. We tend to associate an emphasis on adaptation with British and American psychology, yet, in fact, a dynamic and functional approach has continued to be strongly represented by French speaking psychologists for a good part of this century (notably, Janet, Claparède, and Piaget). The concept of adaptation immediately brings the problems of meaning and value to central importance. Michotte, like Gibson, in treating the adaptive relation between knower and known, achieved an important synthesis of two seemingly conflicting perspectives, for, of course, from the wider evolutionary viewpoint, function and structure are not mutually exclusive but mutually constraining. As a psychologist, Michotte was, in effect, a "structural functionalist" (see Michotte, 1952, p. 235).

Michotte has been both celebrated (and criticized) primarily as an experimentalist. Certainly he was an ingenious and productive researcher, and he was duly reticent about "metatheoretical" issues. As I have tried to explain, however, the status of meaning had preoccupied him for a large part of his career and for several important reasons. He was no simple-minded empiricist, and the perception of meaning was not just another problem (see Michotte, 1952, pp. 234–235).

Frederic Bartlett, a close friend, stressed that Michotte's work on causality—performed during the German occupation—sustained him through this highly stressful time. For Michotte was cut off from the wider psychological community, and also under constant threat. As in the First World War, Michotte and his family had once more been driven from Louvain. Bartlett himself had arranged for him to work at Cambridge, but while on their way to England, Michotte and his party were caught by the Germans and taken back to Louvain. Although neither Michotte nor his family were subjected to any ill-treatment, "his sympathies were well known to be definitely on the English side, and it was impossible for him to feel really safe from one day to another" (Bartlett, 1966, p. 36). Although Bartlett liked to portray himself as a no-nonsense empiricist, he recognized, and respected, the real meaning Michotte saw in his work:

> All of us who saw [Michotte] soon after the end of the war were disturbed and shocked at his appearance. . . . But when he began to talk about his experiments and their results, his manner would change and much of the earlier liveliness come back. I am convinced that these lovely experiments, and his interpretation of their results, had for him a deep, perhaps even religious significance, maintaining as they did his belief in *the integrity of the human mind and its—in a sense—untaught capacity to understand the basic connexion of natural phenomena.* (Bartlett, 1966, p. 36; emphasis added)

THE EXPERIMENTAL PHENOMENOLOGY OF ALBERT MICHOTTE

Georges Thinès

Experimental Phenomenology as a Fundamental Tradition Within Psychology

The founding of psychology as a science is generally acknowledged to have occurred in Germany—its 'founder' being Wilhelm Wundt. Little credit is given to the parallel movement that developed under the influence of Franz Brentano. Yet, the "empirical psychology" proposed by Brentano was intended to be scientific, even if it did not turn to physiology as an ultimate explanatory framework. Brentano's psychology confined itself to phenomena as they appeared to the observer and sought the theoretical interpretation of them at the level of phenomenal organization itself. Brentano's influence in the history of experimental psychology was by no means negligible. In particular, Stumpf (a student of Brentano) developed an original theoretical and methodological approach known as Experimental Phenomenology, which drew upon Brentano's ideas and which, in turn, had a central influence both on Gestalt psychology and on Michotte himself (see Thinès, 1988).

The phenomenologists rejected the method of introspection considered as an analysis of essentially meaningless, "intra-psychic" elements (Giorgi, 1983). Thus, if the observer is presented with an array, such as a complex geometrical figure, the experimenter asks for no more than a description of its appearance, and refrains from insisting on a report of any "internal" reference to so-called elements of consciousness. Such phenomenal descriptions later became a fundamental rule of Gestalt psychology. The description is subjective in the sense that it informs the experimenter about how the objects and events appear to the observer, but it certainly does not imply a separate realm of mental contents, as if consciousness were a "substance enclosed upon itself" (Giorgi, 1983, p. 145). According to the phenomenological perspective, "subjectivity" is not understood as in opposition to "objectivity" but rather in terms of the "subject's" activity as intentionally centred upon an object.

The views of Stumpf and other related views developed by Brentano's disciples within the Graz circle can be summarized as follows (see Thinès, 1977). Firstly, they were concerned to establish a definition of mental phenomena which was not only epistemologically sound but also scientifically fruitful, and thus mark out a distinct field for psychology which would set it apart, to some extent at least, from other sciences and also philosophy. They also adopted a unified approach to both perceptual and cognitive phenomena in their appeal to the concept of form or structure in contrast to the elementaristic units of atomistic psychology. Perhaps most important, however, was their commitment to Brentano's concept of intentionality which insisted that the subjective aspects of consciousness are related to the physical world in an intrinsic way. The implication of this principle is that the study of mental phenomena should not involve a search for meaningless, "intrapsychic" contents.

Thus the Experimental Phenomenology originated by Stumpf, and taken up by Michotte and also by the Gestaltists and other important figures, such as Edgar Rubin and David Katz, should not be confused with introspectionism. It rejected both elementarism and, in its fundamental commitment to the intentionality of consciousness, the view of subjective descriptions as referring to a mental realm of ultimately self-contained, meaningless contents. In short, the reports of the observer are considered to be subjective in the sense that they are informative about how objects and events appear to him or her. Because the experimental method was held to be the most reliable one for obtaining reports of this kind, the approach is properly termed an *Experimental* Phenomenology.

Michotte's own development of the tradition of Experimental Phenomenology can be characterized first of all in terms of the relation between hypothesis and actual experiment. Michotte's starting assumption was that the organization of subjective phenomena can be studied using appropriate arrays of objects and events without attempting to define what these subjective phenomena are in themselves. In other words, given an appropriately designed experiment, the verbal responses of the subjects constitute valid indicators of the subjective organization. Thus the way in which the observer describes a particular display indicates under which class of phenomena it is spontaneously classified. If, for instance, an object such as a small colored rectangle moves on a screen toward another stationary object, and, after they make contact, they move off together, then the observer may describe the event differently according to how long they remain in contact. If the contact is brief, then the event will usually be described as a *causal* action of the first object on the second: "The first object takes the second object with it," or "entrains" it. If they remain in contact, however, the description will then refer to a single movement of one object composed of two differently colored halves. Thus, it would seem that the causal impression is critically dependent on the spatiotemporal conditions of the visual event. Because the "objects" are in fact just small colored surfaces in motion, they have no mass or other physical properties that allow them to be treated as mechanical events in the physical sense. Rather, the response indicates how mechanical events are subjectively experienced. It is not surprising if objects with mass give rise to a causal impression when they collide under certain conditions. But if objects devoid of mass can provoke similar perceptual effects, then, according to Michotte, it may be inferred that the seen relation is due to the subjective organization of the perceiver. Hence, something about the subjective organization of the perceiver may be considered as actively establishing the causal relations between objects. We may conveniently call it the perception of causality. Other aspects of the perceptual world can be revealed in a similar way. Objects may be experienced as having a variable degree of "apparent reality" or as "permanent" or even experienced as "complete," even though only parts of them are physically given in the system of stimulation. Many examples of such effects can be found in the various studies of Michotte reprinted in the present book.

The approach is appropriately described as experimental phenomenology for two reasons. It is phenomenology because it tackles neither the "internal" impressions (as introspectionism would have it) nor the physical components of the situation. It is experimental because, in contrast to pure, philosophical phenomenology (in Husserl's sense), it studies subjective phenomena through descriptions obtained from experimental situations. The subjective organization of perception is experimentally investigated on the basis of what the verbal responses produced by the experiment imply. The experiment, as a physical manipulation, simply allows the analysis of everyday facts and events in more rigorous terms (including the measurement of spatial and temporal variables). Thus, according to this view, the experiment should reveal the functional relations that exist between the subject and his or her phenomenal world.

Having examined the relation between hypothesis and experiment in Michotte's final work, we must consider the question of how the research actually proceeded. Once we take everyday life as the basis for our psychological hypotheses about the subjective organization of experience, then, clearly, the possible directions of investigation would seem to be limitless. In fact, however, once we investigate phenomena in this way, we soon discover that they fall into a limited number of classes. Causality, reality, permanence, and so on, are convenient labels for them. Although Michotte was sparing in his use of such labels, a much greater variety of subclasses needed to be distinguished within each class in the light of actual observations. Thus, within the category of perceived causality, specific effects were discovered, such as "launching," "entraining," "tracing," "pushing at a distance," and so on. In this way, experimentation played as important a role in the specification of major effects and subeffects as the basic reference in Michotte's research to the functional aspects of ordinary life. It was by testing the various possibilities derived both from reflection on real-life situations and also from the concrete possibilities of different experimental situations that Michotte came to devise the various types of experiments he actually performed. This approach reflects Michotte's congenial gift for grasping complexities in apparently simple facts and for then rapidly formulating them into scientific hypotheses. He would immediately start to fiddle with the various pieces of apparatus to try to create a preliminary demonstration, and usually succeed. If, however, the effect was unexpected, he would express his surprise with some force. His conspicuous curiosity about possible effects was central to Michotte's conception of the basic tasks of experimental psychology.

According to Michotte, the experimental data consisted of the verbal responses of the observers. In his view, these were the dependent variables of the stimulation system, and the conditions of stimulation were the independent variables of the experiments. He treated the meaning of the verbal responses by the observer as indicating the functional significance of the subjective phenomena in the subject-world relationship. Michotte repeatedly stressed this role of language in the study of perception (e.g., Michotte, 1959, 1963). Thus, the only clue to the subjective organization of causality is ultimately the causal meaning of the expressions used by the subject to describe the events presented in the experiment. These linguistic data can be treated as true dependent variables because their meaning varies as a function of the physical variations brought about by the experimenter's manipulations of the experimental display. For example, causal responses only occur under very restricted spatiotemporal conditions that concern the relative motions of the objects. Once such responses are obtained, the experimenter is able to use the semantic categories employed by the observer to theorize about the perception of causality. Thus, what characterizes Michotte's experimental phenomenology is first a search for specific links between perceptual displays and the semantic content of the observer's responses, and then the attempt to relate the semantic content to a broader theory.

As Michotte explained in the introduction to his book on causality, "the first requirement was obviously to try to produce experimentally some typical causal impressions and to determine by test the conditions under which they occur" (Michotte, 1963, p. 18). However, when Michotte added that the conditions of stimulation need to be determined empirically, he did not refer to the experimental design itself, nor to some prior notion of what the conditions ought to be. Michotte, it seems, was not primarily testing a previously formulated hypothesis;

rather, he was trying to discover the appropriate conditions by means of a series of trials, initially linked to the technical constraints of the apparatus, to produce immediate perceptual effects.

Michotte's procedure, therefore, was empirical in two senses. His evidence was, of course, based on observation, and his experimental approach proceeded in a highly exploratory way, by numerous, small modifications of the apparatus until the effect appeared to be satisfactory. This kind of approach is present in the initial phase of any research, but in Michotte's case it actually extended throughout the entire experiment.

Stressing this special aspect of Michotte's conception of experimental work does not imply at all that his methodology was poorly devised. In the study of perceptual causality by means of the well-known disc method, for example, it is almost certain that Michotte would not have discovered the manifold aspects of perceptual structures with the wealth of phenomenal characters that he reported if he had used more sophisticated and rigid techniques. The apparatus simply consisted of a disc rotated at a steady speed by an electric motor. Concentric circles and spirals of known angular decrement were drawn on the disc in such a way as to create the effect of movement when viewed through a narrow slit oriented radially in front of the disc. Numerous preliminary trials were performed to determine the optimal speed of the disc for which observers would report a "good" causal action of one object on another. Due to the relative simplicity of the apparatus, it was possible to make minute spatiotemporal changes to the display at any time and then immediately observe their effects on the perceived structure. In purely technical terms, such a straightforward procedure was sufficient to allow Michotte to develop a basic theory of perceptual causality, such as the concepts of *ampliation* and *radius of action* (see Chapter 2). Other concepts, such as *phenomenal permanence* and *reality, phenomenal dependence, quality of movement*, and *amodal presence*, required no more sophisticated procedures to provide a satisfactory basis for theorizing.

There is an interesting parallel between Michotte's Experimental Phenomenology and Husserl's principle of "imaginative variation." According to this principle, the examination of a large number of possible "aspects" of an object or event leads to the discovery of its "essence." One first thinks of a clear example of the relevant concept, and then of the various ways in which it might be changed while still counting as an instance of that concept: "it then becomes evident that a unity runs through this multiplicity of successive figures, that in such free variations of an original image, e.g., of a thing, an *invariant* is necessarily retained as the *necessary general form*, without which an object such as this thing, as an example of its kind, would not be thinkable at all" (Husserl, 1973, p. 341).

In a similar way, Michotte would begin his research by attempting to isolate a clear example of causality (or permanence, or reality) and then investigate the ways in which the display could be manipulated so as either to retain or destroy the effect. Of course, unlike Husserl, Michotte engaged concurrently in variations both at the imaginative and technical level. Furthermore, as an experimentalist, Michotte did not concern himself with the ontological status of facts and events, but attempted only to reveal the organization of subjective effects through variations in verbal meanings.

Given Michotte's approach to research, whereby imaginative variation and actual experimental manipulation continuously interacted, it is difficult to say at what point such "thought experiment" ceased and actual experimentation began—or even to assess their relative importance at various stages of the overall investigation. Michotte's tendency to look for perceptual effects in the manner of an intelligent craftsman did sometimes mean that his experiments were insufficiently controlled. He was perhaps too readily convinced that the study of perception is first and foremost the discovery of novel effects within ordinary experience, and this is why his studies sometimes serve more as demonstrations rather than experiments in the strict sense of the word. Nevertheless, this procedure proved astonishingly productive and resulted in theoretical conclusions of long-standing importance. The concept of *amodal presence*, for example, is a typical example of the fruit of this kind of phenomenologically inspired work (see Chapter 3). This is true for all the important concepts to be found in the studies translated in this book.

Michotte was convinced that a scientific psychology must inevitably involve experimentation; he never supposed that philosophical reflection in itself could be an alternative for solving psychological problems. He was equally convinced, however, that every experimental hypothesis must be founded on a descriptive approach to the spontaneous, functional relation between ourselves and our everyday world. It is ultimately in this sense that his research was phenomenological. Michotte was a phenomenologist who studied subjectivity "from outside," as it were, so that his contribution involves a thorough and rather unique experimental survey of our functional world, a world in which perception and action are never dissociated.

References

Aveling, F. (1931). *Personality and will.* London: Nisbet.

Bartlett, F.C. (1966). Baron Michotte van den Berck (1881–1965). *Bulletin of the British Psychological Society, 19,* 35–37.

Blumenthal, A.L. (1979). The founding father we never knew. *Contemporary Psychology, 24,* 547–550.

Blumenthal, A.L. (1985). Wilhelm Wundt: Psychology as the propaedeutic science. In C. Buxton (Ed.), *Points of view in the modern history of psychology* (pp. 19–50). New York: Academic.

Danziger, K. (1979). The positivist repudiation of Wundt. *Journal of the History of the Behavioral Sciences, 15,* 205–230.

Danziger, K. (1980). The history of introspection reconsidered. *Journal of the History of the Behavioral Sciences, 16,* 241–262.

Elmgren, J. (1939). *Gestalt psychology: A survey and some contributions.* Göteberg: Elanders Boktryckeri Aktiebolag.

Fauville, A. (1947). Discours [Address]. In *Jubilé Albert Michotte* (pp. 14–21). Louvain: Éditions de l'Institut Supérieur de Philosophie.

Freemantle, A. (1955). *The age of belief.* New York: Mentor.

Gilson, E. (1924). *The philosophy of St. Thomas Aquinas.* Cambridge: Heffer.

Giorgi, A. (1983). Concerning the possibility of phenomenological psychological research. *Journal of Phenomenological Psychology, 14,* 129–170.

Guillaume, P. (1937). *La psychologie de la forme.* Paris: Flammarion.

Hall, G.S. (1924). *Founders of modern psychology.* New York: Appleton-Century-Crofts.

Heider, F. (1959) *On perception, event structure, and psychological environment. Psychological Issues, 1(3),* Monograph 3.

Holt, E.B. (1915) *The Freudian wish and its place in ethics.* New York: Holt.

Humphrey, G. (1951). *Thinking.* London: Methuen.

Husserl, E. (1973). *Experience and judgment.* Evanston, IL: Northwestern University Press.

Katz, D. (1947). Address. In *Jubilé Albert Michotte* (pp. 29–33). Louvain: Editions de l'Institut Supérieur de Philosophie.

Kenny, A. (1980). *Aquinas.* Oxford: Oxford University Press.

Kenny, A. (1984). Aquinas: Intentionality. In T. Honderich (Ed.), *Philosophy through its past* (pp. 82–96). Harmondsworth: Penguin.

Koffka, K. (1924). Introspection and the method of psychology. *British Journal of Psychology, 15,* 149–161.

Koffka, K. (1928). *The growth of mind* (2nd ed.). London: Routledge & Kegan Paul.

Köhler, W. (1930). *Gestalt psychology.* London: G. Bell.

Leichtman, M. (1979). Gestalt psychology and the revolt against positivism. In A.R. Buss (Ed.), *Psychology in social context* (pp. 47–69). New York: Irvington Publishers.

Lindenfeld, D. (1978). Oswald Külpe and the Würzburg school. *Journal of the History of the Behavioral Sciences, 14,* 132–141.

Lundh, L.-G. (1983). *Mind and meaning.* Uppsala: Acta Universitatis Upsaliensus, Studia Psychological Upsaliensia, Vol. 10.

Michotte, A. (1907). A propos de la 'Methode d'Introspection' dans la psychologie expérimentale [Concerning the method of introspection in experimental psychology]. *Revue Néo-Scholastique, 14,* 507–532.

Michotte, A. (1927). Rapport sur la perception des formes [On the perception of form]. *VIIth International Congress of Psychology, Groningen 1926: Proceedings and Papers* (pp. 167–174). Groningen: Noordhoff.

Michotte, A. (1929). Quelques aspects de la psychologie de la perception négligés dans les recherches expérimentales [Some neglected aspects of the psychology of perception within experimental psychology]. In *IXth International Congress of Psychology, held at Yale University, New Haven, Connecticut, 1929: Proceedings and Papers* (pp. 307–308). Princeton, NJ: Psychological Review Company.

Michotte, A. (1936). Psychologie et philosophie [Psychology and philosophy]. *Revue Néoscholastique de Philosophie (Louvain), 39,* 208–228.

Michotte, A. (1946). *La perception de la causalité* [The perception of causality]. Louvain: Institut Supérieur de Philosophie.

Michotte, A. (1950). The emotions regarded as functional connections. In M.L. Reymert (Ed.), *Feelings and emotions: The Mooseheart Symposium* (pp. 114–126). New York: McGraw-Hill.

Michotte, A. (1951). La psychologie néothomiste: Échange de vues [Neo-Thomist psychology: An exchange of views]. *Revue Philosophique de Louvain, 49,* 713–718.

Michotte, A. (1952). Albert Michotte van den Berck (Autobiography). In E.G. Boring, H.S. Langfeld, H. Werner, & R.M. Yerkes (Eds.), *A history of psychology in autobiography* (Vol. 4, pp. 213–236) Worcester, MA: Clark University Press.

Michotte, A. (1953). La participation émotionelle du spectateur à l'action representée a l'écran. Essai d'une théorie [The emotional participation of the spectator in the action represented on the screen: An approach to a theory]. *Revue Internationale de Filmologie, 4,* 87–96.

Michotte, A. (1959). Reflexions sur le role du langage dans l'analyse des organisations perceptives [Reflection on the role of language in the analysis of perceptual organization]. *Acta Psychologica, 15,* 70–91.

Michotte, A. (1963). *The perception of causality.* (T.R. Miles & E. Miles, Trans.) London: Methuen. (Original work published 1954)

Michotte, A., Piéron, H., & Piaget, J. (1955). Discussion entre les trois rapporteurs [Discussion among the three contributors]. In *La perception: Deuxième Symposium de l'Association Scientifique de Langue Française, Louvain 1953* (pp. 47–61) Paris: Universitaires de France.

Michotte, A., & Prüm, E. (1910). Étude experimentale sur le choix voluntaire et ses antecedents immédiats [Experimental study of voluntary choice and its immediate antecedents]. *Archives de Psychologie, 10,* 113–320.

Michotte, A., & Ransy, C. (1912). Contribution à l'étude de la memoire logique [Contribution to a study of logical memory]. *Études de Psychologie* (Louvain), *1,* 1–96.

Mischel, T. (1970). Wundt and the conceptual foundations of psychology. *Philosophy and Phenomenological Research, 31,* 1–26.

Misiak, H., & Staudt, V. (1954). *Catholics in psychology: A historical survey.* New York: McGraw-Hill.

Nuttin, J.R. (1947). Carrière scientifique de M. le Professeur A. Michotte van den Berck [Michotte's scientific career]. In *Miscellenea Psychologica Albert Michotte* (pp. xxv-xl). Louvain: Editions de l'Institut Supérieur de Philosophie.

Nuttin, J.R. (1966). Albert Edouard Michotte van den Berck: 1881–1965. *American Journal of Psychology, 79,* 331–341.

Ogden, R.M. (1951). Oswald Külpe and the Würzburg School. *American Journal of Psychology, 64,* 4–19.

Pieper, J. (1963). *Introduction to Thomas Aquinas.* (R. Winston & C. Winston, Trans.). London: Faber & Faber.

Pillsbury, W.B. (1947). *Fundamentals of psychology* (3rd ed). New York: Macmillan.

Spiegelberg, H. (1960). *The phenomenological movement.* (Vol. 2). The Hague: Martinus Nijhoff.

Strasser, St. (1951). Désiré Mercier et le probleme de la psychologie néothomiste [Désiré Mercier and the problem of neo-Thomist psychology]. *Revue Philosophique de Louvain, 49,* 699–713.

Thinès, G. (1977). *Phenomenology and the science of behavior.* London: Allen & Unwin.

Thinès, G. (1988). The phenomenological background of Michotte's experimental investigations. *Journal of Phenomenological Psychology, 19,* 19–58.

Waterhouse, R. (1981). *A Heidegger critique.* Brighton: Harvester.

Woodworth, R. S. (1924). Four varieties of behaviorism. *Psychological Review, 31,* 257–264.

ALBERT MICHOTTE: BIOGRAPHICAL SUMMARY

1881 Albert Edouard Michotte born in Brussels on October 13, the son of Edmond Michotte and Maria Bellefroid.

1894 Foundation at the University of Louvain of the *Institut Supérieur de Philosophie.* The founder, Désiré Mercier, becomes its first president. Armand Thiéry, a Belgian student of Wundt, organizes a small laboratory of Psychology at the *Institut Supérieur.*

1897 Michotte enters the University of Louvain as a student of philosophy at the *Institut Supérieur de Philosophie,* where he makes the acquaintance of Désiré Mercier.

1899 Michotte graduates with a degree in philosophy with the title of *Licencién Philosophie.* The subject of his Licence memoir is the physiology and psychology of sleep (*Étude sur la physiologie et la psychologie du sommeil*).

1900 Michotte becomes doctor in philosophy with a thesis on the aesthetics of Herbert Spencer. He enters the Faculty of Science, where he makes the acquaintance of Arthuer Van Gehuchten, a prominent Belgian neurologist.

1902 Michotte obtains the degree of Candidate in Natural Sciences, section of zoology.

1902–1904 Research in nervous physiology at Louvain under A. van Gehuchten.

1904 First published works: "La fibre nerveuse et sa bifurcation dans les ganglions", *Le Nevraxe,* 1904: 201–215, and: "Contribution a l'étude de l'histologie fine de la cellule nerveuse", *Bull.Acad. Royale de Médecine Belg.*, 1904: 515–556.

1905 Michotte obtains the degree of *Maître agrégé de l'Institut Supérieur de Philosphie* with a thesis on Regional signs (*Les Signes Régionaux*) prepared under Armand Thiéry's direction.

Teaches a practical course at Louvain in experimental psychology.

Attends the 5th International Congress of Psychology in Rome, where he meets Felix Krueger, then Wundt's assistant.

Michotte works under Wundt in Leipzig.

1906 Further work with Wundt in Leipzig during the summer term. Meets in Wundt's laboratory Spearman, Wirth and Klemm.

Lecturer (*Chargé de course*) at the University of Louvain.

Attends the Congress of the *Deutsche Psychologische Gesellschaft* in Würzburg where he meets Oswald Külpe. The acquaintance with Külpe will be a turning point in Michotte's career. Dissatisfied with Wundt's teachings, Michotte will turn from then on to the *Denkpsychologie* of the Würzburg School.

1907 Michotte spends a term at Würzburg where he works under Külpe. Teaches during the other term at Louvain.

Desiré Mercier, founder of the *Institut Supérieur de Philosophie,* becomes Cardinal of Belgium.

1908 Michotte spends a further term at Würzburg and teaches during the other terms at Louvain.

Michotte becomes Extraordinary Professor at Louvain.

Attends the Congress of the *Deutsche Psychologische Gesellschaft* in Frankfurt. His contribution to the psychology of memory attracts Ebbinghaus' attention. Ebbinghaus proposes to Michotte to that he should write a monograph on memory for the series *Die Psychologie in Einzeldarstellung,* a project never realized.

1909 Marriage with Mademoiselle Lucie Mulle.

1910 Attends the Congress of the *Deutsche Psychologische Gesellschaft*. His contribution on the immediate antecedents of voluntary choice was noted by Külpe, who placed Michotte among the leading psychologists of his time, based on this piece of research.

1912 Michotte ordinary Professor at Louvain. Teaches to students of philosophy, science and medicine. He is attached to the Faculty of Medicine.

1913 Michotte co-director with A. Thiéry of the Laboratory of Experimental Psychology.

1914 The war sets an end to the activities of the laboratory. Michotte emigrates to Holland with his family. He works at the University of Utrecht with Zwaardemaker and lectures there and in Amersfoort to Belgian students detained in Holland, though, interestingly, not on psychology, but in meteorology.

1918 Returns to Belgium.

1920 The Louvain laboratory resumes its activities after two years of reorganization.

1923 Michotte meets Wolfgang Köhler and Kurt Koffka for the first time at the International Congress of Psychology held at Oxford. First fundamental acquaintance with Gestalt psychology.

Foundation of the Psychological Institute at the University of Louvain. Michotte will be head of the Institute until his retirement in 1952.

1928 Michotte attends a private scientific meeting organized by David Katz at Rostock to discuss the fundamental issues of Gestalt psychology. The other participants are Wertheimer, Koffka, Lewin, Werner, Köhler, Heider, and Rubin.

1929 Spends a term at Stanford University as visiting professor.

Michotte attends the International Congress of Psychology at Yale University. First outline of his conception of the links between perception and action, to be fully developed later in *La Perception de la Causalité* (1946).

1927 Honorary Fellow of the British Psychological Society.

1935 Michotte attends the meeting organized in Santander by the Spanish government on contemporary problems of psychology. The other participants are Claparède, Germain, Janet, Lahy, Langfeld, and Myers.

1936 Elected member of the Pontifical Academy of Sciences.

1937 Lectures at the Collège de France on the psychology of action.

1946 Elected member of the Académie Royale de Belgique.

Publication of *La Perception de la Causalité.* The English translation will appear in 1963.

1947 Michotte founds the Société Belge de Psychologie and becomes its first president. Celebration of his professorial jubilee, with contributions from his ex-students P. Fraisse, J. Nuttin, and G. de Montpelier and from other well-known figures in psychology (e.g. J. Piaget, W. Köhler, F. C. Bartlett, E. Thorndike, and H. Langfeld.)

1952 Retirement of Michotte. He will still lecture on perception until 1956. He will also remain active in his laboratory until 1962. From 1956 to his death in 1965, Michotte will carry out several experiments and develop his theory of perceptual causality. The four last collaborators with which he will work during this last period are M.P. Mandy, A. Coen-Gelders, G. Crabbé, and G. Thinès.

1965 Michotte dies on June 2.

AUTOBIOGRAPHY OF PROFESSOR A. MICHOTTE VAN DEN BERCK[1]

My first reaction, on being invited to contribute to the series, *History of Psychology in Autobiography,* was to decline the honor. My academic and scientific life, as much as my personal life, has developed in such a simple, regular, and even logical way that there seemed little to interest anyone outside of my immediate circle. However, on reflection, I came to the conclusion that it might be appropriate that this series should include the most diverse examples of different "life-styles" among contemporary psychologists.

[1]Translated by A. P. Costall from A. Michotte "Autobiographie de M. Le Professor A. Michotte van den Berck." *Psychologica Belgica,* 1954, *1,* 190–217.

Because we are concerned here with the history of psychology (even its more incidental, personal aspects), "life-style" refers exclusively to scientific life. As I see it, what is required is an account of my contribution to the discipline so as to describe, and explain the reasons for, the individual development of my ideas. This is the way in which I have approached the following task.

I was born in Brussels in 1881, the second and last child of a wealthy, intellectual family. There was a tradition of involvement in the arts and the sciences, and so I grew up in a cultured environment. (My brother, Paul, was also a professor at the University of Louvain, in geography, and founded the Institute of Geography, which is named after him.) All my known ancestors were sincere Catholics, as I myself have been throughout my life.

I commenced my studies in 1897 at the University of Louvain where I studied philosophy and science until 1905. I had the good fortune to encounter two great teachers. The first was the incomparable man who was later to become the eminent Cardinal Mercier and who was then Professor and President of the Institute Supérieur de Philosophie. From the very start he treated me kindly with true fatherly concern and affection. His influence was crucial to both my intellectual and "human" development, and I feel its good effects even to this day.

The second was the great neurologist, Arthur van Gehuchten, who introduced me to scientific work, and directed my first researches (Michotte, 1904).

Mercier took a keen interest in psychology, and so when he founded the Institut de Philosophie he sought to introduce the teaching of psycho-physiology. This was achieved by the collaboration of Professor Armand Thiéry who had worked with Wundt at Leipzig and who organized a small psychology laboratory at the institut. It was there that I learned the rudiments of our science. However, Thiéry was very preoccupied with philosophical and theoretical issues and was not a laboratory man. Once my scientific and philosophical training had sufficiently advanced, therefore, Mercier provided strong support for my plan to specialize in psychology. And so I began to do some research, on the distribution of tactile sensitivity under Thiéry's direction (Michotte, 1905).

I then made my way to Leipzig where I spent two semesters in 1905 and 1906. It was there that I really began to become acquainted with psychology since the Louvain laboratory was still in a rudimentary condition and its library was even more so. I immersed myself in Wundt's *Grundzüge der physiologischen Psychologie* and introduced myself to the experimental technique. Although I had a great admiration for

FIGURE 1.1 Albert Michotte presenting the Presidential Address at the 15th International Congress pf Psychology, Brussels, July 28–August 3, 1957.

FIGURE 1.2 Visit to the Cambridge Psychological Laboratory by Professor Albert Michotte and members of the Department of Psychology, University of Louvain, 1948. Frederic Bartlett is first on the left, and Michotte is fifth to his right.

FIGURE 1.3 Rostock, 1928. Left to right: Kurt Lewin, David Katz, Heinz Werner, Madame Katz, Wolfgang Köhler, Albert Michotte, Edgar Rubin, and Max Wertheimer. (Fritz Heider also attended this meeting but does not appear in this photograph.)

FIGURE 1.4 Albert Michotte with apparatus for the study of rhythm, 1939.

FIGURE 1.5 Some of the participants at the 1953 symposium of the Association de Psychologie Scientifique de Langue Française, held at the University of Louvain. Left to right: Piaget, two visitors, Vin Bangh, Michotte, and Germain.

Wundt's system, I felt it was inadequate since I had already read the works of Binet and had been struck by his emphasis on the study of "higher processes" and by his wide application of introspection.

In 1906 I first met Külpe, at the Congress for the German Psychological Society at Würzburg. I immediately realized that I would discover in him just what was lacking at Leipzig. This is why I decided to move to his laboratory where I spent some months in 1907 and 1908. It was a real revelation, and I was perfectly content there. For it was thanks to Külpe that I really developed as a psychologist, not only as the result of my personal contacts with him during his seminars and research, but also because it was he who led me to "discover" the works of Brentano, Meinong, Husserl, Stumpf, von Ehrenfels, etc.

In 1909 I married Lucie Mulle. Our home has always been a source of complete happiness, and our six children have been a delight. I am profoundly grateful to my wife. Although she never became an academic herself, she has shown a remarkable appreciation of the duties that fall on me as a professor and a scientist and has constantly sought to free me of other concerns.

Another event should be mentioned at this point since it had a great impact upon my career by freeing me to concentrate my efforts on the rather specialized field in which I was most keenly interested. After the 1914 war, the academic authorities and especially Cardinal Mercier, then Chancellor of the University, had decided to modernize the teaching of education at Louvain and kindly sought my support. This opportunity gave me the chance to found with my former student, Professor Fauville, the "École de Pedagogie et de Psychologie appliquée a l'Education" in 1923. This allowed the development and diversification of psychology teaching, which had previously been restricted to the courses I myself taught. From that time, the University offered courses conducted by specialized teachers that included individual psychology, mental testing, and the psychology of childhood and adolescence. Little by little, the appointment of new professors allowed us to enlarge the curriculum even more, and in 1944 our school was transformed into an Institut de Psychologie appliquée et de Psychologie. This provided a full practical and theoretical training in all branches of psychology and was entitled to award academic degrees up to the level of the Doctorate in Scientific Psychology.

This leads me naturally to say a few words about the factors that have directed the course taken by my scientific work, that is, my own personal dispositions and the conditions under which I have worked.

A central idea has guided my activities (perhaps overly so). To ensure maximum effectiveness, everyone should first take account of his or her personal abilities and especially their limitations, and then ensure, wherever possible, to concentrate every effort on the kind of work that promises to achieve the optimum effect.

Since childhood my interests as well as my aptitudes have, above all, led me to be an experimenter. Furthermore, I have been especially attracted towards the exact sciences and that is why my preferred field of activity has always been that of experimental psychology in its strict sense. Other branches of psychology, such as social psychology as it existed at that time, the application of mental tests, which was then still finding its feet, and especially psychoanalysis failed to correspond to my ideal of precision. Nevertheless, I have always been convinced—and I have stressed this point in my teaching—that social psychology is of fundamental importance in the study of behavior, since it is perfectly obvious that behavior is primarily determined by the human environment within which the individual lives. This essential complement of psychology must be postponed for the future and the discovery of adequate methods of study.

However, there is no point in attempting to establish a scale of values in purely scientific matters, since every real problem, that is, every problem that, when solved, truly enriches our knowledge in some field or another, warrants the effort required for its investigation.

I will also add that it seems to me that, given the degree of development at that time (and perhaps even now), it was premature to try to construct theories. As far as I was concerned, there were too many theories of a remarkably shaky kind in the works of psychologists. I was therefore convinced that the primary task was to achieve the most exact knowledge possible about the facts and their underlying laws (but see my comments below under the heading "Overview").

As I have just indicated, my initial teaching at Louvain was restricted to scientific psychology, and, furthermore, my courses were addressed to students of the Institut de Philosophie for whom this field was subsidiary and of value mainly as background information. Some of the students, however, did show a special interest and wished to conduct research, but unfortunately they had been given no technical preparation in the use of experimental methods. As a result, we relied on a kind of collaboration that has persisted throughout my career, no doubt through force of habit, even after the creation of the École de Pedagogy when certain students had achieved a higher level of training.

In fact, I have always taken charge of the technical and instrumental side of the experiments, as well as their organization, and have always participated in them, either as an observer or an experimenter. Over the last 30 years, I have had a first-rate technical collaborator, M.L. Roland, who is well known to many psychologists. Thanks to his remarkable talent as a mechanic, he has not only enriched our laboratory with many instruments, but has also provided invaluable assistance in the course of my research. But I have never had an assistant in the strict sense of the word, partly because the need to extend our teaching into new fields took up the time of our best young talent, but also because of financial restrictions. I do not have cause to complain because this way of working has infinitely enriched my own experience and has given my laboratory the character of a kind of old-fashioned workshop for artists or craftsmen, in which the training of "apprentices" was ultimately based on the experience they derived from their active cooperation with the "master." This has been a great delight to me and has given rise to friendships between myself and students that have been one of the joys of my life.

There is, however, a darker side to this story. All this work took an enormous amount of time, and no sooner had the research been finished and the results analyzed than I found myself having to turn to different issues with new students. Consequently, although I have conducted a tremendous number of experiments throughout my life, and therefore learned a great many things that I have used in my teaching or for conferences abroad, a relatively important part of our work has never been published. But it should also be confessed that, given my overwhelming passion for research, my enthusiasm waned once the experiments themselves had been completed and I had found the answer to the question that had originally aroused my curiosity. The idea of committing myself to the tedious task of publication had no appeal for me, since I then mistakenly believed that this task could teach me nothing more.

Perhaps, when I retire soon, I may be able to publish the most interesting material that we accumulated.

What I have written so far should be sufficient to indicate the nature of my scientific work and to demonstrate that I am, above all, a laboratory researcher. My ideas have been generated not only during the course of my researches but in direct relation to them, and this is also true for the development of my fundamental views on the major problems that have concerned me. It follows, therefore, that the most effective way to present the development of my psychological ideas is by following the progress of the research that I have conducted with my students over the last 40 years. I shall, of course, restrict myself to the principal studies, and, in relation to each, try to identify those conclusions that, in my view, are of general interest.

Experimental Research

My research can be readily divided into three phases, during which it has taken a rather different character: the first extends up to the First

World War; the second between 1920 to 1939; and the last from 1939 to the present day. (Some of our laboratory work, especially that extensive enough to provide the basis for a volume, has been published in the series "Études de Psychologie" published by Éditions de l'Institut Supérieur de Philosophie of Louvain. Six volumes have appeared so far, and the series is now continued under the name "Studia Psychologica.")

Systematic Introspection: 1905–1920

By 1905 I had already been put in charge of the direction of the Louvain laboratory as an assistant (then as lecturer in 1906, and as professor from 1907). After some trial and error at the outset, our research took the direction adopted by the Würzburg school and by Binet, and concentrated primarily on the study of "higher processes:" logical memory, recall, cognition and the establishment of logical connections, the development of verbal meaning, voluntary choice, etc.

We made extensive use of "systematic introspection," but we always made every effort to complement introspection with a degree of objective confirmation, by trying to discover a correlation between the data provided by the observers and certain objective indices, such as reaction times, or else the frequency of occurrence of certain sequences of these phenomena under controlled conditions. In fact, in many cases, we discovered such correlations and this led us towards many interesting findings, notably in our studies of logical memory and voluntary choice.

Thus, for example, differences in reaction time led us to discover the integrative role of thought in memory where the items to be memorized become embedded in a complex relational whole (a Gestalt!) so that the reactivation of one aspect leads to the reproduction of others or allows an intentional search for them, and hence gives rise to the "restoration" of the entire configuration (Michotte & Ransy, 1912; Michotte & Portych, 1914).

The result was to provide me with my own empirical grounds for my views on the autonomy of thought processes, as well as on the limitations of traditional associationism and an "elementarist" approach to mental life. Our research on thinking and on the meaning of words reinforced this attitude and was especially effective in highlighting the importance of mental processes in the origin of "symbols."

From this time, I was convinced that the empirical findings justified, regardless of any metaphysical considerations, the distinction between two levels of mental activity: first, "sensory experience" and everything related to it (the formation of units, associations, emotions, etc.) and second, the higher level of thought. In my view, this higher level did not involve the intervention of new mental "elements," but rather the enrichment of sensory experience by means of special functions that allow the use of symbols and the formation of more comprehensive syntheses, as well as relational thought and reasoning.

The most important work of this period, however, was that on voluntary choice in 1910 (Michotte & Prüm, 1910; Michotte, 1912). This described the different forms taken by either voluntary or involuntary choice between two possible actions and attempted to determine the different motivational conditions under which these forms occurred. To do this, we conducted both a descriptive and (very primitive) statistical analysis of the motivational state and examined how it developed with subsequent repetitions of the situation in which the subject was placed.

These researches gave rise to the conclusion that we have an immediate experience of our own activity (which we termed "awareness of action"). This conclusion was in accord with Ach's findings, though we had arrived at it independently.

Furthermore, the study of the role of what was then termed "determination" (or "determinative tendency") led me to a dynamic conception of psychology that has dominated all my work and made me recognize the central importance of persistent, unconscious dispositions in the formation of the personality.

This work was generally well received by the critics, and Külpe wrote me a long letter on the topic that was extremely flattering. I still treasure it because it had an important role in reinforcing my self-confidence and was invaluable in stimulating my later efforts.

Then the war came in 1914, and the burning of Louvain, and, alas, the death of my father in tragic circumstances. I therefore moved with my family to Utrecht to join my friend Professor Zwaardemaker. I remained there until 1918, having been appointed by the Belgian government to teach the young university students who, as members of our army, had been interned in Holland. I kept myself busy with a variety of scientific work, primarily the measurement of acoustical energy at Zwaardemaker's laboratory (Michotte, 1922).

Reaction to Behaviorism: 1920–1939

My ideas had matured during the war, and I had reflected a good deal, especially on the problem of introspection. The numerous discussions that had arisen in Germany and the United States about the work of Külpe's school, particularly the criticisms by Titchener and the new Behaviorist Movement, had shaken my confidence in the scientific value of the method employed at Würzburg and by myself up until that time.

What justified all this skepticism was not only the theoretical objections but also the fact that experiments conducted under apparently identical conditions, by well qualified people but with different training and especially different "schools", produced contradictory results. Furthermore, it was clear that everyone remained convinced of the soundness of his own "observations" despite the criticisms of his opponents.

Since there was no higher authority to which to appeal to decide what was right and wrong, I concluded that such experiments had only an individual value in supporting one's personal beliefs, and that being incapable of yielding to any general verification they could not be treated as "scientific."

By then, I had come to see that there was no point in trying to "describe" internal events or "analyze" them into their elements, and that introspection only played an *informative* role. What I mean by this is that the verbal responses of the observers must be considered as "differential reactions" that simply reveal the presence or absence in the subject of an event *x*, the nature of which necessarily remains hidden and unknowable to the experimenter.

Nevertheless, in my view, general information of this kind about the state of mind of the subject, about how he "understands" the situation in which he finds himself, and his own reactions to that situation are essential in all psychological research, even in research intended to bear exclusively on the external, objective behavior of the individual.

Such information is especially important in the study of perception where it is possible to establish a relation between the relatively simple and limited responses of the observers and the stimulus or complex system of stimulation. Then, one can determine by applying the principle of concomitant variations, the conditions under which the phenomenon *x* occurs, whatever it might be "in itself." This is what is always done in experiments in psychophysics and is clearly applicable to the study of form perception (Michotte, 1936).

Most of our research between the two wars was concentrated on the field of perception. The topics included constancy phenomena in the tactile-kinesthetic domain, "sensory synthesis" in the same domain, relations between visual and tactile-motor localization, the relations between the reproductions of irregular figures presented either visually or in the tactile-motor mode, the influence of overall form of an object and the localization of its parts in depth, induced movement, and the development of visual forms when their parts are presented successively. In addition, there were tachistoscopic experiments and extensive studies of the stroboscopic phenomenon, and so on. It would be tedious to present a complete list, and this should be enough to indicate what they involved.

Our earliest studies along these lines yielded results and conclusions entirely analogous to those fundamental to Gestalt psychology, though I was then unaware of this because I had been deprived of access to publications after the destruction of the University library in the war.

I first discovered the similarity between my views and those of

Gestalt psychology when I met Koffka and Kohler at the International Congress of Psychology at Oxford in 1923. There were, however, a number of differences between us, particularly in relation to the importance of past experiences, as well as the role of needs and attitudes in the structural organization of perception. My ideas have since changed, especially during my recent research, and I have come to realize that the influence of acquired experience is less powerful in principle than I had previously thought. It now seems to me that past experience only achieves maximum importance in ambiguous cases (which are nevertheless frequent) where several different types of structuring are almost equally probable so that "objective factors" of organization (proximity, similarity, symmetry, etc.) are not necessarily powerful enough to impose a definite form.

This question of the role of acquired experience and of needs is connected with a thesis that has remained central for me. It is futile to study perception "in itself;" instead, it should be treated as a "phase of action" in relation to the motor and intellectual activity of the individual.

When considered in this way, the role of perception does not rest solely in the detection of objects of a certain color or shape. A completely isolated object lacks any meaning and, therefore, any relevance. An object only affects behavior in so far as it has meaning (Michotte, 1926), and this arises from its relations to other objects, such as spatial and temporal relations, causal relations, and those of finality. The problem of meaning, therefore, ultimately has priority over that of form. One might wrongly conclude that, in principle, meaning has nothing to do with perception, because, as has been long assumed, all meaning is an extrinsic addition to the data provided by perception. However, this is not the case, and one must reconsider the question in light of the fact that it is also possible to perceive certain functional relations (as I later showed in my work on the impression of causality) and hence certain complex experiences have an intrinsic significance.

In any case, it was these views on the importance of the meanings that certain actions or objects could have for a person or animal observing them that prevented me from supporting an extreme form of behaviorism. I had become convinced that psychology was not a science of mental life but rather a science of behavior or action. It also appeared obvious that a thorough study of behaviour must take into account the way in which people and animals "understand" the situation in which they are placed and the actions of other people and animals, as well as those they perform themselves.

On the other hand, it was certainly the development of behaviorism that led me to concentrate on motor reactions in 1924 and for many years after, this work forming a complete series of very closely connected studies.

The first study arose from an unusual observation I had made concerning the speed with which one can perform a chain of movements involving reaching at a number of targets arranged irregularly on a surface and separated by a rather large distance from one another (van der Veldt, 1928). I had, in fact, discovered that the speed was practically the same whether the subject had performed this activity a great many times or for the first time, as long as sufficient time was given for an examination of the targets in advance. This finding raises the question of the exact role of motor training as such.

To resolve this issue, I used a technique based on an old procedure devised by Marey so that it was possible to obtain a photographic record of the trajectory followed by the subject's hand (or finger). We also recorded times, etc. These photographic records, "kinesigrams," provided an objective basis for a systematic study of the variations that occurred in the form of the trajectories.

It was immediately apparent that training involved profound changes in the movements. The appearance of the trajectories had quite a different character after training. It was clear that the orientation, extent, and form of each movement had become adapted to those of the movements that followed, and vice-versa. All the parts were integrated into a continuous whole and varied in relation to the entire group. This was an objective demonstration of something that had been recognized for a long time: that exercise leads to the development of unitary, global motor reactions and that these are triggered all at once. Furthermore, they were no longer "controlled" by a visual schema, and the sight of the targets merely served as a command analogous to the order to salute or to pick up something lying on a table.

Further experiments complemented this finding by revealing that the forms of the trajectories became stereotyped, being identical on successive occasions, and that they could also remain the same even when the subject was required to perform the task in another plane or on a different scale (i.e., the forms showed the Gestalt property of transposition).

Because the forms represented on the photographic records were the mechanical effect of the movements performed by the subjects, their characteristics must indicate certain properties of the movements themselves. One can conclude, therefore, that motor practice leads to the development of motor forms that are global and autonomous and possess similar properties to perceptual forms. This is an experimental demonstration of the relevance of Gestalt principles to the realm of motor movement and hence was a fresh contribution to Gestalt psychology, which, at that time, had only really been applied to the sensory domain.

This first study, however, had been concerned with many other issues, and the use of kinesigrams had been rather incidental. Later, however, they became central to our work concentrating on motor forms as such, and the study of temporal and spatial structures which I termed "the morphology of movement" (Michotte, 1938).

In 1931, we used an improved technique to study the way in which the trajectories become deformed when the movements had to be performed more and more quickly (Montpelier 1935). As is familiar in the case of handwriting, the trajectory could deviate very profoundly from the "mode," and the task was to discover which factors determine its form.

An initial point needs to be made in relation to this topic. The model presented visually to subjects can naturally be structured in various ways by different individuals, and they are able to provide an introspective description of how they "see" it. Our research showed that the form of the trajectory literally replicated the sensory structure as described, without the subjects being aware of it. Therefore, this constituted an actual objective record of the subjective organization and, furthermore, evidence of the importance of organization in determining the reaction.

There are, however, factors of a more purely motor nature. I noticed that many trajectories executed at high speeds and strongly deformed were strikingly similar to Lissajous figures. This led me to conclude that the movements of our limbs that control the trajectory are probably pendular movements. This was eventually confirmed in 1938 during new research conducted with other collaborators; using film to analyze the movements of different parts of the limbs, we found that the trajectories were in fact of the required form. The results served to show very clearly that continued movements of the segments of the limbs were of a pendular form.

As is well known, movements of this kind correspond to familiar physiological mechanisms, which enable them to occur under optimal conditions and particularly economically. From this, we concluded that such combinations of movements should be seen as preferred or "pregnant" forms that occur spontaneously if the conditions are appropriate. So here we have a further analogy between motor and sensory forms!

Furthermore, we found that subjects tended to organize their movements rhythmically and that these not only had a spatial but also a definite temporal structure, which was determined by the form of the model.

A new study, conducted in 1938 (Montpelier, 1946), required subjects to touch targets in time with a rhythm that was presented auditorily. This showed that the need to perform the movements rhythmically caused modifications in their trajectories that were specific to each rhythm. These changes were so characteristic that even after 3 month's delay, each rhythmic structure remained clearly the same, and there was no significant effect of practice.

Regardless of their basis, these deformations of the trajectories raised a further problem. It seemed obvious that they should cause a decrease in the accuracy with which the targets were touched, and so we turned out attention to this issue. In 1933 we used new techniques, notably so-called typtograms, which record the distributions of taps, along with kinesigrams (MacNeill, 1934). The results confirmed our hypothesis in a general way and showed that the accuracy of performance was a function of its rhythm as much as its speed. They also showed, however, that the forms of the trajectories traced by various subjects who responded with the same degree of accuracy could differ profoundly from one another.

Other studies performed in 1936 and the following years were devoted to the following topics: the improvement in accuracy for rapid movements; the morphological characteristics of automatic motor reactions of everyday life; movement acceleration; the transfer of motor training; etc.

In our work on motor reactions, we constantly encountered the problem of rhythm, and so, in 1935, we began a systematic study of rhythm as such (Fraisse, 1946). This confirmed that rhythm must be treated as a temporal form, analogous to spatial forms, and occurs in various sensory domains, as well as in motor activity.

Moreover, an intensive study of the spontaneous development of rhythm revealed that the rhythmic meter is internally organized to a really surprising extent in terms of its structural complexity, as well as its extraordinary precision and stability.

Although a lengthy discussion would be distracting, I should at least say that in spontaneous rhythm the "beats" constituting the complex "measures" are of two kinds: simple successions and durations, which are combined in various ways. These "beats" are functionally integrated, for a change in one is associated with a change in all the others so as to maintain the structure of the whole group. Certain types of organization, therefore, are favored, and, when an attempt is made to impose a different rhythmic form on the subjects, their reactions tend to move towards a pregnant structure at the cost of systematic deviations from the given model.

Finally, the favored temporal structure occurs spontaneously, and always in the same way, even when the total duration of the "measure" is varied to a quite considerable extent, or when the reactions are brought about by different parts of the body, such as the hand, the foot, or the head. There is, therefore, transposition.

These studies count as a novel contribution to Gestalt psychology, and, as far as I know, are the first intensive experiments on particular aspects of temporal form.

Our work on motor activity gave us the chance to make numerous observations concerning learning, and this led my research into two new directions: the law of effect, which I will discuss shortly, and the traditional problem of "association."

In relation to the latter problem, our initial work of 1924 had neatly confirmed the views of Lewin on the ultimately dynamic nature of "associations through contiguity" for they showed that connections established in this way were never sufficient in themselves to give rise to the associate following the mere presence of the "inducing" item. Instead, reproduction seemed to depend on distinct dynamic factors, such as the effect of the "task" undertaken by the subject. Furthermore, we also found that the errors in reproduction, which involved learned reactions different from those required from the subject, occurred when the appropriate form of response was similar or almost identical to that of previously learned movements.

This was reminiscent of our early study on logical memory since, in both cases, the unitary, global form established during training was completely restored at the moment of reproduction, as long as a sufficiently characteristic part of it was present.

In all these respects, there was an obvious analogy here with the Gestaltists' view of the "laws of association" as being ultimately inseparable from the laws that govern the formation of global structures.

To understand this matter more precisely, I devised some new experiments in 1937 to compare the probability that one item (a familiar object or meaningless geometrical figure) would be elicited by another when they had simply been presented at the same time, either spatially juxtaposed at the time of learning, or else organized into a global unit. This unit was sometimes purely spatial or formal such as the partial superposition of the two; at other times, their relation was "internal" in the form of a picture representing certain functional relations between the two items, such as an-axe-chopping-wood. The general result could be readily predicted, in that the probability of arousal was much greater when the organizing factors during learning were stronger; the temporal relations seemed to have no special priority in this respect.

These experiments clearly revealed the need to correct a general principle. In order for rearousal to be possible, it is obviously essential that the "part" to be reproduced should not be absorbed into the entire unit when it was established, but rather should retain its own phenomenal existence. This being so, it would appear that the general principle should be reformulated as follows: the optimum conditions for rearousal are those where the formation of the strongest units are compatible with the persistence of sufficient autonomy among the parts that constitute the whole. This principle, by the way, goes far to explain the superiority of so-called "logical memory."

Turning now to the "law of effect," we had already established that during motor training of rapid responses the form of the trajectories changed successively at critical points so that their execution became easier; this was an absolutely unconscious process. It was clear that the law of effect could be applied to this phenomenon.

Therefore, I investigated the extent to which the recollection of rewards and punishments could influence intentional learning; the aim was to discover if the law of effect could be explained, in part at least, by the effect of conscious recall. These experiments, which were similar to Thorndike's in design, examined the respective frequencies with which subjects recalled the rewards and punishments that had been assigned to particular "connections" at the time of training. The results showed that rewards were recalled more frequently, but what was really significant was that this superiority primarily arose from false recollections, that is, cases where the subjects wrongly believed that the connection had been rewarded when in fact it had been punished. Thus, the conclusion was ultimately negative: It could not be the recollection of the rewards which led the subjects to make intentional connections that had actually been rewarded during successive trials in training.

Other studies on the law of effect attempted to resolve the contradiction, which, as I saw it, existed between the general principle of the positive effects of satisfaction in Thorndike's sense, and the fact, confirmed by Lewin, that the interruption of an activity leads to its improved fixation in memory, as the latter would seem to count as a kind of punishment. This led to an interpretation of the law of effect, which was very different from Thorndike's; according to this alternative view, reward does not serve to reinforce a connection, but rather to maintain the state of tension created by the instructions concerning training (see Nuttin, 1942). I will not discuss this conception any further; it was mainly developed later on by Professor Nuttin and formed the basis for a whole series of studies.

Experimental Phenomenology: 1939 Onwards

The year 1939 was a turning point in my career and marks the beginning of a period when, still employing experimental methods, I confronted some problems fundamental to phenomenology: the problems of causality, permanence, and apparent reality in our experience of the external world.

Phenomenal causality. Having been asked to write an article for the *Tijdschrift voor Philosophie* (Michotte 1941; see also Michotte, 1946), I decided to treat the problem of the perception of action, which had already provided the topic of a paper presented to the International Congress of Psychology at Yale, and of lectures given at the Collége de France in Paris in 1937.

On the basis of incidental observations, I had long been convinced that we can perceive the "actions" performed by objects or animate beings on one another in the same way as we can see simple movements. However, since I wanted to provide confirmation for this claim and subject it to critical examination, I attempted to find a means of experimental proof.

Fortunately, I then thought of a way of producing combinations of movements of several objects in a systematic fashion. This was based on the well-known movement illusion, which occurs when a line is moved behind a screen with a slit such that the slit forms an angle to that line. Using this technique, I was immediately able to perform an experiment intended to represent the case of the impact between two billiard balls (by two patches of color). The result was obvious. All the observers agreed that they *"saw one of the objects strike the other and push it away."*

This result was just the first step, for it hardly went further than casual observation. It was then necessary to vary the experimental conditions so as to determine the factors responsible for this kind of response from the subjects (genetic analysis) (Michotte, 1963, p. 18).

The conditions were shown to be extraordinarily precise and specific, not only spatially (in terms of the length and direction of the trajectories) but also in terms of the temporal aspect (the duration of contact) and the kinetic aspect (the absolute and relative speeds of the two objects). By applying the method of concomitant variations, it was possible to confirm that there was a direct relation of dependence between a definite system of stimulation and the presence in the observers of an impression *x*, which they characterized by expressions referring to a causal relation. This argument, and others also based on experimental data, demonstrated that, whatever else, this impression *x* must be a specific Gestalt; it was quite different from a mere combination of movements to which an external meaning had become attached in the way, for example, that meaning becomes attached to the visual form of words in language.

I then made every effort to go further than this conclusion (and the views on introspection I had adopted in the middle phase of my career) and sought to clarify the nature of the impression as such.

Reflecting on all the data I had obtained in my work, I was able to formulate the theory of "ampliation of movement," which implied that the impression obtained is one of genuine production of the displacement of the moved object by the blow it receives (Michotte, 1963) and thereby possesses an intrinsic meaning.

It was natural to extend what I had found in relation to vision to the tactile-kinaesthetic field and hence to the impression of the causal influence that we exert on external objects by means of limbs. This research extended and complemented my early work on the awareness of activity in inner experience (in voluntary choice) by now stressing a new aspect of the question: the perception of the action of our own bodies.

All these findings clearly contradicted the classic thesis of Hume, which denied the possibility of perceiving the production of one event by another. In so far as this is a factual matter, the point now seems settled. However, since my research is based solely on the phenomenological approach, it implies no fixed stand on the epistemological status of causality. I need to stress this because there have been various misunderstandings.

The research on the perception of causality turned my attention to two questions about the perception of the actions of living beings.

The first concerned the particular appearance of living movements. Do they show certain special characteristics that make us treat them as being produced by the animal itself (i.e., as immanent)? The answer was clear once we showed that it was easy to produce combinations of movements of passive objects (color patches), which yielded an impression completely analogous to the crawling of an animal, such as a worm for example. Appropriate variations of the kinetic conditions showed that the impression was tied to some of them, and hence that we were once again dealing with a specific perceptual form. We later found that it was possible to formulate a fairly satisfactory theory of the nature of this perceptual form (Knops, 1947).

The second question concerns a different point that is theoretically of much greater importance. Given that some writers hold that it is possible to "perceive" the intentional character of human and animal actions, the question arises of whether this too might be a rather primitive, specific impression based on particular configurations of movements. Supposing these movements were combined so as to give the observer the impression of actions involving several (in this case, inert) objects, it was plausible that, under specific conditions, certain phases might seem to occur "in order to lead to what followed" or, at least, as "preparing for them," etc. The results of our earlier experiments and many observations concerning successive Gestalts indicated that such a hypothesis was not ridiculous and well worth investigating.

We therefore conducted trials in which combinations of rather complex movements of colored patches served as a schematic representation of human or animal actions, such as pursuit, flight, or detour. Forty different combinations which were as diverse as I could imagine, were used, but the result was negative as long as I studied observers who were unaware of the purpose of my research; the perceived chain of events seemed purely mechanical.

As soon as they were given the slightest hint that human actions were being represented, however, finalistic interpretations were elicited from them, and these interpretations naturally showed themselves to be predominantly independent of the systematic variations made to the system of stimulation. The significance of the responses of the observers was therefore quite different from that in the experiments on causality; this case evidently involves "extrinsic meanings."

Of course, this conclusion is restricted to the context of our own experiments; but, in any case, it would seem that they serve to show that if there really is a phenomenal character of intentionality inherent in the perception of certain activities, then it must occur under thoroughly different conditions from those that give rise to the impression of causality. Furthermore, one can appreciate the need for caution in these matters and the care needed to distinguish by adequate criteria what is a phenomenal character, in the proper sense, from an extrinsic meaning. This may be especially difficult in the present case, since such intentional significance could probably often arise from a process of projection that will only be detected with difficulty.

Phenomenal permanence. In the course of my work on the impression of causality, I studied different forms it could take. This led me to wonder if it would be possible to use my method to produce the impression of one object compressing another. The experiments were performed as follows: A moving object A (an elongated rectangle) moved towards an object B of the same shape; after they had made contact, A continued to move in the same direction while B decreased in length as A advanced.

To my great surprise, no observer perceived the shortening of object B. Instead, everyone agreed that it was merely covered by A, which slid in front of it and progressively concealed it. This was extremely interesting because the hidden object seemed to remain present, and retain its identity, even though certain parts of it had become invisible (or had even disappeared entirely).

I immediately decided to conduct a systematic investigation of this remarkable case of phenomenal permanence. Some very diverse experiments were performed and showed that this was a special phenomenon and not (as one might have imagined) a case of "interpretation," or even an "assimilation" arising from acquired knowledge or the direct effect of past experience. The "theory" of this phenomenon was easy to formulate and confirm by numerous findings. According to the theory, this phenomenon, too, involves the principles of structural organization, particularly those controlling whether a boundary separating two objects seems to belong to the first or second object (Sampaio, 1943; Knops, 1947).

We then investigated other examples of apparent permanence, as well as cases of nonpermanence, where one either has the impression of "creation" or "annihilation" (for example, bubbles of air at the surface of a liquid). I realized that the whole problem had to be approached in terms of the psychology of time. "Creation" and "annihilation" imply that the object or event has its own temporal limits, whereas permanence occurs when there are no such intrinsic temporal boundaries (Michotte, 1950).

Thus, the problem of the "belongingness of boundaries" occurs both in the temporal and spatial domain. The further my research developed, the more I came to see how crucial it is for the understanding of the phenomenal world. The following is a new example of this.

The problem of permanence is also connected with that of the perception of change (such as a change of shape, size, or color), since there can only be change to the extent that the "thing" that changes remains in some respects the same; if not, there is simply a substitution of one thing by another. We have therefore devoted some new studies to this phenomenon.

Our attention was especially drawn to the case in which an object or group of objects becomes larger by the addition of new parts. This is an important example since it appears to constitute the intuitive foundation of the arithmetical concept of addition, and thus the fundamental starting point of mathematics. Here again permanence is essential, for true addition is only possible as long as the "parts" continue to exist in the "whole."

The findings led to the conclusion that such addition gives rise to a process of structural reorganization, which includes an apparent displacement of the external boundary of the object so that it appears to get bigger. This enlargement (temporarily, at least) preserves the object's identity and thus its permanence. I have termed this phenomenon "incorporation;" it probably has an important role in the understanding of addition in mathematics, although this could only be established, of course, by a different kind of investigation.

Apparent Reality. My work on the impression of causality also led me in a third direction. I had been struck by the fact that the subjects had the impression that the impact between the objects was real (in the physical sense) rather than just a mere representation of such a collision. Yet, of course, they were aware of the technique employed and therefore knew that it only involved an optical illusion. This observation aroused my curiosity, and so I attempted to investigate the apparent reality of perceptual data by experimental means. I felt that a good method would be to compare systematically cases that involve apparent reality and those which do not. The most obvious example is that of a volume represented in a perspective picture compared with the corresponding solid object itself (Michotte, 1948a, 1948b).

I can summarize the essential results of these studies as follows. The same combination of lines that form a perspective representation of a volume and hence are objectively restricted to the plane of the picture surface, can, according to the conditions, either give the impression of an unreal volume (a picture) or of a volume with the same degree of apparent reality as that of a solid, physical object used as a comparison.

The first effect occurs when the structural organization of perception is such that the lines seem to be traced upon, and to belong to, a surface. However it is possible by a suitable technique to apparently detach the lines from any surface of support and hence apparently release them into the third dimension; once this is achieved, there is the impression of the reality of the volume.

This result clearly allows the variations of the conditions of the experiment so as to obtain at will either effect and to shift gradually from one to the other. This demonstrates that the character of reality, in the example investigated, can occur to different degrees.

It seems we can conclude therefore that this character of reality must be treated as a special *dimension* of perceptual experience, which, as in the other cases, corresponds to a definite kind of structural organization.

Summary

We have gradually accumulated a great deal of data, which I am still trying to extend. (This is why only a part of our findings has been published up until now.) But these results make it possible to envisage a general framework, the outlines of which are already reasonably clear.

It now seems certain that our sensory experiences (and by this I mean all the impressions corresponding directly to rather complex systems of stimulation) are infinitely richer in content than could have ever been anticipated.

It also seems that this richness does not arise from learning alone. In my view, at least, all our findings suggest the contrary. The fundamental structure of the phenomenal world is ensured directly by the influence of those laws that control the organization of the perceptual field. Although the importance of acquired experience is not denied, it serves to complement, supplement, confirm or correct the structure already formed.

Our research suggests that this primitive structure occurs in the form of a world of "things" that are separate from one another and are either passive or else animate bodies ultimately endowed with specific "vital" movements.

These things normally possess a character of *reality* which differentiates them from the unreal or imaginary.

Furthermore, most of them are *permanent,* in the sense that their apparent existence is not solely determined by the *actual* action of the corresponding sensory stimulation, since they persist either before or after such stimulation.

Finally, these things, and the processes they enter into, are linked to one another not only by their relations in space and time, but also by all kinds of functional relations. These include the multiple forms in which mechanical causality occurs, the Screen effect (the phenomenal persistence of an object which "disappears" behind another), pursuit, flight, etc. Thanks to these functional relations, objects as well as events have an intrinsic significance prior to any extrinsic meaning they might later derive as a result of increasing experience.

In brief, in the phenomenal world, or world of "appearance", there seems to be a kind of "prefiguration" of abstract concepts, the mental "categories" of substance, reality, and causality, which underlie the conception that human beings spontaneously develop concerning the physical world which surrounds them (Michotte, 1948c).

This possibly throws some light on the origin of these concepts, but we ought to stress the biological importance of such spontaneous organization of the phenomenal world since only such organization could enable the individual (whether human or animal) to adapt its reactions before any individual experience had the opportunity to provide it with any structure.

Furthermore, it should be clear that such prefiguration justifies the profound analogies that exist between the behavior of animals and humans despite the absence, presumably, in the case of animals of those "higher" functions that enable humans to comprehend intellectually the world in which they live.

Overview

Having mentally retraced the entire course of my scientific life, which is now drawing to a close, I think I can say that I have remained faithful to the views I arrived at in my youth and to which I referred at the beginning of this account. I considered that I had special ability at experimental research, and I have remained an experimenter throughout my career. I have always attempted to gather material that is as reliable as possible and hence capable of supporting the general syntheses that I felt must wait for the future and, perhaps, for minds better suited than my own.

Nevertheless, my work in no way seems to me a mere "hunt for facts" or the simple collection of observations, for this would have been a rather sterile enterprise.

The experiments I have performed, as well as my efforts at deriving conclusions, have always been dominated by the concern to contribute to the study of one or another of the large questions that has continued to preoccupy me. If my work has been productive it is precisely for this reason, for I have thought again and again about the questions that intrigue me. These have developed in my mind, and their solutions, although initially vague, have gradually been transformed and settled. Finally, after many long years, long-standing problems have suddenly appeared in a quite different light. I am profoundly convinced—and I am sure this is no exaggeration—that my work of the last 10 years on phenomenology represents the outcome of an entire life of research and reflection.

Teaching and Other Activities

My teaching has, by force of circumstances, extended well beyond my own field of research, although it has been constantly nurtured by the latter. In the light of what I have been saying, it should be easy to appreciate that the views I have presented in my lectures have been rather eclectic and have developed a great deal during the course of my career. However, if I were to identify their dominant feature and provide an appropriate label, I would be tempted to call "my" psychology dynamic and, at once, both functionalist and structuralist. I have, in fact, approached every problem with reference to action, stressing the directing and motivating roles of needs and dispositions, as well as the characteristic attitudes of the active individual. On the other hand, of course, I have also especially emphasized the principles of structural organization (the Gestalt) of action itself. This organized structure constitutes a veritable "cell" of behavior and of the events that it involves: perception, emotion, thought, and motor reactions.

My teaching has not been restricted to the University of Louvain. No doubt because of my knowledge of different languages, a large part of my professional career has been taken up by lectures and courses presented at other universities. I have been honored by invitations to teach in Holland, England, Germany, France, Switzerland, Italy, Spain, and the United States. I will mention in particular the invitation from Stanford University to teach as a visiting professor during the summer session of 1929.

Furthermore, I have, on many occasions, presented my ideas and the results of our work to the International Congress of Psychology, which I have regularly attended since 1905, as well as to certain meetings of foreign psychological societies.

Finally, we have recently established contacts between different laboratories involving collective visits lasting several days between the members of one department of psychology and another. These have already occurred between Amsterdam and Louvain, as well as Cambridge (England) and Louvain. Such exchanges have proved so useful and stimulating that it seems highly desirable to extend the scheme as far as is practical.

It is in this same spirit of collaboration that I founded with the generous support of my colleagues the Belgian Psychological Society in 1947. This new society was required, as I saw it, given the growth of psychological research in Belgium.

Before concluding, I wish to stress most strongly the immense value of my many personal contacts with my colleagues abroad. These have allowed me to discuss topics of common interest, to see their work more closely, . . . and also to sort out my own ideas when I have had to present lectures. This has contributed tremendously to the development of my scientific work, not to mention the many invaluable friendships that have arisen in the course of all these contacts.

References

Fraisse, P. (1946). Contribution a l'étude du rythme en tant que forme temporelle [A contribution to the study of rhythm considered as a temporal form]. *Journal de Psychologie, 39,* 280–304.

Knops, L. (1947). Contribution a l'étude de la "naissance" et de la "permanence" phénoménales dans le champ visuel [A contribution to the study of phenomenal "coming into being" and "permanence" within the visual field]. *Miscellanea Psychologica A. Michotte.* Louvain: Editions de l'Institut Supérieur de Philosophie.

MacNeill, H. (1934). Motor adaptation and accuracy. *Études de Psychologie, 5,* 1–303.

Michotte A. (1904). Contribution a l'étude de l'histologie fine de la cellule nerveuse [Contribution to the study of the detailed histology of the nerve cell]. *Bulletin de l'Académie Royale de Médecine de Belgique, 53,* 515–556.

Michotte, A. (1905). *Les signes régionaux* [Local signs]. Louvain: Institut Supérieur de Philosophie.

Michotte, A. (1912). Note à propos de contributions récentes à la psychologie de la volonté. [Note concerning recent contributions to the psychology of will]. *Études de Psychologie* (Louvain), *1,* 193–233.

Michotte, A. (1922). Note sur la mesure de l'énergie acoustique au moyen du miroir de Rayleigh [Note on the measurement of acoustic energy with the Rayleigh mirror]. *Archives Néerlandaises de Physiologie, 7,* 579–587.

Michotte, A. (1936). Psychologie et philosophie [Psychology and philosophy]. *Revue Néoscolastique de Philosophie* (Louvain), *39,* 208–228.

Michotte, A. (1926). Rapport sur la perception des formes [Address on the perception of form]. *Congrès International de Psychologie de Groningen,* pp. 89–97.

Michotte, A. (1938). L'étude morphologique des réactions motrices [The morphological study of motor reactions]. *Onzième Congrès International de Psychologie, Paris,* pp. 29–41.

Michotte, A. (1941). La causalité physique: est-elle une donnée phénoménale? [Is physical causality a phenomenal datum?]. *Tijdschrift voor Philosophie, 3,* 290–328.

Michotte, A. (1946). La perception de la causalité [The perception of causality]. *Études de Psychologie* (Louvain), *4,* 1–296.

Michotte, A. (1948a). L'énigme psychologique de la perspective dans le dessin linéaire [The psychological enigma of perspective in line drawings]. *Bulletin de la Classe des Lettres de l'Académie Royale de Belgique* (5me serie), *34,* 268–288.

Michotte, A. (1948b). Le caractère de "realité" des projections cinematographiques [The character of 'reality' in cinematic projections]. *Revue Internationale de Filmologie, 1,* 249–261.

Michotte, A. (1948c). La préfiguration dans les données sensorielles de notre conception spontanée du monde physique [The prefiguration within sensory data of our spontaneous conception of the physical world]. *Comptes-rendus du XXIIme Congrés International de Psychologie à Edinburgh.*

Michotte, A. (1950). A propos de la permanence phénoménale: Faits et théories [On phenomenal permanence: Facts and theories]. *Acta Psychologica, 7,* 298–322.

Michotte, A. (1963). *The perception of causality.* (T.R. Miles & E. Miles, Trans.) London: Methuen.

Michotte, A., & Prüm, E. (1910). *Étude expérimentale sur le choix volontaire et ses antécédents immédiats* [The experimental study of voluntary choice and its immediate antecedents]. Louvain: Éditions de l'Institut Supérieur de Philosophie.

Michotte, A., & Ransy, C. (1912). Contribution a l'étude sur la mémoire logique [Contribution to the study of logical memory]. *Études de Psychologie, 1,* 1–96.

Michotte, A., & Portych, T. (1912). Deuxième étude sur la memoire logique [A second study of logical memory]. *Études de Psychologie, 1,* 237–346.

Montpelier, G. de. (1935). Les altérations morphologiques des mouvements rapides [Morphological changes in rapid movements]. *Études de Psychologie, 4,* 1–251.

Montpelier, G. de. (1946). Note sur le rythme dans les mouvements volontaires de la main [Note on the rhythm of voluntary hand movements]. *Journal de*

Psychologie, 39, 467–473.

Nuttin, J. (1942). De Finalitet in het menselijk handelen en het Connectionisme: Een Studie over der wet van het Effect [Finality in human behavior and connectionism: A study of the law of effect]. *Tijdschrift voor Philosphie, 4,* 235–268.

Sampaio, A.C. (1943). La translation des objets comme facteur de leur permanence phénoménale [The translation of objects as a factor in their phenomenal permanence]. Louvain: Éditions de l'Institut Supérieur de Philosophie.

van der Veldt, J. (1928). L'apprentissage du mouvement et l'automatisme [The training of movement and automatism]. *Études de Psychologie, 3,* 1–350.

[illegible]

2
Phenomenal Causality

PHENOMENAL CAUSALITY
Alan Costall

The term "positivism" has come to embrace so many different issues that it defies simple definition. As Raymond Williams has noted, it is now hardly more than a "swear word, by which nobody is swearing" (Williams, 1983, p. 239). Indeed, in recent psychology, and especially social psychology, the term is identified with the very idea of an experimental psychology. There have been two episodes in the history of psychology, however, where the methods (and prestige) of experimental science were themselves directed against some of the main foundations of positivism in psychology, and Michotte participated, as a significant figure, in each of these developments. The first was the Würzburg research of Külpe and his students on "imageless thought"; their work explicitly challenged the sensationalist assumption of positivistic psychology by showing that human awareness is not restricted to sensory contents. The second challenge to positivism involved the psychology of perception, and was directed, to a remarkable degree, against a single assumption of traditional theory, the "constancy hypothesis." According to this hypothesis, the sensory effects of local stimulation are supposed to be fixed, and hence uninfluenced by the wider context. The Berlin Gestaltists (Wertheimer, Köhler, and Koffka) tend to be given the main credit for this particular challenge to the atomistic and mechanistic basis of positivistic psychology, yet, in fact, it involved a much wider and disparate group of researchers (including Rubin, Katz and Michotte).

The psychology of perception provides a wide range of examples that run counter to the constancy hypothesis: "reversible figures", where the same stimulation gives rise to distinctly different effects; geometrical and other illusions, where the wider context can have a profound effect on the appearance of a part of the display; and a diverse set of cases where what is experienced transcends any local property of the visual field. For example, David Katz's (1935) classic work on surface color perception describes numerous examples of colour effects, such as transparency, shadow, and glossiness, that do not hold for isolated patches of colored light. Many of these cases involve "scission" or "phenomenal duplication" so that in transparency, for example, the same region of the visual field is simultaneously experienced as a transparent surface and as the opaque surface it happens to overlay.

As Metzger (1928) has noted, we tend to associate the notion of *Gestalt* with static form or shape and yet the research often involved movement and change. In fact, the term *Bildung,* rather than *Gestalt,* would often be more appropriate since it implies the idea of an evolving or transforming structure. Indeed, the textbook example of the research directed against the constancy hypothesis is, of course, the early work by Wertheimer on apparent movement (see Kolers, 1972, for a very useful discussion). Wertheimer sought to demonstrate that the perception of movement is not the mere experience of the (remembered) change of location of an object; indeed, he showed that, under certain conditions, "pure movement" can occur where one continues to see movement even though the object undergoing the movement can no longer be recognized as such. Movement, Wertheimer concluded, is a phenomenon in its own right and not derivative.

In a similar way, Michotte attempted to show that causality is a phenomenon in its own right, distinct from the experience of mere succession. In doing so, however, he was not merely questioning the constancy hypothesis but also challenging the specific claim of positivistic psychology that causality is not perceived. Michotte was not the first to suggest that causality is a qualitively distinct experience; the issue had even been raised in the context of the earlier Würzburg research (Pillsbury, 1904). Previously, however, the perception of causality had usually been explained as the effect of projection or attribution of the perceiver's own feelings of muscular effort to inanimate objects. Michotte, however, contended that causality can be immediately experienced through vision alone. This claim is remarkable because it implies that visual stimulation does not simply give rise to an emergent structure but one that is meaningful and in no obvious sense "visual" at all. For this reason, the fundamental question addressed by Michotte in his work on causality is bound to sound rather paradoxical: What does mechanical causality *look like*?

Michotte's first step was to devise schematic displays that would produce a clear example of causality. He found that under appropriate spatiotemporal conditions a colored square would appear to move toward a second square and give it a "push" so that the second square only appeared to move because of the movement of the first square. The second step in his research then involved the manipulation of the stimulus conditions in various ways so as to determine the optimal conditions for the impression of causality and those conditions which led to the destruction of the effect. What impressed Michotte (and others subsequently) about the outcome of these two phases of his work was, first, that such a schematic display could produce a vivid impression of causality, and, second, that this effect could be completely destroyed by minimal changes of the spatiotemporal conditions of the displays.

The third step depended upon the observers' careful descriptions of the displays—on the contrast between the appearance of the causal and noncausal conditions. Michotte relied on such descriptions to establish a psychological account of perceived causality, the theory of ampliation. According to this theory, the appearance of the "productivity" of the active object in a causal event arises from the phenomenal extension of its own movement to another object, the latter seeming to be merely "displaced" in a passive way by the movement of the agent. (For Michotte's own comments on his methods, see Michotte, 1963, pp. 18–19, 307–313.)

As Michotte himself acknowledged, his theory of ampliation drew upon Katz's concept of phenomenal duplication (Michotte, 1947). After the collision of the two objects, the passive object is seen to move and yet the movement appears to belong, not to that object, but rather to the now static, active object. Michotte's insistence on trying to capture descriptively what it is that characterizes a particular phenomenon, allied him not only with Katz but also with Rubin. He had little interest in the physiological speculations of the Berlin Gestaltists, and their talk of cortical fields and isomorphism. In addition, however, his work on causality was prompted by an issue he felt the Gestaltists had neglected, if not ignored: the problem of how we relate adaptively to the world in which we find ourselves.

The Primacy of Functional Relations

Several aspects of Michotte's own development encouraged his commitment to what he called the "action perspective." Functionalism itself was a dominant movement among French-speaking psychologists at the beginning of this century (Guillaume, 1937, pp. 216–17). Then, as Michotte explained in his autobiography, his early research with the Würzburg school also turned his attention in this direction. Just as his later work sought to undermine the positivists' denial of the psychological reality of causality (Klein, 1970), so some of his earliest research (Michotte & Prüm, 1910) attempted to show that the "self" and the "will" were more than mere fictions, and that we are conscious of our own *agency* (Michotte, 1963, p. 11; cf. Pillsbury, 1904). Finally, although Michotte never explored the issue in his writings, his own research was conducted in a Catholic university (indeed, he himself was a devout Catholic). In fact, the institute in which Michotte worked for most of his career had been established by the Catholic Church with the specific purpose of promoting the philosophy of St. Thomas Aquinas. An important aim was to challenge Cartesianism, and, in particular, the idea that we are, by nature, set apart from the world and somehow acquire knowledge in spite of, rather than by means of, our body (Gilson, 1924; Pieper, 1963, pp. 121–132). All these influences reinforced Michotte's view that objects are experienced ultimately in terms of their functional significance for our activities:

> It is futile to study perception "in itself." It must be treated as a "phase of action" in relation to the motor and intellectual activity of the individual. . . . An object only affects behavior in so far as it has meaning, and this only arises from its functional relations to other objects, be they spatial or temporal relations, or relations of causality or purposiveness, etc. The problem of meaning, therefore, ultimately has priority over that of form. (Michotte, 1954, p. 200)

The Perception of Causality

Michotte's research on phenomenal causality was an attempt to substantiate the claim he made many years before, that certain functional relations between objects can be immediately experienced or, as he put it, "directly lived," and hence that some experiences can be *intrinsically* meaningful (see Gavin, 1972).

His book on the perception of causality (Michotte, 1946/1963) was recognized as a classic from the outset. What was valued about this work was its attempt to go beyond the rather introverted and straitlaced kind of experimental psychology in which experimentation is promoted to the position of end rather than means. The reviewers stressed the refreshing flexibility of its approach, such as the extensive use of subjects' spontaneous reports, in order to address a genuinely significant problem (see, for example, Gogel, 1964; Guillaume, 1947; Ogden, 1949; Oldfield, 1949; Vernon, 1963; Zangwill, 1963).

An old friend of Michotte's, Frederic Bartlett, wrote to him on receiving the American edition of the book, emphasizing its value as a corrective to the narrow vision of the current experimental psychology:

> I hope that its appearance in English in the USA will distract some at least of the brighter young people there, away from some of the rather fruitless and trivial things they seem to do now, towards the vital and basic problems that you have shown how to tackle. . . . Sometimes it seems to me that we have got into a jam, with overmuch information theory which tends towards preoccupation with interminable somewhat small detail and conducts most of us away from a study of the more humane interests. (Bartlett, 1963)

Wolfgang Köhler, in a letter written to Michotte toward the close of World War II, went even further, stressing that Michotte's studies of causality had implications well beyond psychology itself:

> My dear man, I cannot think of any discovery that would be so apt to start things in a better direction as this finding is. Naturally, the repercussions will extend far beyond our special discipline. For, if I am not mistaken, the doctrine that we experience nothing but facts of concomitance and mere sequence is one of the ultimate factors behind the present scepticism and the corresponding crises in every field, including that of ethics and politics. . . . I admit, the Positivists have meant no harm. They have none the less almost succeeded in destroying human culture. Am I mistaken in believing that you see your discovery in this wide context? (Köhler, 1944)

Clearly, Michotte's work on causality was valued as much more than a mere exercise in experimentation for its own sake. I have stressed this point because recent criticisms have suggested the contrary: that Michotte's work was regarded primarily for its experimental rigor, and that this rigor was illusory.

Michotte's Experimental Methods

In the 1970s, the credibility of Michotte's research was called into serious question (Beasley, 1968; Joynson 1970, 1971 but see also Boyle, 1972, 1973; Montpelier & Nuttin, 1973). The basic criticism was that although Michotte had taken great care to specify the details of the displays used in his research, "the factors connected with the subjects and their reports were neglected or mishandled" (Joynson 1971, p. 293).

To some degree, Michotte had anticipated these criticisms. He supervised some extensive research by Geneviève Crabbé, comparing trained and naive observers, which essentially confirmed his main conclusions about the generality and immediacy of the basic causal effects (Crabbé, 1967; see also Boyle 1973; Vernon 1972). Yet the question still remains: Why had Michotte himself not taken greater care? Most of his own studies were conducted not only with very few people, but usually these people were colleagues and students well aware of the purpose of the experiment and perhaps under some obligation to conform (Beasley, 1968; Boyle 1972; Joynson, 1970, 1971). In addition, he seems to have been rather cavalier about the use of statistical techniques, and was little perturbed by "analytical observers"—or, to use Richard Walk's nice term, "Titchenerians" (Walk, 1984, p. 214)—who failed to report causal effects even under the optimal stimulus conditions.

Boyle has suggested that Michotte's experiments should really be understood as "demonstrations" along the lines of the familiar examples found in texts of Gestalt psychology (Boyle, 1972). Yet Michotte certainly thought of himself as an experimenter, and, furthermore, his studies of causality were performed toward the end of a long career in which he had already established a reputation as an important experimental psychologist. It is tempting to excuse Michotte (after all, his causality research was conducted during the most difficult, not to say threatening, of times—during the German occupation of Belgium). But I believe this would avoid the basic issue. What did Michotte himself understand by experimentation, and how did his conception of experimentation relate to his fundamental purpose?

As I have explained at the beginning of this section, the role of the observers in his experiments was not simply to provide responses but to offer descriptions that would warrant the use of causal terms. Thus, to a degree unusual in modern psychology, the observers were themselves *meant* to be involved in the process of theory development. Given these objectives, it should be clear why Michotte felt it natural to enlist the help of reliable observers, such as colleagues and students who appreciated the nature and point of his research. Within Michotte's own terms of reference, the use of expert observers was not a question of carelessness at all, but was in accord with his own idea of the nature of psychological experimentation and the relation between the experimenter and the "subject." Moreover, his view of experimentation was hardly idiosyncratic. The underlying premise of Michotte's critics in their charge of carelessness—that there has been (or could be) only one notion of the experimenter-subject relation—is simply mistaken. As Danziger (1985a) has recently explained, from its inception, experimental psychology has possessed two basic models for the social structure of the psychological experiment. One, which derives from early clinical work on hypnosis ("the Paris model"), now largely dominates our discipline and presupposes a rigid distinction between experimenter and subject. However, the kind of experimentation to which Michotte had been introduced in his earliest research with Wundt and Külpe ("the Leipzig model") assumed the interchangeability of these roles; indeed, it was often the "subject" in such experiments who eventually published the results of the investigation!

The point is that we can only properly assess the charges of casualness (or worse) on Michotte's part by reference to his own intellectual context, and not by imposing our current canons of good practice. This point also holds with respect to Michotte's apparent disregard of so-called "analytic observers" and his neglect of group statistics. As Buytendijk has noted, Michotte was a living example of his commitment to the principle that functional relations are essential in giving significance to the objects in our surroundings. In describing Michotte's approach to research, he made reference to Goethe's *Faust:* "What Nature does not make manifest to your spirit cannot be forced from her with levers and screws" (Buytendijk, 1947, p. 27). According to Buytendijk, Michotte was convinced that the meaning of objects and events in our surroundings was manifest and could be revealed to any attentive observer by arranging the conditions appropriately. As far as Michotte was concerned, the failure of any particular observer to report causality under the supposedly optimal conditions did not constitute evidence against the proposition that there is "an immanent order in which we can participate" (Buytendijk, 1947, p. 27). What impressed Michotte was that *some* observers could indeed respond lawfully to the various conditions of his causality displays to the degree previously only found in the research on "sensory psychophysics." His critics, however, were committed to the quite different conception of perception as necessarily probabilistic and to a corresponding statistical method that simply *assumes* that the variability of group data is representative of the individual case (Danziger, 1985b). Failing to consider the suitability of Michotte's methods to his purposes, they could only question his competence and good faith.

New Directions in Causality Research

The primary purpose of the preceding has been to provide an insight into the intellectual context of Michotte's work to help contemporary readers appreciate its purpose and significance, and to counter some of the criticisms leveled against Michotte as an experimenter. But how do Michotte's findings and ideas now stand, in the light of subsequent research and theory?

Michotte's basic purpose was to establish that causality can be *seen*, that there is something *visually distinct* about such events; but he seems to have been confused about exactly what this claim implies. He often argued that the restriction of perceived causality to highly critical spatiotemporal conditions in itself proves that our experience of causality is innate, learning having a merely predisposing role. However, the fact of *specification* of certain properties and events does not explain how perceivers come to discriminate them as such; the latter issue requires proper developmental investigation (see Gibson & Gibson, 1955). This point was stressed, from the perspective of phenomenology, by one of Michotte's closest colleagues:

> In the detailed and exact investigations of Michotte on the perception of causal relations . . . the external stimulus-factors for the attribution of meaning to perceived objects were exactly determined. But one can also study the genesis of this attribution of meaning, that is, the modalities of signifying, interpreting, valuing; and this leads to a knowledge of *what*, to the essence, the idea, the *eidos* of a causal relation. . . . (Buytendijk, 1987, pp. 39–40)

The point, of course, is that Michotte was hardly alone in this confusion of the questions of specification and development. It was fundamental to the position he challenged. His opponents, committed to the empiricist tradition of perceptual theory, insisted (and continue to insist) that the perception of causality depends on our prior experience as though this countered Michotte's claim that causal events are perceptually distinct. Thus, Weir (1978), for example, has argued that we make sense of Michotte's abstract displays by assimilating their structure to templates based on our past experience of real causal events. Yet Michotte himself had intended that his schematic displays should "abstract" the relevant structures of real events (Michotte, 1962, pp. 99, 109) for his ultimate purpose was to determine what it is that real causal events share in common, and what, therefore, differentiates them visually from other kinds of events. This, surely, is a basic issue for the empiricist theorist, too, for even an appeal to prior experiences implies some similarity among those experiences:

> The systems of stimulation which correspond to the objects and events occurring in our surroundings are very often such that the kinds of perceptual structures I have been studying [with schematic displays] should occur under objective conditions. (I deliberately chose these cases for this reason.) Thus, we naturally encounter limitless examples where such structures occur in our everyday experience. Hence, it is hardly surprising that we are tempted to attribute a leading role to these recurrent

experiences in the actual organization of sensory data. Yet this begs the question of precisely why these types of structures occur in the first place. In my view, this is the fundamental problem. (Michotte, 1955/1962, p. 554)

An appeal to inference or past experience can serve as no proper reply to this question. As Reed and Jones 1978 have stressed:

[I]f we have to explain the normal case of perception in terms of knowledge already had, in terms of data to be processed, or in terms of inferential processes, we are lost—for any such knowledge presupposes perception on which it is based. (p. 526)

As for the further question of the development of the perception of causality, the recent research suggests that the ability to distinguish events involving mechanical collisions and also animate movement is present, to some extent, in babies in the earliest months of life (e.g., Bertenthal, Proffitt, Spetner, & Thomas, 1985; Fox & McDaniel, 1982; Kaiser & Proffitt, 1984; Leslie, 1982, 1984a, 1984b; Leslie & Keeble, 1987).

The most striking evidence of Michotte's continuing importance is the lively research now being conducted on the perception of inanimate, animate, and social events, research deriving from the pioneering work of Michotte, as well as that of Fritz Heider and Gunnar Johansson (e.g., Heider, 1959; Heider & Simmel, 1944; Johansson, 1950). Michotte respected the distinction between *proximal stimulation* (the pattern of energy falling on the receptors) and *distal stimulation* (the object or event as such). His purpose in using schematic displays was to permit the easy variation of the proximal stimulation, but there remains the question of how the proximal stimulation might be constrained in the normal environment by the structure of the world in which we live (for an early discussion of this general issue, see Heider, 1959, p. 82; in relation to causality, see Oldfield, 1949; Ryan, 1935). An important development of Michotte's ideas has involved the examination of essentially this question, though it is now formulated in terms of James Gibson's concept of information (structure available in light that specifies environmental properties and events). Recent researchers have considered the extent to which there is information to specify environmental events, given the physical and biophysical constraints that operate upon those events. Thus, Runeson and Frykholm (1983) consider the relation that holds between movements (the realm of kinematics) and what causes and constrains them (i.e., the dynamics), such as force, mass, and even, they suggest, intentions and emotions:

What information could be available for perceiving dynamics? The science of mechanics typically provides equations for how given dynamic condi-

> tions determine the kinematic properties of events. For our purpose it will be necessary to reverse the analysis and, given the kinematics, try to solve for dynamic factors. . . . To the extent that such reversals are possible, kinematics can be said to specify dynamics and hence contain the sort of information sought for. (p. 588)

An impressive body of work is beginning to develop that involves the identification of informative structures specifying the properties of both inanimate and animate events and the investigation of their effectiveness in perception (e.g., Runeson, 1983; Runeson & Frykholm, 1983; Todd & Warren, 1982; Kaiser, 1987; for a review, see Johansson, Hofsten, & Jansson, 1980). (An issue arising from these researches is the extent to which observers rely on information as opposed to local "heuristics"; see Gilden & Proffitt, 1989.) It will be interesting to see how this line of research can be extended to the traditional topic of social perception (McArthur & Baron, 1983).

Michotte's own contribution was primarily phenomenological. Although he certainly was aware of the connection between the structure of his schematic displays and of real cases of causality, he tended to emphasize negative and paradoxical cases, that is, examples of real causality that do not yield the causal impression, and impossible cases that do, such as a beam of light "hitting" a solid object and sending it flying (cf. Runeson, 1983). His important purpose was to establish that certain events in our surroundings are "directly lived" (Michotte, 1963, p. 15) and to describe the qualities and dimensions of such experiences.

The Following Papers

As we have explained, our aim in this book is to make available to English readers previously inaccessible aspects of Michotte's experimental phenomenology of perception. His work on causality is generally well known, thanks to the publication of the translation of his book on this topic (Michotte, 1963). In this section, therefore, our concern has been to present additional material on perceived causality, as well as the papers in which Michotte extended his treatment beyond the cases of simple collisions.

The first paper is a translation of Michotte's earliest statement of his views on the perception of causality and "functional relations." It is a summary of an unpublished paper he presented at the International Congress of Psychology at Yale in 1929. Despite its brevity and early date, it provides a clear account of Michotte's view of perception as a phase of action, and his misgivings about the unnaturalness and reductionism of much experimental research.

The second paper is important in that it presents Michotte's final statement of his theory of perceived causality in the light of the available research. It was written in collaboration with Georges Thinès.

Michotte extended his treatment of functional relations beyond the basic example of "launching" where one object appears to strike a second object and set it in motion. The third paper is concerned with the "tool effect." In this case, an object seems to serve simply as an intermediary between the action of the agent object and the recipient of that action.

In his studies of causality, Michotte was interested to find that observers would often personify the schematic objects and ascribe intentions to them. Using appropriate displays, he found that he could produce a vivid impression of animate movement, such as crawling or swimming; such impressions of immanent activity, he argued, were phenomenally distinct from cases of pure causality:

> Besides their relation with external objects, the movements made by a man or an animal possess a special character which, in the normal way, differentiates them clearly from the movements of inanimate objects, and makes it easy to recognize the presence of animal life, an important fact from a biological view. These movements are not only spontaneous, . . . they also have the appearance of being activities of which the object itself seems to be *the source.* (Michotte, 1963, p. 184; emphasis in the original)

The last paper in this chapter considers an important aspect of animate movement, its expressive character. This paper has been available in English translation, though in a relatively inaccessible source for most readers. We reprint it here because it represents Michotte's attempt to extend his ideas on the perception of functional relations to the case of social perception. For, in this paper, he argued that we can properly be said to *see* the meaning of another's actions: "this is not a "meaning" *attributed* to the literal, step-by-step translation of a table of stimuli; they are primitive, specific impressions which arise in the perceptual field itself" (Michotte, 1950, p. 120).

References

Bartlett, F.C. (1963, August 18). Letter to Michotte (Cambridge, U.K.).

Beasley, N.A. (1968). The extent of individual differences in the perception of causality. *Canadian Journal of Psychology, 22*, 399–407.

Bertenthal, B.I., Proffitt, D.R., Spetner, N.B., & Thomas, M.A. (1985).The development of infant sensitivity to biomechanical motions. *Child Development, 56*, 531–43.

Boyle, D.G. (1972). Michotte's ideas. *Bulletin of the British Psychological Society, 25,* 89–91.

Boyle, D.G. (1973). Letter. *Bulletin of the British Psychological Society, 26,* 82.

Buytendijk, F.J.J. (1947). Address. In *Jubilé Albert Michotte* (pp. 22–28). Louvain: Éditions de l'Institut Supérieur de Philosophie.

Buytendijk, F.J.J. (1987) Husserl's phenomenology and its significance for contemporary psychology. In J.J. Kockelmans (Ed.), *Phenomenological psychology: The Dutch school,* (pp. 31–44). Dordrecht: Martinus Nijhoff. (Original work published 1959)

Crabbé, G. (1967). *Les conditions d'une perception de la causalité* [The conditions for the perception of causality]. Paris: Centre National de la Recherche Scientifique.

Danziger, K. (1985a). The origins of the psychological experiment as a social institution. *American Psychologist, 40,* 133–140.

Danziger, K. (1985b). The methodological imperative in psychology. *Philosophy of the Social Sciences, 15,* 1–13.

Fox, R., & McDaniel, C. (1982). The perception of biological motion by human infants. *Science, 218,* 486–487.

Gavin, E.A. (1972). The causal issue in empirical psychology from Hume to the present, with emphasis upon the work of Michotte. *Journal of the History of the Behavioral Sciences, 8,* 302–320.

Gibson, J.J. (1979). *The ecological approach to visual perception.* Boston: Houghton-Mifflin.

Gibson, J.J., & Gibson, E.J. (1955) Perceptual learning: differentiation or enrichment? *Psychological Review, 62,* 32–41.

Gilden, D.L., & Proffitt, D.R. (1989). Understanding causal dynamics. *Journal of Experimental Psychology: Human Perception and Performance, 15,* 372–383.

Gilson, E. (1924). *The philosophy of St. Thomas Aquinas.* Cambridge: W. Heffer.

Gogel, W.C. (1963). Origin and nature of the causal impression. [Review of *The perception of causality*]. *Contemporary Psychology, 9,* 241–242.

Guillaume, P. (1937). *La psychologie de la forme.* Paris: Flammarion.

Guillaume, P. (1947). "La perception de la causalité" d'Albert Michotte ["The perception of causality" by Albert Michotte]. *Journal de Psychologie Normale et Pathologique, 40,* 112–128.

Heider, F. (1959). On perception, event structure, and psychological environment. *Psychological Issues, 1* (3), Monograph 3.

Heider, F. & Simmel, M. (1944). An experimental study of apparent behavior. *American Journal of Psychology, 57,* 243–259.

Hochberg, J. (1957). The effects of the Gestalt revolution: The Cornell Symposium on perception. *Psychological Review, 64,* 73–84.

Johansson, G. (1950). *Configurations in event perception.* Uppsala: Almqvist & Wiksells.

Johansson, G., Hofsten, C. von, & Jansson, G. (1980). Event perception. *Annual Review of Psychology, 31,* 27–63.

Joynson, R.B. (1970). The breakdown of modern psychology. *Bulletin of the British Psychological Society, 23,* 261–269.

Joynson, R.B. (1971). Michotte's experimental methods. *British Journal of Psychology, 62,* 293–302.

Kaiser, M.K. (1987). Observers' sensitivity to dynamic anomalies in collisions. *Perception and Psychophysics, 42,* 275–80.

Kaiser, M.K., & Proffitt, D.R. (1984). The development of sensitivity to causally relevant dynamic information. *Child Development, 55,* 1614–1624.

Katz, D. (1935). *The world of colour.* London: Kegan Paul, Trench, Trubner, & Co.

Katz, D. (1947) Address. In *Jubilé Albert Michotte* (pp. 29–33). Louvain: Éditions de l'Institut Supérieur de Philosophie.

Klein, D.B. (1970). *A history of scientific psychology.* London: Routledge & Kegan Paul.

Koffka, K. (1938). Reply to V. Benussi. In W.D. Ellis (Ed.), *A sourcebook in Gestalt Psychology* (pp. 371–378). London: Routledge & Kegan Paul. (Original work published 1918).

Köhler, W. (1944, November 28). Letter to Michotte, Swarthmore College, PA.

Kolers, P.A. (1972). *Aspects of motion perception.* Oxford Pergamon Press.

Leslie, A. (1982). The perception of causality in infants. *Perception, 11,* 173–186.

Leslie, A. (1984a). Spatiotemporal continuity and the perception of causality in infants. *Perception, 13,* 287–305.

Leslie, A. (1984b). Infant perception of a manual pick-up event. *British Journal of Developmental Psychology, 2,* 19–32.

Leslie, A., & Keeble, S. (1987). Do six-month-old infants perceive causality? *Cognition, 25,* 265–288.

McArthur, L.Z., & Baron, R.M. (1983). Toward an ecological theory of social perception. *Psychological Review, 90,* 215–238.

Metzger, W. (1928). Certain implications in the concept of *Gestalt. American Journal of Psychology, 40,* 162–166.

Michotte, A. (1929). Quelques aspects de la psychologie de la perception négligés dans les recherches expérimentales [Some aspects of the psychology of perception neglected in experimental research]. In *IXth International Congress of Psychology, held at Yale University, New Haven, Connecticut, 1929: Proceedings and Papers* (pp. 307–308). Princeton, NJ: Psychological Review Company.

Michotte, A. (1962). La causalité physique est-elle une donnée phénoménale? [Is physical causality a phenomenal datum?]. Reprinted in A. Michotte, *Causalité, permanence et realité phénoménales* (pp. 91–127). Louvain: Publications Universitaires. (Original work published in 1941)

Michotte, A. (1947). Address. In *Jubilé Albert Michotte* (pp. 39–50). Louvain: Éditions de l'Institut Supérieur de Philosophie.

Michotte, A. (1950). The emotions regarded as functional connections. In M.L. Reymert (Ed.), *Feelings and emotions: The Mooseheart Symposium* (pp. 114–125). New York: McGraw-Hill.

Michotte, A. (1952). Albert Michotte van den Berck (Autobiography). In E.G. Boring, H.S. Langfeld, H. Werner, & R.M. Yerkes (Eds.), *A history of psychology in autobiography* (Vol. 4, pp. 213–236). Worcester, MA: Clark University Press. Pp. 213–236.

Michotte, A. (1954). Autobiographie de M. le Professeur A. Michotte van den Berck [Autobiography]. *Psychologica Belgica, 1,* 190–217.

Michotte, A. (1955). L'influence de l'expérience sur la structuration des données sensorielles dans la perception [The influence of experience in the structuring of sensory data in perception]. *Deuxième Symposium de l'Association de Psychologie Scientifique de Langue Française* (pp. 31–45). (Louvain, 1953). Paris: P.U.F.

Michotte, A. (1963). *The perception of causality.* (T.R. Miles & E. Miles, Trans.) London: Methuen. [Original work published 1946]

Michotte, A., & Prüm. E. (1910). Étude expérimentale sur le choix volontaire et ses antecedents immédiats [An experimental study of voluntary choice and its immediate antecedents]. *Archives de Psychologie, 10,* 113–320.

Montpelier, G. de., & Nuttin, J.R. (1973). A note on "Michotte's experimental methods" and "Michotte's ideas". *British Journal of Psychology, 64,* 287–289.

Ogden, R.M. (1949). [Review of *La perception de la causalité* and *Miscellenea Psychologica Albert Michotte*]. *American Journal of Psychology, 62,* 127–133.

Oldfield, R.C. (1949). La perception de la causalité [Review of "The perception of causality"]. *Quarterly Journal of Experimental Psychology, 1,* 104–105.

Pickford, R.W. (1963). [Review of Michotte (1963)]. *British Journal of Psychology, 54,* 369.

Pieper, J. (1963). *Introduction to Thomas Aquinas.* London: Faber & Faber.

Pillsbury, W.B. (1904). The psychological nature of causality. *Philosophical Review, 13,* 409–419.

Reed, E.S., & Jones, R.K. (1978). Gibson's theory of perception: A case of hasty epistemologizing? *Philosophy of Science, 45,* 519–530.

Runeson, S. (1983). On visual perception of dynamic events. *Acta Universitatis Uppsaliensis: Studia Psychologica Uppsaliensia,* (Serial No. 9). [Doctoral dissertation, first published in 1977.]

Runeson, S., & Frykholm, G. (1983). Kinematic specification of dynamics as an informational basis for person-and-action perception: Expectation, gender recognition, and deceptive intention. *Journal of Experimental Psychology: General, 112,* 585–615.

Ryan, T.A. (1938). Dynamic, physiognomic, and other neglected properties of perceived objects: A new approach to comprehending. *American Journal of Psychology, 51,* 629–650.

Todd, J.T., & Warren, W.H. (1982). Visual perception of relative mass in dynamic events. *Perception, 11,* 325–335.

Vernon, M.D. (1964). [Review of Michotte (1963)]. *British Journal of Social and Clinical Psychology, 3,* 74–75.

Vernon, M.D. (1972). Letter. *Bulletin of the British Psychological Society, 25,* 254–255.

Walk, R.D. (1984). Event perception, perceptual organization and emotion. In W.R. Crozier & A.J. Chapman (Eds.), *Cognitive processes in the perception of art* (pp. 211–221). Amsterdam: North-Holland.

Weir, S. (1978). The perception of motion: Michotte revisited. *Perception, 7,* 247–260.

Williams, R. (1983). *Keywords.* London: Fontana.

Zangwill, O.L. (1963). [Review of Michotte (1963)]. *Quarterly Journal of Experimental Psychology, 15,* 224.

SOME ASPECTS OF THE PSYCHOLOGY OF PERCEPTION NEGLECTED IN EXPERIMENTAL RESEARCH[1]

Albert Michotte

1. Most experimental studies in human psychology seem to be premised on the following assumption: Perception constitutes a sort of "terminus", the final stage of processes triggered by stimulation. In fact, far from being a "terminus," perception should be considered as a beginning; it initiates and directs our activities and is appropriately treated as a simple "phase" of the complete process of an action. As a phase of action, perception develops under the pressure of dispositions and needs that dominate the individual at the moment when the external stimulation occurs, and it ought to depend on these factors.

However, the dispositions at work within classical laboratory experiments are very limited and usually quite weak in comparison with those that occur in everyday life. Furthermore, "laboratory perception" only begins to approximate the functional role served by perception in real life. Therefore, research needs to be extended in the following direction: (a) to study perception in its natural setting (as is done, of necessity, in animal psychology), and (b) to determine systematically the extent to which the needs and dispositions of the individual influence perception and the underlying principles involved.

2. Despite the new direction taken by research in perception in recent years, the power of the analytical approach within psychology is still such that certain categories of complex phenomena are hardly investigated even today. This is especially the case for the perception of the physical actions that objects perform on one another and the resulting transformations, such as, for example, the perception of the impact between two objects and the corresponding mechanical effects of breaking, deformation, and so on.

Can the perception of these "processes" be reduced ultimately to the elementary percepts of movement and of qualitative and quantitative change, in accordance with the classical approach? Or might it not be the case that these percepts are dynamic syntheses of a higher order and obey laws somewhat different from those that govern simpler aspects of experience? This would be more consistent with the data actually obtained in the psychology of perception (and demonstrated by certain findings pointing in this direction). The investigation of these "percep-

[1]Translated by Alan Costall from A. Michotte. Quelques aspects de la psychologie de la perception négligés dans les recherches expérimentales. In Ninth International Congress of Psychology, Yale 1929, *Proceedings and papers*. Princeton, NJ: Psychological Review Company, 1929. pp. 307–308.

tions of process" (which are obviously linked to our experience of manipulating objects) is interesting for a variety of reasons. These perceptions seem to play an essential role in the development of the "meaning" of objects and even words, and, furthermore, they determine our behavior to a large extent, since they constitute the basis for our use of the objects around us, such as tools and other instruments.

PERCEIVED CAUSALITY[2]

Albert Michotte and Georges Thinès

The continuous changes that occur both in our surroundings and within our own body are revealed in the perceptual field in the form of event sequences, which can be classified in various ways, either by properties that are directly apparent, or on the basis of previous experience of a more or less extensive kind.

These categories are very different in nature. Sometimes events occur one after the other while being, or seeming to be, separate from one another. In contrast, in other cases they seem to be strongly linked by various ties. Events may be integrated within a global perceptual structure, as, for example, the sound of a melody; one event may act as a signal for another; a means/end relation may exist between the two; one may be the condition of the production of another, etc. Finally, there are causal relations as such (i.e., efficient causality), which are the topic of the present paper. These include, in the usual sense of the word, the "production" of a change by a preceding event, as for example, the reddening of an iron bar after heating, the displacement of a body after an impact, the various changes resulting from the motor activities of man and animals, such as: pushes, pulls, compressions, launchings etc. Other changes manifest themselves over much longer periods, such as the erosion of stones by wind or waves, the effects exerted on organisms by pharmacological agents, etc.

It is hardly necessary to stress that causal relations are essential to our knowledge of the world, since they seem to provide valid explanations of the changes that occur both around and inside us. Moreover, they allow us both to predict the occurrence of certain events and ultimately to control or adapt to them. It is therefore hardly surprising that philosophers have preoccupied themselves with the search for the basis of the concept of causality and have consequently proposed various

[2]Translation by G. Thinès, A. Costall and G. Butterworth from A. Michotte and G. Thinès, La causalité perceptive, *J. Psych. Norm. Path.*, 1963, 60: 9–36. The same text was published in German in the *Handbuch der Psychologie*, Band I/1 (W. Metzger, Ed.), 1966: 954–977.

solutions to this problem, all of them depending on their own viewpoints, such as Descartes' rationalism, Hume's empiricism, Kant's apriorism, and Maine de Biran's inner experience, to mention only the most famous (see Michotte, 1963).

However, in spite of the diversity of these conceptions, all the authors hold the assumption, usually attributed to Hume, that we have no direct experience, as far as "external" experience is concerned, of the influence exerted by one event or another. This was also assumed by the first experimental psychologists, as a result of their belief in a strict correspondence between sensory stimuli and resulting "sensations." According to this viewpoint, the "influence" exerted by a physical or mechanical event on the production of another cannot result in a particular "sensation" because such events cannot be said to correspond to any specific sensory stimulation.

However, after the Gestalt psychologists and their immediate forerunners had shown that there was no point to point correspondence between sensations and local stimuli, but rather that perceptual structures were global units endowed with specific properties, it was possible to tackle the problem of perceived causality from a new point of view.

This is what Köhler and Michotte did simultaneously, though independently, in 1929 (see Köhler, 1929). In his *Gestalt Psychology,* Köhler asserted the existence of immediate causal impressions in outer experience. Michotte, in a paper delivered to the International Congress of Psychology at Yale, defended the thesis that "mechanical action" (causal action) could be visually perceived as directly as forms or movements. Similar ideas were later developed by Koffka (1935), Duncker (1945) and Metzger (1941). In the same year the problem was tackled experimentally, when Michotte published the first results of his experiments on perceived causality (Michotte, 1941), and since then, numerous investigations have been devoted to this problem. The present paper reviews the facts and the theories in this extensive field of perceptual research.[3]

The experiments performed in this field are obviously limited to the presentation of events whose connections can be directly perceived. This necessarily excludes all cases in which the action of a cause can only be grasped after a long delay so that the causal link between the perceived events can only be established in an indirect fashion. Apart from this restriction, however, there remains a limitless number of cases where direct succession can be perceived, namely successive qualitative or quantitative changes of objects of their positions in space, etc.

[3]Piaget became interested in the problem of the development of causal responses in children in 1925, a topic which led him to formulate his own theory of the notion of causality. (see especially Piaget, 1937).

Michotte's first investigations were devoted to mechanical causality. These were initiated by two basic experiments called respectively "entraining" and "launching."[4]

Entraining

In the entraining experiment, subjects see two immobile 8 × 5 mm rectangles of different color on a uniform white background (behind a horizontal slit 60 × 5 mm). One of the rectangles (Object A) stands in the vicinity of the left end of the slit, and the other (Object B) stands 30 mm right of object A. At the experimenter's signal, Object A starts moving for example at a speed of 5 cm/sec, towards Object B. When A reaches B the latter also starts moving at the same speed, so that from then on, both objects are moving in contact with one another and disappear behind the right end of the slit (Figure 2.1).

Launching

The launching experiment differs from entraining in only one respect: When Object A has reached Object B, it stands still while the latter starts to move a short distance before disappearing behind the right end of the slit. It should be noted that the best results are obtained when the speed of A is relatively high (30 cm/sec, for instance) while that of Object B is much lower (5 to 10 times, for instance) (Figure 2.2).

Either of these displays are presented to subjects who are asked to look at the slit of the apparatus and describe what they see as if observing an ordinary event in everyday life.[5] Even though the subjects are unaware of the purpose of the experiment and unfamiliar with psychological research, the great majority of the responses on the very first presentation are endowed with causal meaning. In the case of entraining, subjects say that "Object A carries Object B along," that "it takes it with it," that "it pushes it," etc. In the case of launching, the responses mention that "Object A chases B," that "it launches it," that "it projects it ahead," etc.[6]

However, because these experiments replicate, though obviously in a

[4]All technical details concerning these experiments can be found in A. Michotte (1963), p. 27–40 and in G. Thinès (1962), p. 13–20. The numerical values quoted in the following descriptions are only given as examples and do not exclude the use of other values, granted certain *ratios* between the spatiotemporal values of the two successive phases of the experiment are maintained within well-defined lower and upper limits. (see also Fraisse, 1956).

[5]Concerning the use of subjects' verbal reports in the experiments of Michotte and of his collaborators, see Michotte (1962).

[6]According to recent unpublished experiments by G. Crabbé, causal responses were

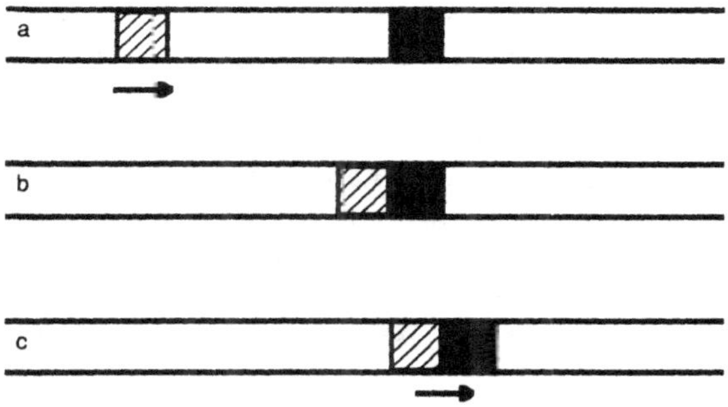

FIGURE 2.1

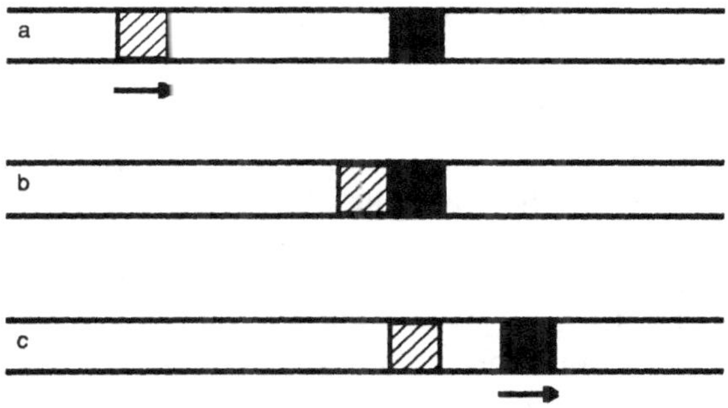

FIGURE 2.2

Figures 2.1 and 2.2. Schematic representation of the two basic experiments. Letters a, b, and c indicate the positions of the moving objects at different moments of the experiment. Arrows under objects indicate that they are in motion in a given direction at the moment considered. The position of objects at the crucial moment of impact is represented without arrows, even when one of the objects or both are in motion at that moment. There were movable blinds at the ends of the slit, allowing the experimenter to vary its length in particular experiments.

simplified form, cases of mechanical causality currently met in everyday life, it is clear that obtaining causal responses in such conditions does not suffice by itself to establish the existence of a "specific" causal character at the level of perceptual structures themselves. The responses of subjects may possibly be dictated solely by their previous knowledge of a causal link between the movements of two objects in similar spatiotemporal conditions.

---

given in the conditions just described by 95% of subjects (N = 50) on first presentation in the launching experiment and by 60% to 65% of subjects (each time N = 50) in four slight variations of the entraining experiment. (The unpublished results quoted here should be compared with the final results published by G. Crabbé [1967]).

Subjects do agree in stating that they really see one object chase or push another as immediately and patently as they see, for example, two vehicles cross or overtake each other in a street; but this cannot be taken at face value. Only through systematic research relying upon a schematic display that allows manipulation of all its conditions does it become possible to demonstrate the existence of proper causal perceptual structures and to define their properties. The first step in this direction involves determining the relations existing between the properties of the stimulation system and the causal responses.

Conditions of Emergence of Causal Responses in the Type Experiments

Temporal Conditions

First among the relevant temporal conditions is the value of the time interval between the moment of contact of objects A and B and the moment when the latter begins to move. The systematic variation of this time interval causes progressive modifications in the responses of subjects. In the case of launching, direct launching is only reported constantly for intervals up to 50 milliseconds, though it may still be reported occasionally up to 100 milliseconds. For higher time values other types of responses occur, which although indicative of definite impressions of launching, suggest that it takes place with a certain "lag" or that "B sticks to A." For delays of 150 to 200 milliseconds and more, reports nearly unanimously indicate a succession of two entirely independent movements.[7]

The same is true for entraining also, the only difference being that, when there is a delay between the contact of objects and their common movement, they generally unite in a group, and it is this group that then seems to be moving independently.

Second, the duration of presence of Object B in the field before the moment of contact is also of some importance. Thinès was able to show that the prior presence of this object greatly enhances causal responses of entraining, although it is not absolutely necessary. Thus, definite cases of entraining have been observed, when B suddenly appeared in motion in the vicinity of Object A, at the place where subjects *expected* the two objects to make contact (Thinès, 1962, p. 109 et seq).

[7]See Michotte (1963), p. 91 et seq. It should be mentioned in this respect that time intervals of the order just mentioned seem to apply to all kinetic structures (causal or not) implying an integration of successive movements. Temporal discontinuity is most evident for time intervals of .1 or .2 second.

Size and Shape of Objects

The size and shape of the objects may vary considerably without appreciably affecting causal responses, so long as discrimination of the objects remains possible at the point of impact. In view of this, the relative size of the objects is not very important. Thus, the motor-object may be much smaller than the projectile and either can even be reduced to a small spot (Michotte 1963, p. 83).

Similarly, there is a great deal of tolerance as far as the shape and the "nature" of objects are concerned. In the basic experiments, various plane, mostly rectangular, figures were used, either painted (surface colors) or projected onto a screen (film colors). Thinès even used triangular arrays of light spots (Thinès 1962, p. 14). *A fortiori,* of course, the objects may be solid. It is worth noting, in this respect, that, if Object A is a real three-dimensional object, for example, a marble, but Object B is just a shadow or a light ray, definite launching responses may still be obtained (Michotte 1963, p. 84).

These observations suggest that causal responses are largely dependent on the movement combinations realized in these experiments, the nature of the moving objects being of only secondary importance. This conclusion is supported by further findings.

Kinetic Conditions

Absolute speed. When the speed of the two objects is the same, causal responses of launching may be maintained for a velocity range of about 10 to 110 cm/sec, although they undergo some qualitative modifications (Michotte 1963, p. 107). However, launching disappears for higher velocities, the subjects reporting that a single object (A) seems to pass along the whole length of the slit in continuous motion, the Object B being seen as motionless while A passes it (tunnel effect). This lack of distinction between the two phases of the experiment indicates a complete kinetic integration and may be largely ascribed to a lack of visual discrimination within the area where contact between the objects takes place; similar reports are obtained under ordinary velocity conditions, when subjects are required to fixate a point from which the contact area can be seen only peripherally (Michotte 1963, pp. 46–47 & p. 107).

Conversely, when absolute speed is low (e.g., less than 3 cm/sec), the structure of launching again tends to fade away.

Ratio of speeds. The ratio of speeds is of utmost importance in the case of launching. The causal character of the structure is considered best and is also most frequently reported when the movement of Object B is slower than that of Object A. In the reverse case, that is, when the velocity of B is definitely higher than that of A, very different reports are given, viz, the movement of B is seen as simply "triggered" by the contact of A. In other words, the movement of Object B seems to be *autonomous* in its execution, while remaining *dependent* on the contact of A at its point of departure.[8]

Length of paths. The respective lengths of paths of objects A and B should be considered separately. In the case of launching (and certainly in the case of entraining), the length of the path covered by A may be considerably reduced, up to a length corresponding to a visual angle of about 10′, without eliminating causal responses (Michotte 1963, p. 57). This means that such responses can be obtained as soon as the length of the path is sufficient to allow a clear perception of the movement of A towards B.

In the case of the length of path of B, various issues need to be considered. First, in the case of entraining, there is the question of whether causal impressions are reported as soon as Object B begins to move at the same speed as A, or only after a certain interval of common movement. The experiments of Thinès on entraining and those of Crabbé on traction show that this time interval is much higher than one would suppose at first sight, namely, a path length of 20 to 30 mm in the case of Thinès and of 15 mm in Crabbé's conditions (Thinès, 1962, p. 105; Crabbé, 1962, p. 272). and time intervals of 100 to 200 milliseconds or more according to both authors. Moreover, Thinès was able to show that the value of the path length was a function of the speed of movement (Thinès, 1962).

A second problem concerns a typical phenomenon, which Michotte has termed the *radius of action*. Lengthening of the path of B (in launching) or of AB (in entraining), brings about a radical change in the subjects' reports; they report that, from a certain distance on, the displacements of B lose their passivity and seem to become autonomous movements. The threshold value corresponding to this change can be determined experimentally and is found to vary as a direct function of the speed of movement (Michotte, 1963; p. 53 et seq; Yela, 1954; Boyle, 1961). We will return to this important finding in our theoretical discussion.

Direction of paths. The main experiments of Michotte were performed using horizontal paths, the movements of Object B continuing along the

[8]See Michotte (1963), Chapter VII and VIII and *infra*, sect. III. The fact has been confirmed by all authors who performed similar experiments. Concerning the speed ratio in entraining, see Michotte, Knops, and Coen-Gelders (1962).

same path of movement as A. However, the overall orientation of either movement does exert some influence on the launching effect (Michotte 1963, p. 102). Piaget has performed experiments using vertical presentation and has found that the reports differ from those obtained for horizontal presentations (Piaget & Lambercier, 1958). Generally speaking, in the case of launching, subjects stress the "passivity" when it is moving downwards and its "activity" when going up, the passivity during descent being accompanied by reports of "braking" which subjects ascribe to the surroundings. In the case of downward entraining, similar responses are given, but in the case of upward entraining, B remains passive, the stress being laid on the pushing action of A. Piaget attributes the peculiarities in the responses to an apparent "gravity" effect introduced into the system by the vertical orientation of paths.

In terms of relative orientation, the best results are obtained when the paths of A and B are in line. When a vertical shift is introduced between the horizontal paths, so that A stops above B, these conditions are found to be very unfavorable to reports of launching. Similarly, when the respective paths are oriented at an angle, the greater the angle, the fewer the launchings reported. They almost completely disappear for an angle of 90° (Michotte, 1963; cf. Kanizsa & Metelli, 1959). A number of investigations have tried to test whether certain movement combinations of two objects were liable to provoke "attraction" responses, by making one object move towards another, the latter moving in its turn towards the former as soon as the distance between them was sufficiently reduced. Kanizsa, Metelli, and Tognazzo have performed various experiments in this field and have obtained frequent causal responses in these conditions. However, according to Michotte, these results were probably due largely to a "contextual" influence in these experiments (Metelli & Tognazzo, 1958; Kanizsa & Metelli, 1957, 1961; see also Michotte, 1963; pp. 102 & 219; Thinès, 1962; p. 78 et seq.)

Continuity and discontinuity of paths. It is possible to elicit causal responses in experiments on launching or entraining at a distance, that is, without direct contact between the objects at the moment B begins to move (Michotte, 1963, p. 99, & 1962, p. 59).

This distance may be completely "empty," as Yela has shown for launching. His experiments employed a stereoscopic device in which the objects appeared as two discs "floating" in an empty space (Yela, 1952, p. 142). In other experiments, Crabbé was able to produce similar effects for entraining with the help of two rods moving in different planes.

On the other hand, Yela, using the ordinary disc method, observed that the reports of launching decreased for greater distances. According to Michotte, however, the frequencies for a given distance are dependent on the speed of the objects (Michotte, 1963, p. 99). Moreover, according to Yela, when causal effects are reported, the responses depend on the same temporal conditions of immediate succession as in the case of a contact, a fact that indicates that there is no apparent propagation of movement through space. In addition, other factors enhancing causal responses, such as absolute and relative speeds, etc., also operate here. Finally—and this is of great importance—the radius of action of B is of the same order of magnitude in both ordinary launching and in launching at a distance. This has led Yela to conclude that the radius of action is the manifestation of a temporal factor, and, as we shall see, this hypothesis seems to be fully justified (Yela 1952, p. 148).

Piaget and Lambercier compared the responses of children and adults in the conditions of launching at a distance and found that causal responses were much less frequent in children, the contact playing, in their case, a much more decisive role (Piaget & Lambercier, 1958. p. 90 et seq.).

Causality at a distance is, in some ways, akin to the phenomenon that Michotte has termed the "tool" function, the simplest case being obtained by introducing a third object between *A* and *B* (Michotte, 1951). In the case of launching, three objects, *A*, *I*, and *B* are set apart by a certain distance. *A* is set moving towards *I* and when it reaches it, stops and then I starts moving towards *B;* when *I* reaches *B*, it stops in its turn, and *B* starts moving and disappears behind a screen after having moved on a certain distance. In fact, these conditions produce two successive launchings, that of *I* by *A*, and that of *B* by *I*. Nevertheless, this duality is only reported by the subjects when the displacement of I extends beyond its radius of action, since only in these conditions is its displacement perceived as autonomous. Conversely, when the *I-B* distance is smaller than the radius of action of *I*, subjects report that A is the only active object, that it launches *B through I*, the latter seeming inert, whatever its own distance of travel may be. In these conditions, *I* appears to be a "tool," that is, a mere means of transmitting the impulse given by *A*, exactly as happens when a tool is manipulated by humans.

Causal Responses and Mental Development

It would be interesting to study the relations existing between casual responses and the intellectual level of the subjects. Until now, however, there are no definite data on this matter, except from developmental studies of the causal responses of children at different ages (Jassogne, 1947; Olum, 1956; Piaget & Lambercier, 1958; Piaget & Maroun, 1958). The clearest results available from this approach indicate that children older than 7 years respond to the type experiments of launching and entraining in the same way as adults, but below 7 years the frequency of positive answers diminishes down to 4 years old, which represents the lower age limit at which such experiments can be attempted. It is impossible, however, to tell to what extent this change is due to the development of vocabulary, to general development of intelligence, or to other conditions.

Finally, there is the result (previously mentioned) to which Piaget attached so much theoretical significance: The direct contact of the objects at the time when the projectile begins to move is much more critical for children than for adults.

The "Causal" Perceptual Structure

The research reviewed here would seem to render one hypothesis highly unlikely. According to this hypothesis, which can hardly be rejected *a priori*, the immediacy of the impression is illusory, the display simply evoking a meaning "acquired" in some way or another. Such an explanation is difficult to reconcile with the correlation between the variations of the display and the response of the observers, the distribution of response frequencies generally showing the usual pattern for psychophysical functions. In the case of acquired meanings, on the other hand, the link between stimulation and response is usually much weaker. In any case, the observers themselves often contrast such cases with the "immediacy" of the causal impression (Levelt, 1962; Michotte, 1962, p. 72).

Further evidence comes from so-called "negative" and "paradoxical" cases, which can be easily produced once the stimulus conditions necessary for eliciting causal response are known. Thus, in negative cases it is possible to combine conditions so that the events displayed fail to give rise to a causal response even though the observer knows perfectly well that these events involve a physically causal action, as in the *transport effect* (Michotte, 1963, pp. 152–153). Conversely, in the paradoxical cases, it is possible to establish conditions that give rise to a causal response even though these conflict with everyday experience. For example, launching responses are obtained when the simple experiment is modified so that Object B, which is already moving at the moment of impact, slows down following the blow it received; a similar effect can be obtained for entraining (Michotte, 1963, pp. 71 & 159). Entraining responses also occur if A accelerates at the moment it begins to push B, etc. (Michotte, Knops, & Coen-Gelders, 1962).

In view of these results, it is necessary to consider whether an hypothesis other than that of acquired meaning might not conform better with the facts. To be specific, should we assume in accord with the comments of the observers, that casual responses reflect characteristics of the perceptual structures arising from particular stimulation configurations? It is necessary, first of all, to define what these special characteristics might be, and then how they could arise from the particular pattern of stimulation.

If the first stage is eliminated from the entraining-type experiment, so that *A* and *B* are joined and begin simultaneously to move with the same speed and in the same direction, then by virtue of the principle of common fate, both objects appear to form a single shape (e.g., a two-colored rectangle) or to constitute a highly integrated group; in both cases, there appears to be only one movement, performed by the rectangle or by the group as such.

However, in the normal entraining experiment, this stage is preceded by a stage in which *B* is stationary and *A* moves towards it; this considerably alters the effects of common fate since, as Michotte has demonstrated in a variety of experiments, the perceptual structures established in the first stage tend to remain during the second stage (i.e., there is a tendency towards phenomenal permanence) (Michotte, 1962. p. 35 et seq.).

The first stage is characterized by the presence of two distinct objects, Object *A*, which is moving, and Object *B*, which is stationary. After impact, however, A continues on its way, but now B begins to move next to it, and so common fate should begin to take effect. From this point on, therefore, there is a conflict between the tendency towards the permanence of the features of the first stage and the effects of the change in the stimulation. As a result of this conflict, a brief, transitory, perceptual structure is formed that constitutes the normal phase of the experiment. This occurs between the initial structure and the visual result of the effects of common fate, which is consequently delayed and appears as only the third phase of the entire perceptual transformation.

In terms of causality, therefore, the second phase is the crucial one. Fortunately, thanks to the particularly clear responses made by the observers, it is relatively easy to infer the characteristics of this phase and to test the resulting hypothesis.

Briefly, according to our hypothesis (see Michotte et al., 1962) the structure in question is a compromise between two opposing tendencies. It involves a phenomenal duplication (of which many examples are known in the psychology of perception), whereby two aspects of the common movement of objects on similar trajections are simultaneously perceived after their impact, both as a "continuation of the movement of *A*" and as a "simple displacement of Object *B*."

If the displacement of B is indeed identified with the continued movement of *A* after this impact, it is clear that the movement of *A* must from then on seem also to displace *B*. Michotte called this apparent extension of the movement of *A* to *B* the *ampliation of movement*. He considered it to be the crucial element of his theory, but such a structure could only be transitory because it is only formed under the influence of the first phase (of the movement), an influence that necessarily fades with time. Consequently, we believe that it is the duration of this influence (a fraction of a second) that determines the value of the somewhat enigmatic radius of action mentioned earlier.

One point in this account may nevertheless seem strange, that is, the distinction made between "displacement" and "movement." Clearly this distinction is only valid from a phenomenal point of view; that is, usually the quality of "movement" is a special property assigned to the displacement of objects, but sometimes, as when a group of objects is integrated within a "perceptual complex", the displacement of one member may seem to occur by its participation in the movement of one or more of the objects to which it is structurally bound.

This distinction can be justified in many ways.[9] It is clear, for example, that a movement physically performed by an object does not necessarily appear to belong to that object. For a convincing demonstration of this, it is sufficient to observe a collection of objects (for example, light spots) moving at the same speed and along different but parallel trajectories. In these conditions, only one movement is seen, that of the group in which each object participates as co-carrier, by executing its own *displacement*.

Another example, closer to entraining, is the "transport effect," which occurs when an object is seen to be carried by another. Though both objects are distinct, it is apparently the carrier that moves, whereas the carried object usually seems intrinsically immobile. Indeed, as it does not move with respect to the carrier, which constitutes its frame of reference, it has no proper movement; but nevertheless, it is obviously displaced in space. The relationship between this case and that of entraining is immediately evident, but they differ in an essential way because, in the case of the transport effect, it is a matter of a *stationary* state of the structure eliciting no causal response. What characterizes

[9]See Michotte (1963, p. 135 et seq and 150 et seq.) as well as A. Michotte et al., (1962, p. 22 et seq). This distinction seems to be related to the speed of objects. According to Michotte, the movement "quality" would be all the more powerful to the subjects to the extent that the movement of the stimulus is quicker; conversely, it would progressively disappear for slower movements and be replaced by a "simple displacement" when the conditions of structuration require it (causal structures, transport effect, etc.). This could explain why the slowing down of speed enhances the causal character of launching, whereas an increase of the relative speed of the projectile favors the apparent autonomy of its movement (ie, the triggering effect.)

entraining is ampliation, which is restricted to the period in which the structure is established; and the causal responses are restricted to this period (Michotte, 1962; p. 149 et seq Michotte et al., 1962).

It seems possible to provide a theoretical explanation of the launching effect along the lines just described. In this case once again, from the point of impact on, a conflict occurs between the tendency towards permanence of the first stage and the current conditions of stimulation: Object *A*, which was moving before the impact, stops at that moment, while Object *B* alone then begins to move.

However, according to Michotte, after the impact, though before the movement executed by *B* appears as being its own movement, there is again a short intermediate phase during which phenomenal duplication occurs. The movement executed by *B* would appear to have two aspects, both as the simple displacement of this object, and as the extension of the preexisting movement of *A*. Thanks to this duplication, there would once again be a momentary identification of the "displacement" of *B*, with (in this case) the apparent continuation of the "movement" of Object *A*. This should be considered as an example of the principle of "good continuation" (rather than that of "common fate" that occurs in entraining). Furthermore, it is noteworthy that a slight modification of the experiment, by the reduction in one way or the other of visual acuity, is enough to change the successive movements of the two moving bodies into a single uninterrupted movement of the first along the slit of the apparatus (Michotte 1963; Michotte et al., 1962, pp 55 et seq.).

It seems that entraining and launching can be considered as the two basic structures of perceptual causality (Michotte, 1963, p. 218), and other kinds of sequence can be related to them. These include "traction" (entraining in which the agent object precedes the moved object during their common displacement), "propulsion" (combination of a translation with one of the components of a change of shape, as in throwing an arrow by loosening a bow), "tracing and erasing", and even the movements of "animal locomotion" (which are characterized by the animal appearing to produce its own movements) (cf. Michotte, 1963. Chs. 10, 11 and 12, and Appendix). In these cases and many others, the same basic structure of ampliation can be found, of the kind that constantly occurs in our perception of combinations of movements in everyday life.

Now, and this is a crucial point, it is this structure that gives rise to the actual *phenomenal generation* of the new event constituting the displacement of the projected objects since once it is set up, the movement of the motor objects seems also to displace the projectile after the impact. Also, since on the other hand, it is the character of "generation," or "productivity," which is generally considered the essential component of the common, nonscientific concept of causality, one sees how the presence of the ampliation structure justifies the "causal" response of the subjects (Michotte, 1963, p. 221 et seq.). It remains to be seen if it is possible to study experimentally at least some aspects of this theory.

Among other things, it has been shown that causal responses can be eliminated when the "character of movement" is assigned to the "displacement" of *B*. This result can be obtained in various ways. Notably, one can combine the conditions of the basic experiments with other movements providing integration of the movement of B into kinetic complexes different from the causal structures, for example, successive movements of a group of objects to which *B* belongs, symmetrical movements of *B*'s group with a third object, series of to-and-fro movements, etc. (Michotte, 1963, p. 73 et seq). The experiment can also be carried out so that B suddenly appears just before the impact, and this is accompanied by gamma movements of expansion of the object, which also favors the autonomy of its later movement of translation (Thinès, 1962, p. 38 et seq).

Another way to make the causal response disappear lies in counteracting the tendency towards permanence of the duality of the objects during the second stage of entraining, by introducing other configurational factors that establish phenomenal unity to the objects (Michotte et al., 1962, p. 53 et seq.).

These various experiments (and many others) fully confirm what has been said about the existence of specific "causal" structures, about their dependence on a determined system of stimulation, and about the basic features characterizing them.

So far, our comments have only concerned the visual perception of causality; but they also apply to the tactile-kinesthetic field, where perceptual causality constantly appears in the relations between our limbs and outside objects as pushes, traction, launching, propulsion, etc. It can be seen, therefore, that the stimulus systems leading to causal responses are, in theory, similar to those of the visual domain (Michotte, 1963). In the course of this research, Piaget and Maroun began comparative experiments on children and adults, in which the subjects had to push, with a kind of rake, boxes of different weights, with eyes closed or open. They found, among other things, that the "tool" effect clearly appeared when a box first pushed then met a second one, etc. Furthermore, the authors obtained some very interesting findings, not only on impressions of weight or resistance and the corresponding "dynamic" impressions of pushing, but also on the interaction of visual and tactile-kinesthetic perception observed by comparing experiments carried out either with eyes closed or open. Visual perception apparently reinforces aspects of resistance and effort within tactile-kinesthetic experience (Piaget & Maroun, 1958). It seems that these last experiments contributed greatly to the development of Piaget's theory of perceptual causality (Piaget, 1961), which in spite of many points of agreement is rather different from that of Michotte. The difference is fundamental in that, in Piaget's view, "a strict form of causality" must imply the *conservation* of movement, and consequently an "exact compensation". (Piaget, 1961, p. 301). He therefore linked perceptual causality to the "constancy" phenomena (shape, size, color) and, in a general way, to his personal conception of perceptual compensation schemes.

According to him, such compensation exists on the phenomenal level, that is, there is an apparent equivalence between effect and cause, which he represented by an ingenious system of equations where he introduced, on one side, the loss of speed of the agent object at the moment of impact, and a "dynamic" impression he terms "pushing;" and, on the other side, the gain in speed of the passive object and an impression of resistance (Piaget & Lambercier, 1958, p. 151). By assigning different values to these factors, the author succeeded in representing symbolically the different cases of causality previously described.

This system nevertheless seems rather artificial and presents unquestionable difficulties, particularly in the visual field. First, if the principal character implied in the causal answers is the production of a new event (displacement of *B*), it is difficult to consider this as a case of "constancy." Next, it is essential to specify what is meant by the dynamic character of the "push." One of the essential points of Michette's theory consists in the explanation of how, thanks to phenomenal duplication, ampliation implies an aspect of "productivity" consistent with the fundamental sense of the word "dynamic," understood as "cause of the movement." Piaget, on the other hand, defines the dynamic character to which he appeals as being "the impression of pushing" (force), or simply of action exerted on B at the moment of the impact (Piaget & Lambercier, 1958). One may wonder exactly what is this "impression of exerted action." Strictly speaking, it seems to be simply perceptual causality as Michotte understands it. Indeed, this "exerted action" includes simultaneously the movement of *A* (because it is only in moving that there can be an action from it), the movement of *B* (because it is only in so far as *B* is moving that an action is exerted), and the connection that phenomenally binds these movements. Finally, this "impression" can only with difficulty find its place in the left hand side of the equations, as it already includes the effect produced by the cause (the movement of *B*).

It could be, however, that the impression of "pushing" is conceived as the equivalent in the visual field of the impression of effort observed in the kinesthetic field, which varies according to the resistance met by our movements, especially by our voluntary movements. Now, a parallel may certainly be established between this effort and the more or less pronounced character of violence of the visual impact; but, if it is true that these aspects of the event give a special character to perceptual causality, it also seems clear that they are not at all basic to it.

Indeed, kinesthetic effort, just as in the case of a visually violent impact, has its maximum value when the obstacle met remains stationary and, as such, has no perceptible effect. On the other hand, clear causal responses can be provoked in the absence of visual impact, just as when the movement of a limb (e.g., the hand) entrains an object so lightly that, though being tactually perceived, its displacement is not accompanied by any discriminable increase of effort. According to the subjects, the entraining is as clear in such a case as in the one in which they push an object with a distinct weight; it is only the fact of displacement of the object that counts (Michotte, 1962 p.69 et seq.).

As far as the impression of resistance is concerned, the subjects practically never mention it in the visual type of experiments, and it seems rather arbitrary to assume that it is only a matter of omission on their part, since they report many details of other aspects of the experiment (Michotte, 1963. p.68).

These divergences between Piaget's and Michotte's views also occur in their conceptions of the origin of causal structures. Of course both authors recognize that the stimulus conditions favoring the formation of causal structures of pushing, traction, etc., usually occur in the tactile-kinesthetic rather than in the visual field. In addition, they both hold the hypothesis that the perceptual causal structures are initially established in the first of these fields (Michotte, 1963; p. 275; Michotte, 1962, p.71). The major difference stems from the fact that Piaget proposes a genetic tie between the tactile-kinesthetic and visual causal structures, the latter developing only by virtue of the former. According to Michotte, however, these structures are formed independently in each of the two domains as soon as the subject has reached a sufficient degree of maturation and is exposed to the appropriate system of stimulation; this occurs simply by virtue of the general laws governing the structural organization of perception.

Piaget's arguments are primarily based on two considerations: the role he attributes to resistance, weight and pushing, etc.; and the necessity for contact between the objects for children (Piaget & Lambercier, 1958, Piaget, 1961). But "resistance" etc. only comes to be important within the framework of Piaget's own hypothesis of "compensation." The superiority of adults in the case of visual causality at a distance could be interpreted in a variety of ways, in particular, by the effect of learning in the formation of causal structures when the conditions of stimulation are inadequate.

Briefly, what primarily distinguishes the views of the two authors, is as follows: first, the different meanings they give to the word "causal" applied to the subjects' answers, and second, the fact that Piaget emphasizes perceptual tactile-kinesthetic causality, whereas Michotte started from researches on visual causality. This allowed Michotte, in his opinion, to study the phenomenon under its simplest, most reduced form and to avoid in particular the complexities introduced by the effects of effort, resistance, weight, etc. in the kinesthetic field.

In any case, it is clear to both authors that the causal perception of manual activities in daily life occurs at one and the same time under both aspects and that there must be an interaction between them, as in the cases studied by Piaget and Maroun.

The Structures of "Dependency"

If causal responses can be explained, in the cases of entraining, launching and their derivatives, by the properties of the ampliation structure, there are other cases in which subjects also assert that perceptual evidence imposes answers with causal significance, in the absence of any ampliation structure.

Some interesting evidence for this can be found in the more or less detailed answers describing the phenomenon of triggering (see previous discussion).

These indeed allow us to assert that the movement executed by B shows the "character of movement" and not simple "displacement" and that it appears as the object's own movement; on the other hand, the origin of this movement seems to be bound to the fact of the impact. It is thus an autonomous, but not a spontaneous, movement: Its start appears "dependent" on the first contact between both objects.

Moreover, it is important to note that, since the nature of this "dependency" remains undetermined, the subjects try to explain it by intervention of factors they have come to know some way or another, but which are not present in the situation (an electric shock, a hidden mechanism, etc.). This is noteworthy because nothing similar is pointed out in the cases of launching nor of entraining with direct contact with objects. Indeed since one sees *A* pushing, pulling, or launching *B*, there is no reason to look elsewhere for the explanation of the displacement of *B*.

In the case of triggering, and when the relation of dependence is rather unusual, the explanations offered vary widely, of course, as a function of the previous experience of the subjects. Often, however, the total situation directly elicits an effect of physical causality that is well known, and then the perceived "dependence" takes on a definite sense, which though acquired applies so well to the situation that it seems to be intrinsic to it (in the way that meaning of words in language seems to be inherent to them). According to Michotte, this explains the causal response to attraction previously discussed or to withdrawal of a support followed by the fall of a body, and so on.[10]

In any case, it seems legitimate to admit that the character of "dependency" is a phenomenal character, which can affect some sequences of events in the same way as the character of belonging or "appurtenance," for example, and of many others.

It must still be determined, however, under which conditions of stimulation this occurs. Rapid succession is required of course as in all the cases of successive integration; but the nature of the events also has an influence because it seems that a dependence structure cannot be established between just any events. At least this is what Michotte's investigations on what he calls qualitative causality indicate—investigations that include, for example, experiments on successive changes in colors of adjoining objects, or objects included one within the other, auditory experiments, etc. (Michotte, 1963 p. 229 et seq). Furthermore, it is rather striking to discover that all the cases of dependency considered authentic up until now always involve combinations wherein the events include at least one kinetic aspect (changes of shape, sizes, gamma movements, etc.).

Another thing to point out about the formation of these structures is the influence of the "preparedness" of the subjects. It is clear that "causal" answers are favored when a more or less ambiguous situation is presented during experiments including many cases of clear causality.

Likewise the instructions given to the subjects and leading questions can cooperate in the formation of such structures in the case of inappropriate stimulation systems. All this offers only a few indications; the problem of the general conditions determining dependence structures is still far from solved.

---

[10]As far as attraction is concerned, see Metelli and Tognazzo (1958), Kanisza and Metelli (1956), Kanisza and Metelli (1961), Michotte (1963), pp. 102, 219, Thinès (1962, p. 78 et seq).

For the fall of bodies see the following studies: Gruber, Fink, and Damm (1957) and Ono (1960). What this last author calls the "liberating effect" of the suppression of support corresponds obviously to the notion of "dependence." For a general discussion of this point, see Michotte et al., (1962, p. 72 et seq).

General Conclusions

All the facts discussed in these pages indicate that the causal responses given by the subjects in certain experimental situations correspond to *specific perceptual structures.*

The structures are established under the influence of definite systems of stimulation that seem, in the present state of our knowledge, limited to combinations of a kinetic type. This is true in the visual field, as well as in the tactile-kinesthetic field. The conditions of formation of these structures are fulfilled at almost every moment of life, either after changes in the external environment or after the continuous movements of our body, of our limbs, and principally during all our manual activities.

These structures are of two kinds. The first kind includes launching, entraining, traction, and their derivatives. This structure is an evolving one, which Michotte called "ampliation" of movement; it arises as a result of phenomenal duplication, the displacement of the projected object following the impact of the motor object being momentarily identified with the movement of the motor object so that it also appears to displace the projectile. Ampliation is thus responsible for the apparent "generation" of the displacement of the projectile, an aspect of "productivity" that is essential to the naive notion of causality.

The second kind of "causal structure" is that of simple, unspecified "phenomenal dependence." It differs from the previous one in that the duplication included in ampliation and the character of "generation" are lacking. So these "dependencies" correspond from a logical point of view, to the idea of *conditions* of intervention of intrinsic causes in the presented situation (Michotte et al., 1962). It is these causes, as far as knowledge of them has been previously acquired by the subjects, that gives a definite meaning to the dependence in question (effects of magnetism, gravitation, etc.).

The existence of these cases of perceptual causality, considered as authentic by the subjects, introduces a new element that theories of the origin of the concept of causality will henceforth need to take into account. However, this problem belongs to the psychology of ideation and of thought and is also situated in a framework of epistemology that goes beyond the scope of this study and we cannot deal with it here (see Michotte, 1963, Ch. 17; Piaget, 1961).

Nevertheless, it is perhaps necessary to emphasize some aspects of the question, which the results given in these pages do allow us to specify. First, it seems clear that the most salient result of the researches made until now concern the relation between "efficacy" and the properties of certain perceptual structures. Now, if the formation of specific concepts of launching, entraining, traction, etc., from the perception of these events does not create major difficulties, it is not the same as soon as one passes on to more elaborate generalizations, such as the idea of "mechanical" causality, for example, which covers all the previous cases and many others, and above all, the "universal" concept of "efficacy" (efficiency).

The concept of efficacy is indeed constantly applied to sequences of events that present no kinetic or mechanical aspect and that are qualitatively widely diverse. Moreover, these events are often separated one from the other by considerable delays, in such a way that any possibility of formation of a structure of ampliation or even of dependence is totally excluded (Michotte, 1963).

Consequently, we may wonder whether the notions of "productivity" or of "efficacy" can also be acquired in other ways and if so, what they may be. How is it that one or the other leads to a convergent result, to a basically identical concept?

On the other hand, if ampliation of movement is the only source of "efficacy," other difficulties arise because it is then a matter of determining how and why this notion is extended to the cases just mentioned and what the psychological conditions of perception are that allow this extension, without being entailed by the perceptual structures themselves.

References

Boyle, D. G. (1961). The concept of radius of action in the causal impression. *British Journal of Psychology, 52,* 219–226.

Crabbé, G. (1962). Rivalité entre différents types d'organization structurale de causalité perceptive. [Rivalry between different types of structural organization for perceived causality.] In A. Michotte et collaborateurs, *Causalité, permanence, et réalité phénoménales.* (Studia Psychologica.) (pp. 259–274). Louvain: Publications Universitaires.

Crabbé, G. (1967). Les conditions d'une perception de la causalité. [The conditions for the perception of causality.] Paris: Centre National de la Recherche Scientifique.

Duncker, K. (1945). On problem solving. (L. S. Lee, Trans.). *Psychological Monographs, 58,* No. 5.

Fraisse, P. (1956). *Manuel practique de psychologie expérimentale.* [Practical manual of experimental psychology.] Paris: Presses Universitaires de France.

Gruber, H. E., Fink, C. D., & Damm, V. (1957). Effects of experience on perception of causality. *Journal of Experimental Psychology, 53,* 89–93.

Jassogne, M. T. (1947). Etude sur l'effet écran et les impressions causales chez l'enfant. [Study of the screen effect and causal impressions in the child.] Unpublished thesis, University of Louvain, Louvain.

Kanizsa, G. & Metelli, F. (1957). Connessioni di tipo causale fra eventi percettivi: l'effeto attrazione e l'effetto lancio inverso. [Causal connections among perceived events: the attraction effect and the inverse launching effect.] *Atti dell'XI Congresso degli Psicologi Italiani Milano, 1956* (pp. 131–140). Milano.

Kanizsa, G. & Metelli, F. (1959). L'orientation relative des mouvements dans la peception de la causalité. [The relative orientation of movements in the perception of causality.] *Actes du XV Congrès Internationale de Psychologie (Brussels 1957)* (pp. 290–291). Amsterdam: North-Holland Publishing Co.

Kanizsa, G. & Metelli, F. (1961). Recherches expérimentales sur la perception visuelle d'attraction. [Experimental research on the visual perception of attraction.] *Journal de Psychologie Normale et Pathologique, 58,* 385–420.

Koffka, K. (1935). *Principles of gestalt psychology.* New York: Harcourt Brace & Co.

Köhler, W. (1929). *Gestalt psychology.* New York: Liveright.

Levelt, W. J. M. (1962). Motion braking and the perception of causality. In A. Michotte et collaborateurs, *Causalité, permanence, et réalité phénoménales.* (Studia Psychologica.) (pp. 244–258). Louvain: Publications Universitaires.

Metelli, F. & Tognazzo, D. (1958). *Risultati di una serie di esperimenti sull'effeto di attrazione fenomenica.* [Results of a series of experiments on the effect of phenomenal attraction.] Istituto di Psicologia sperimentale di Padova.

Metzger, W. (1941). *Psychologie.* [Psychology] Leipzig: Steinkoff.

Michotte, A. (1941). La causalité physique est-elle une donnée phénoménale? [Is physical causality a phenomenal given?] *Tijdschrift voor Philosophie, 3,* 290–328.

Michotte, A. (1951). La perception de la fonction "outil". [The perception of the "tool" effect.] In *Essays in Psychology, Dedicated to David Katz.* Uppsala: Almqvist & Wiksells, 193–213.

Michotte, A. (1962a). Théorie de la causalité phénoménale: Nouvelles perspectives 1961 [The theory of phenomenal causality: New perspectives 1961.] In A. Michotte et collaborateurs, *Causalité, permanence, et réalité phénoménales.* (Studia Psychologica.) (pp. 9–90). Louvain: Publications Universitaires. (Available in English as Appendix II in A. Michotte, *The perception of causality.* London: Methuen 1963.)

Michotte, A. (1963). *The perception of causality.* (T. R. & E. Miles, trans.) London: Methuen. [English translation of Michotte, 1946.]

Michotte, A., Knops, L. & Coen-Gelders, A. (1962). Étude comparative de diverses situations expérimentales donnant lieu à des impressions causales d'entraînement. [A comparative study of the various experimental conditions which give rise to causal impressions of "entrainment."] In A. Michotte et collaborateurs, *Causalité, permanence, et réalité phénoménales.* (Studia Psychologica.) (pp. 231–243). Louvain: Publications Universitaires.

Olum, V. (1956). Developmental differences in the perception of causality. *American Journal of Psychology, 69,* 417–425.

Ono, A. (1960). An investigation on the perception of causal relations. *Tohuku Journal of Experimental Psychology, 2,* 164–172.

Piaget, J. (1937). *La construction du réel chez l'enfant.* [The construction of reality by the child.] Neuchâtel and Paris: Delachaux.

Piaget, J. (1961). *Les mécanismes perceptifs.* [The mechanisms of perception.] Paris: Presses Universitaires de France.

Piaget, J. & Lambercier, M. (1958). La causalité perceptive visuelle chez l'enfant et chez l'adulte. [The perception of causality by children and adults.] *Archives de Psychologie, Genève, 36,* 77–201.

Piaget, J. & Maroun, J. (1958). La localisation des impressions d'impact dans la causalité perceptive tactile-kinesthetique. [The localization of impressions of impact in tactile-kinaesthetic causality.] *Archives de Psychologie, Genève, 36,* 202–235.

Thinès, G. (1962). *Contribution à la thèorie de la causalité perceptive: Nouvelles recherches sur l'effect entrainement.* [Contributions to the theory of perceived causality: New research on the entraining effect.] Louvain: Studia Psychologica, Publications Universitaires de Louvain.

Yela, M. (1952). Phenomenal causation at a distance. *Quarterly Journal of Experimental Psychology, 4,* 139–154.

Yela, M. (1954). La nature du 'rayon d'action' dans l'impression de causalité mécanique. [The nature of the 'radius of action' in the impression of mechanical causality.] *Journal de Psychologie Normale et Pathologique, 51,* 330–348.

THE PERCEPTION OF THE "TOOL EFFECT"[1]

Albert Michotte

In my research on the impression of causality, I restricted my investigations to isolated instances of causality: launching, entraining, and propulsion. Yet we constantly encounter complicated sequences of successive, causal interactions, which are coordinated in such a way that as a group they form a global process. This is typical of human activities, for example; we can always see people using tools of some kind, be it a hammer, a screwdriver, a fork, a knife, a broom, or a pencil. They move the tool, and then the tool in turn acts upon another object, by, for example, driving a nail, turning a screw, slicing a loaf of bread, or by creating a trace on a sheet of paper.

It is clear that in such cases we attribute quite different roles to the respective effects of the initial mover and the intermediary: The latter is essentially subordinated to the former. The tool is only the means of performing the action of the user. This subordination of the "means" to the "principal cause" is fundamental to the concept of an instrument. It was particularly emphasized by the early philosophers in their concept of "instrumental causality."

---

[1]Translated by A.P. Costall from "La perception de la fonction 'outil' " in *Essays in Psychology,* dedicated to David Katz, Almqvist & Wiksells, Uppsala, 1951, pp. 193–213.

In fact the scope of the term "instrument" is very general. It applies to scientific instruments, musical instruments, kitchen utensils, work tools, and so on. Of course, the particular role of the instrument varies in each of these cases, and our knowledge of this role can be acquired in quite diverse ways. Thus, in order to know that an ammeter can measure the intensity of electrical current, it is necessary to have acquired a good deal of previous knowledge, even when it is being put to empirical use by someone unfamiliar with the laws of electricity.

In complete contrast, however, there are many mechanical actions, such as the use of a hammer or a broom, where, it seems, the actual function of the tool can be directly observed through simple inspection. We need to consider such examples because they raise a problem for the psychology of perception.

Is the perception of the tool function direct? In other words, does the causal intervention of the tool possess a specific phenomenal character that differs from that of an isolated cause and from that of the intervention of the initial agent? To take a particular example, does the causal effect of a hammer knocking in a nail appear the same if we see the hammer handled by a user, or, as a result of some kind of trick, we see the same hammer moving spontaneously? Of course, the question is purely psychological and relates exclusively to the field of sensory perception. Yet, considered from this perspective, the answer is by no means obvious *a priori*. It is possible that there is no perceptual difference between the two cases; if so, we should simply witness two successive causal events—the movement of the hammer by the user, then the hitting of the nail by the hammer. The introduction of a relation of subordination would then be a matter of intellectual elaboration separate from what is perceptually given. It is just as possible, however, that there is an actual difference at the level of perception as such, and that the hammer manipulated by the user gives us a direct impression of being an intermediary, that is a means of execution, which is itself devoid of any initiative.

If this second hypothesis were confirmed, it would not only enrich our knowledge of the phenomenal world and help to fathom the problem of "the perception of causality," but would also be certain to throw some light on the origin of the concept of "instrumental causality." For these reasons, we have attempted to investigate the problem experimentally. We have studied very simple chains of causal interactions in the form of schematic displays. These were presented to different observers, and we noted how they described what they saw and how their descriptions changed as the conditions of the experiment were systematically varied.

The studies were of the same type as those reported in my work on causality, and we employed the disc method described there (Michotte, 1963). The following served as the starting point of our investigation.

Experiment 1. The subject saw two objects, which we called *I* (the intermediary) and *B*, set at a certain distance from one another behind a slit in the apparatus. *I* was a small red square (5 × 5 mm), and *B* was a black square of the same size to the right of *I*. At a given moment, a third object, *A*, appeared. This was a black rectangle of 8 × 5 mm. It came from behind a screen that covered the slit on its left side and headed towards the object *I* which it contacted after moving 40 mm. *A* then stopped, while *I* began to move and head towards *B*. When it reached *B*, it stopped, and *B* then began to move in its turn, traveling a distance of 10 mm before it disappeared behind a screen, which restricted the slit on its right side.

Clearly, this display involves a simple combination of two launching experiments. We used different speeds in the various studies, but they always decreased from *A* to *B* so as to ensure the best conditions for the causal impression (Michotte, 1963, chapt. 7). The combinations used are given in Table 2.1.

The distance separating objects *I* and *B* also varied across the series of experiments, ranging, in gradual steps, from 5 to 75 mm.

The observer was located at a distance of about 1.5 meters from the apparatus, and there were no restrictions concerning the point of fixation. The observer was only asked to "look at" the slit and describe what was seen to occur there. These latter comments apply to all the following studies, and will not be repeated in this discussion.

The results were a function of the magnitudes of the speeds selected and the distance between *I* and *B*. They allow us to distinguish two typical cases.

1. In the first case, one has the impression of a single complex operation which is the action of *A* and essentially consists in the launching of *B*.

The subjects were in total agreement in stating that there was in no

Table 2.1

Speeds	A	I	B
(cm/sec)			
	58	20	6
	30	11	3
	12	4	1

sense an impression of two successive launchings, but rather a single global action. Furthermore, it is clear that it is *A* "which does everything," and is the sole agent.

However, despite the unitary nature of the entire action, the subjects saw distinctly two impacts, and perceived the displacement of *I*.[2] What, then, is the role of *I*? The descriptions leave us in no doubt about the passive aspect of its intervention; its movement is neither spontaneous nor autonomous, and it certainly is not the case that *I* launches *B* through its own power. In the words of one observer, "*A* launches *I against B*," and this form of words seems rather appropriate; it indicates, in fact, that *A* immediately appears as responsible for the impact *I-B*, which launches *B*. Others say much the same thing; that *I* simply serves to transfer the blow that it received to object *B*. It should be emphasized that this is certainly not a case of the "relay effect," the passing on of movement by a carrier object to another (see Michotte, 1963, p. 57). The present case is infinitely more dynamic in that it involves the actual transfer of impulse. *I* is thus the mere agent of transmission of the blow, and it is apparently the same blow given by *A*. This counts as special confirmation of the unitary nature of the action and of the way it is centered on the launching of *B*.

Such, then, is the phenomenal aspect of the event. We will return to it later, when we will explain the reasons why, in our view, it necessarily occurs in this way. For the moment, we will note that this phenomenon occurs for different distances between *I* and *B* as a function of the speeds. For the combination in which the speed was 58 cm/sec, it could be observed for distances ranging from 10 to 30 or 40 mm; when the speed of *A* was 30 cm/sec, it occurred for distances between 20 or 30 mm; and, finally, when the speed of *A* was only 12 cm/sec, we observed it for distances between 5 and 10 mm.

2. When these distances are increased, the experience takes on a different character. This becomes progressively more marked while passing through all kinds of subtle changes that are difficult to describe. However, in every case, there is some distance between the locations of the two impacts beyond which the observers have the impression of two successive events. This distance increases for greater speeds.

The blow delivered by *A* launches *I*; *I* then travels for some distance, during which its movement becomes autonomous and begins to belong

[2]The results were always as follows: For the fastest speeds and the smallest distances between I and B (particularly when it was 5 mm), the structural organization was often rather confused, and the impression approximated that of simple launching. Either B seemed to be launched by A directly, as if I did not exist, or else one did not perceive any clear succession between the impacts between A and I and between I and B, but rather one had the impression that A launched I and B *en bloc*, and so on.

to itself; then *I* strikes *B*, which is launched in its turn. There are two different actions that are separate from one another. Yet this separation is not complete, as if it involved two totally alien events. There is a clear continuity as a result of the continuity of the movement of *I* and the persistence of its identity. However, this continuity is in no sense a relation of dynamic dependence between two actions, analogous to the preceding case. There is no impression that the impact of *A* against *I* influences the launching of *B*. *A* simply serves to set *I* in motion and nothing more.

The differences between these two cases is rather easy to appreciate when one contrasts the following examples: (a) watching a billiard player launching a ball against another, which happens to be close enough that it could be grasped in the fingers (e.g., 1 or 2 cm away), and (b) observing a skittles game, where the ball travels a long distance before reaching the "target." The impressions are in every respect analogous to those we have described.

Perhaps we should emphasize that these differences in the role of the intermediary occur at the level of perception; clearly, they do not exist from the point of view of mechanics.

What we have found so far is sufficient to show that not every causal interaction that we perceive necessarily appears as a mere succession of events (as in this second case). Under certain conditions (of speed and distance, etc.), the intermediary link between the initial impulse and the final effect can take on a specific character of "transmission." The object that effects this transfer then seems inert and passive, and in no way seems to be the source of the effect that follows its intervention.

The answer to our initial question, therefore, is clear; but it is now relevant to investigate whether the property of "agent of transmission" can be understood as deriving from some of the concepts that have already been developed in the field of causal perceptions. Can the unitary nature of the action, the impression that object *A* ultimately launches *B*, be related to the fact of "launching at a distance" (Michotte, 1963, p. 99)? If so, this would allow us to understand why one has the impression that object *A* "does everything."

In fact, our previous research has demonstrated that it is possible to produce impressions of launching when objects *A* and *B* are some distance apart at the moment when *A* stops and *B* begins to move. To determine to what extent this effect can account for the present results, we conducted some new experiments on two experienced subjects in conditions which were analogous to Experiment 1.

Experiment 2. The experimental situation was the same as in Experiment 1, except that object *I* was omitted. At the beginning of the trial, the subject only saw object *B* in the slit, then object *A* appeared and headed towards it and stopped after moving 40 mm. At this moment, *B*, which was a distance ranging from 10 to 80 mm from object *A*, began to move. The speed of *A* was 30 cm/sec and that of *B* was 3 cm/sec.

The impression of launching, which was extremely clear when the distance was minimal, clearly persisted up to a distance of 30 to 50 mm. It would even occur for a distance of 80 mm, but this case was more ambiguous, for it was then just as possible to perceive two successive, independent movements. These results were obtained as long as the delay between *A* stopping and *B* starting to move did not exceed 50 milliseconds. When this interval became much longer, however, the causal impression disappeared. (Compare Michotte, 1963 p. 91 et seq. Note that the results reported there correspond to the case where *A* and *B* make direct contact.)

This result is important, for it is clear that in the case of Experiment 1, the delay between *A* stopping and *B* beginning to move corresponds to the time taken by object *I* to reach *B* and, therefore, varies with the length of its path. The delays that correspond to the speed of *I* and the distance it traveled are given in Table 2.2.

As one can see, this delay is only of the order of 50 milliseconds or less for the two highest speeds and the shortest distances. Yet, as was previously indicated, the impression of a global process in which *A* is the sole mover occurs for distances of 30 to 40 mm when the speed of *I* is 20 cm/sec, and for 20 to 30 mm when it is 4 cm/sec. In other words, the effect of a unitary process occurs for delays that would certainly lead to segregation in the absence of *I*.

We can only conclude that "launching at a distance" could only be effective for the fastest speeds and the smallest distances between *I* and *B*; this perhaps accounts for the fact that one does not generally have the impression of simple launching. In all the other cases, it is clear that the presence of *I* has an effect in ensuring the impression of launching of *B*

Table 2.2

Speed of Object I (cm/sec)	I-B Distances (mm).[2]				
	5	10	20	30	40
20	25	50	100	150	200
11	45	90	180	270	360
4	125	250	500	750	1000

Note. The values for the distances between A and B take into account the fact that those for launching at a distance are 5 mm longer than the distances between I and B since they do not include the length of I itself (5mm).

by *A*, despite the existence of a delay that is incompatible with direct launching.

Furthermore, if launching at a distance constituted the essential factor in our experiments, then it would be quite impossible to see why object *I* seems to play a role in the activity, rather than appearing merely as a kind of irrelevant diversion, as it sometimes does (see Experiment 6b, later in this Section).

Another phenomenon, however, seems to be much more promising in providing some element of explanation. A valuable clue lies in the fact that the presence of *I*'s character as an "agent of transmission" is found to depend on the speeds and on the distance between *I* and *B*. The *I-B* distance over which it occurs varies systematically as a function of the speeds, and, in particular, the speed of object I. The faster the movement, the greater this distance.

This relation naturally suggests the concept of "radius of action," which our research on the causal impression led us to introduce. When, in the case of simple launching, the path of object B excedes a certain length, the projectile gives the impression of "going too far given the impact it received." It only seems to be "launched" up to a certain distance, and beyond this it seems to move with a motion that appears to be its own. As long as the launched object remains within the range of the radius of action, however, it is inert and passive; its displacement is imposed upon it by the blow it received. Experiments have revealed that it is possible to measure the extent of the radius of action, and that it increases with the speed of the motor object (Michotte, 1946/1963 p. 54).

The analogy between this finding and the results of Experiment 1 is immediately striking. Here again, as long as the distance *I-B* does not exceed certain limits, object *I* remains passive; recall the typical comment: "It is *A* that *launches I* against *B*"! To repeat an apparently paradoxical statement we have made elsewhere "it is the movement of *A* that displaces the projectile," and this is the essential point of the "theory of ampliation" (Michotte, 1946/1963 ch. 8).

In the way that we have found that the displacement of the projectile becomes autonomous when it goes outside of the radius of action, so here we find that, when the distance *I-B* is sufficiently large, object *I* no longer acts as the "transmitter of the impulse" but launches *B* "through its own force."

All this conforms exactly to our theory of ampliation. Furthermore, these new findings reinforce our general conception of the causal impression. However, there is more. If one compares the maximum lengths between *I* and *B* for which *I* seems to be a mere agent of transmission, one finds that they are of the same order of magnitude as the values of the radius of action we have recorded for the same speeds in our earlier research (Michotte 1963, Table 1. Radius of action of B, p. 55). Therefore, there can hardly be any doubt that the specific character of agent of transmission that is taken on by *I* under certain conditions corresponds simply to the fact that, within the limits of the radius of action, its displacement seems to be a continuation of the movement of object *A* and that the impact of *I* against *B* occurs within these spatial limits.

However, we need to prevent a possible misunderstanding. One might suppose from what has been said that the passive aspect of the movement of the intermediary could only be assured when the distance separating the two points of impact (*A-I* and *I-B*) does not exceed the bounds of the radius of action, but this would be to misunderstand completely that this concept is defined essentially in terms of the extent of the displacement, or of the movement of recoil, which corresponds to the passivity of the projectile. This is largely independent of the actual size of *I*, as the next experiment reveals.

Experiment 3. This study was similar to Experiment 1 except that object *I* was a rectangle 45 mm long (instead of 5 mm). The distance separating it from object *B* was 5 mm, and the speeds of the three objects were, for example, 12, 3, and 2 cm/sec, respectively.

The results show that the effect produced was similar to that in Experiment 1. Once again, one sees object *A* "launch object B;" once more, therefore, *I* is a mere agent of transmission. However, the distance separating the two points of impact *A-I* and *I-B* is 50 mm, which is considerably greater than the size of the radius of action of *I*, which, at this speed, certainly does not exceed 10 mm. Nevertheless, the displacement of object *I* was only 5 mm and falls within its limits. We are not concerned, therefore, with a geometrical distance between two points but rather with the amplitude of the movement performed by the projectile, which varies, moreover, with its speed as we noted previously.

We will now consider two studies in which we introduced more intermediaries, *Ia, Ib,* etc., between *A* and *B,* thus producing a cascade of impacts; each one of these, in isolation, would give a perfect impression of launching.

Experiment 4. The subject viewed three objects (red, black, and red), which we called *Ia, Ib,* and *B.* Each was 8 by 5 mm in size and set in a horizontal row 10 mm apart from one another behind the screen of the apparatus.

At a given moment, a fourth object, *A,* appeared, which was black and of the same size. It appeared from behind a screen, which curtailed the slit on its the left side, and headed towards *Ia*, which it reached after traveling 40 mm. *A* then stopped, while *Ia* began to move to *Ib*. When *Ia* touched *Ib*, it stopped in turn, and *Ib* moved in the direction of *B*. The same thing then happened when *Ib* made contact with *B*, except that *B*, having traveled about 10 mm, disappeared behind a screen limiting the right side of the slit.

The speeds used for the four objects were either 58, 29, 15, and 6 cm/sec, or 12, 6, 3 and 1 cm/sec respectively. Interestingly, once again, the use of faster speeds had the effect of rendering organization a little confused and tended to simplify it. Usually, for example, *Ia* and *Ib* formed a block and appeared to constitute a single, complex intermediary, which eventually separated and transmitted the impulse to *B*.

At the slower speeds, things were better differentiated. The activity was complex, yet unitary. Once again, *A* generally did everything, and finally launched *B*. *Ia* and *Ib* were passive intermediaries, which were "launched against one another and against *B*."

Experiment 5. This experiment was similar to the preceding one, but we introduced three intermediary objects, *Ia*, *Ib*, and *Ic*. Their sizes and their separations were the same as before. The speeds of the five respective objects were either 58, 29, 20, 15, and 6 cm/sec, or 12, 6, 4, 3 and 1 cm/sec.

The complexity of the situation rendered it rather ambiguous and could give rise to different kinds of structural organizations. Thus, for the faster speeds, some saw *A* form a block with *Ia*, whereas others saw a second block formed by *Ib* and *Ic*, which took the role of intermediary. Other saw the movement of *A* "pass from one to another up to *B*," etc.

At the lower speeds, the organization remained unstable and varied a good deal according to the attitude of the observer. Sometimes one saw a kind of relay effect or else true launchings occurring at the level of certain intermediaries, etc.

In summary, it would seem that multiplying the number of intermediaries does not favor the observation of the phenomenon and that the best results are obtained when only one is used.

Up until now, we have only considered the case of launching. However, we have also performed some studies on the type of causality known as entraining, and the results complement the preceding data very well.

Experiment 6. At the beginning of the trial, the subject saw two objects in the slit of the apparatus, objects *I* and *B*, which were squares 5 × 3.5 mm and colored black and red respectively. These were separated from one another by a distance of either 5, 10, 30, 40 or 70 mm.

At a given moment, a third object, *A*, of the same size and colored

red, appeared from behind a screen situated 25 mm to the left of *I* and headed towards *I* at a speed of either 20, 7, or 4 cm/sec.

When *A* reached *I*, the two objects moved together simultaneously, one beside the other, at the initial speed of *A*, and in the same direction.

When they reached object *B*, this in turn began to move, always at the same speed so that they all moved together as a group. They then disappeared by slipping behind a second screen placed 10 mm to the right of the initial position of *B*.

The results were very clear but varied a little depending on the experimental conditions.

1. At the fastest speed of 20 cm/sec, and for the distances of 5, 10 and even 30 mm, object *A* performed a kind of "sweep" of *I* and *B*. As one of the subjects put it, it "swiped" them, or, more simply, it "removed" them in one go. There was no impression of succession in their disappearances.

2. At the speed of 7 cm/sec, and for the distances of 10, 20, and, to some extent, 30 mm, A successively pushed objects *I* and *B*. This also happened at the speed of 4 cm/sec, for the distances of 5, 10, and possibly 20 mm. Here the succession was clear, but it was manifestly A that did all the work. It was analogous to seeing two beads being threaded by the same needle. Object *I* merely appeared as something interposed "by chance" between *A* and *B*; it played no special role, and one had the impression that the action of *A* on *B* was identical to the action of A on I. This was quite different from what happened in the case of launching, where object *I* at least served as the means of transfer of the movement of *A*. Here it was as if *this object did not exist*.

3. When the speeds were slow and the distance between *I* and *B* was even more considerable, one saw object *A* entrain *I*; then these two objects, while moving beside one another, lost their autonomy beyond a certain point as a result of the influence of their contact and their "common fate." They then formed a rectangular block of two colors, and this block then entrained object B (see Michotte, 1963 chapt. 9). This was absolutely clear when the speed was only 4 cm/sec, and the initial distance between *I* and *B* was 70 mm.

Under these conditions, there was clearly a double activity: the entraining of *I* by *A*, and then, after a certain interval and a certain distance, the entraining of *B* by the block *AI*. However, the two events were far from being completely isolated from one another. As in the analogous case of launching, they were integrated within a global unit, which, although rather weak, was preserved by the persistence of the objects and especially, no doubt, by the continuity of their movement.

However, there was no trace of a causal relation between the two entrainings; *A* itself no longer produced the second entraining, but rather the new object *AI* had become autonomous in the course of its displacement. The global structure, therefore, seems to exist essentially at the temporal and kinetic level.

A final study of entraining relates to what we found earlier for launching. The aim was to provide further evidence that the effect is not determined simply by the separation between A and B.

Experiment 7. This experiment differs from the preceding one in that object *I* was a long rectangle, from 40 to 75 mm in length, situated 20 mm from object *B*. Objects *A* and *B* were similar to those used in Experiment 6. The speeds were respectively 14, 4, and 3 cm/sec.

The results were predictable. It was consistently the case that there were two successive entrainments performed by object *A*, with some subtle differences depending on the speeds. Once again, only *A* was the motor object. It would not be true, however, to say that things happened exactly in the same way as in the preceding experiment, that is, that it was as if the intermediary did not exist. The dimensions of *I* served to give a novel character to the impression. The common motion was certainly too short for *A* and *I* to form a unitary block, and *I* remained unquestionably distinct from *A*. However, from the moment when it was pushed by *A*, and especially when *B* was entrained in its turn, object *I* appeared to be an elongation of *A*, a kind of extension attached to *A*, and the intermediary by which it pushed *B*. Throughout, *I* remained passive. Furthermore, it did not in any way give rise to an impression of transferring the impulse, analogous to the intermediary in the case of launching. Perhaps it would be more correct to say that the push exerted by *A* was made through *I* without *I* having had a hand in it.

These then are the observations that our new researches have allowed us to make. It now remains for me to summarize them, and identify the conclusions which, in our view, they seem to imply.

Discussion

Two of the cases we have described deserve more attention as being the most typical. These are the ones in which the intermediate object either occurs as an extension of the motor object, or as an agent of transmission of its impulse. Furthermore, despite their difference, they are theoretically very close, for it is possible to pass progressively from the one to the other by gradually changing the experimental conditions.

The essential finding of our research is that *the intervention of the intermediary appears to be purely passive and dependent on the action of the motor object with which it is integrated as a constituent part; it is this which gives it a characteristic phenomenal aspect.* We will refer to it as "the tool effect."

The tool effect is particularly impressive when the movements of the intermediary object and projectile are those normally optimal for the appearance of the causal impression, and all the activity that it brings.

Nevertheless, it is easy to provide clear evidence of the difference that exists between the tool effect and the causal impression for similar kinematic combinations. It is only necessary to compare Experiments la or 7, as described in this text, with parallel studies in which the motor object, *A*, is simply removed. When *A* is removed, all its activity is transferred to what was previously only an inert, intermediary object; now it produces the impulse and pushes the projectile "through its own force" after striking it.

We should also recall that the loss of initiative of I under the influence of the prior intervention of *A* only persisted as long as the path traveled by *I* before it reached the projectile did not exceed the radius of action. Similarly, a simple increase in the distance between *I* and *B* was sufficient to ensure its autonomy and apparent activity. This results necessarily from the very nature of the radius of action since it is defined as the zone within which the movement of the launched object (the intermediary) *seems to be passive,* and, phenomenally, not its own. In fact, we think we should have been able to predict the specific experimental conditions for the tool effect on the basis of the results from our work on the causal impression, but this prediction was never actually made. We took an empirical approach, which revealed the fundamental importance of the existence of the radius of action to the theory of the tool effect.

Nevertheless, our work shows that the tool effect must be considered as a special phenomenon, and that its appearance is controlled by the combination of movements presented to the observer (the presence or absence of the movement of object *A*, the distance between *I* and *B*, the speeds, etc.), and, furthermore, that the character of this phenomenon varies gradually in parallel with the changes produced in the experimental situation.

One can conclude that the effect is, in the last analysis, a problem concerning the structural organization of perception. It is determined by the laws that govern the formation of particular types of organization (such as integration within a global unit, the apparent belonging or nonbelonging of the movement of the carrier object, and temporal and dynamic hierarchies, etc.), and it arises from a definite system of sensory stimulation.

Once again, we seem to have encountered a phenomenon that is primitive and nonderivative. This conclusion is in line with those drawn from a whole series of cases we have studied, such as the different forms of the simple causal impression, the screen effect, and so on. This is yet further evidence of the great richness and infinite differentiation that exists in the spontaneous organization of the phenomenal world and that serves to establish an actual prefiguration of the great conceptual categories of our understanding at the level of sensory perception (see Michotte, 1948).

It is certainly interesting to relate these necessarily schematic and artifical laboratory studies to our everyday experiences. In this respect, we need to distinguish two cases: those in which we are observers of actions involving the use of tools and those in which we ourselves are the users.

In the case of visual experience, it hardly needs to be emphasized that we constantly encounter examples of the two types of tool effect. These arise naturally in the objective situations that occur in reality and from the same spatiotemporal and kinematic conditions that we have found to be critical in our studies.

Examples of the "extension type" include the use of a knife and fork in eating, the use of a screwdriver, a file, a pencil, and so on. In each of these examples, the coupling between the instrument and the user is more or less rigid, yet they maintain their segregation in such a way that the tool, as an object, is sufficiently distinct for it not to be identified with the "mover." Sometimes, however, this is not the case, and the fusion is much more complete. An example comes from the use by some ball-players [as in the Basque game of Pelote or Jai-alai] of a kind of elongated scoop that they fix to their hands; as a result of "common fate" it becomes so well integrated to themselves that they give the impression of launching the ball without any intermediary.

Usually, however, the segregation is well marked, and the displacement of the instrument is clearly distinguishable from the movement of the operator, and this corresponds to a common type of causality, which we have termed "propulsion" (Michotte 1963, p. 172). The tool then becomes an agent of transmission. This occurs, in particular, when the form or amplitude of the motion of the tool differs somewhat from that of the limb manipulating it. Examples include a shovel, a broom, a hammer (when used correctly), a mason's trowel, a tennis racket, a croquet mallet, levers, etc. Needless to say, the distinction between these cases and the preceding ones, which lies in the extent of the movements, is only relative; and the use of the same tool can give either the impression of "an extension" or that of "an agent of transmission," depending on the conditions.

However, in both cases, the instrument never appears to act by itself; the person acts by means of the instrument. It is entertaining to recall those rather popular films in the early days of the cinema in which the user was concealed, and one saw a tool move without any apparent cause, and perform the task on its own. This is clearly analogous to the experiment mentioned just now in which object A was eliminated. The result was similar, but the substitution of a character of activity in place of passivity in the case of everyday instruments gives rise to a peculiar effect of surprise and even comedy.

The segregation of the movements of the motor object and the intermediary can, of course, be taken even further. For example, in addition to the game of skittles mentioned earlier, there is also the case of billiards where the impulse given to one of the balls often makes it travel a long distance and change direction several times before it hits a second ball. Of course, the movement of the first ball originates from the blow given to it by the player, yet it is hardly the player who seems to be the immediate cause of the final effect, but rather the "intermediary" ball.

In this case, the continuity of the movement and the persistence of the identity of the objects guarantee the whole group an obvious perceptual identity. This does not always happen, however, and it is possible to reach a degree of segregation sufficient to disrupt this global unity. In fact, this usually occurs, and we must now examine an important case.

Consider, for example, a simple pump, and let us assume an observer is unaware of how it is constructed, and of the physical laws that govern its function. In this case, the perceptual data relative to the movements are discontinuous. One sees, on the one hand, someone moving a lever up and down, and, at the same time, water pouring from somewhere rather distant from the lever. Therefore, one sees two distinct movements, but these are totally segregated because of their separation and their different directions and the form of their motion. The conditions that give rise to the tool effect are hardly satisfied here, and there is no question that the phenomenon occurs. On the other hand, however, the entire situation still forms a perceptual unit, and the simultaneity or the direct succession of the two kinematic events—the operation of the lever and the flow of the water—naturally leads us to make a connection between the two and attribute a functional significance to the pump.

This conclusion relates to what was previously said concerning the different ways in which we can come to know the role of an instrument and even to the more general problem of the discovery of causal relations in the absence of strictly causal impressions. However, we will not return to this latter question here (see Michotte 1963, p. 229).

There can be no question that our knowledge and use of the tool function in everyday life is very often based only on the perception of apparent simultaneity or immediate succession. Empirical knowledge of the recurrent sequence of operating a device and some definite event, therefore, is sufficient to make us consider that object as an "intermediary," even when the nature of the connection uniting the events remains a mystery. Once we have reached a certain level of mental development, we are all convinced, more or less consciously, that there is a causal connection and that the intervention of the intermediary constitutes a link that establishes a real continuity between the events. It is only in this respect that the intermediary object has the right to be considered as an "instrument."

One can now clearly appreciate the exact importance of the results from our experiments. They actually show that, under certain conditions, the entire causal chain, as well as its internal dynamic hierarchy, is manifest (i.e., the exclusive activity of the motor object). In these cases, the tool effect is an immediate datum, which is complete and open to view. When, in contrast, some of the elements of the series are absent (as in the case of the pump or a light switch) there is a break in the perceived chain, and then only by means of hypothesis, or through the application of acquired experience, can the continuity be restored; but this involves a level beyond mere perception and depends on processes of a different order.

All of the preceding discussion has been concerned with the impressions available to an external observer of the activity. We will now briefly consider how things occur for the agent as such, that is from the point of view of the person who is actually using a tool to perform a task. Naturally, this involves a difference in the "material" available to perception, because this time tactile-kinesthetic impressions are added to the visual impressions and become primary.

However, these impressions are clearly governed by the same structural laws as the visual ones; once again, therefore, these laws determine the degree of segregation of the tool in relation to the agent, the 'belonging' of the movement to the tool or the agent, the formation of a unitary activity, the internal hierarchy of perception, etc. Consequently, all that was said above concerning the spatiotemporal and kinematic conditions should apply in this case as well.

Nevertheless, in the present case, past experience possesses a special characteristic as a result of the intervention of "the bodily self" (*moi corporel*) that proprioceptive impressions bring into play. It is "me" who acts by means of the tool, who turns the screw, knocks in the nail, hits the tennis ball, slices the bread, and so on.

Again, the tool is passive; but, as in the case of purely visual experience, its passivity is a function of the degree of its dependence relative to the mover. Thus, to return to our example of skittles, it is obviously "me" who launches the ball, but it is no longer "me" who knocks over the skittles but rather the ball that I had rolled in their direction. Such cases are particularly interesting because they clearly bring to light the importance of the kinematic continuity. In fact, despite the duality of the actions, the player considers himself as the agent responsible for the result because he perceives "himself" as the original source of the entire process.

I should stress again that all this is not the outcome of a more or less direct "interpretation" of what is perceptually given in this case any more than it is for other experiences. From the structural point of view, the "bodily self" should in fact be considered as one object among others; it is natural that it should appear as the sole mover when we are using tools just as object *A* does in our laboratory experiments, and for just the same reasons.

Having concluded this research, we believe we are now in a better position to reconsider two suggestions we had already formulated in relation to the simple impression of causality.

The first concerns the origin of the concept of tool or instrument (Michotte, 1963, Ch. 17). It seems logical to suppose that the primary source of this concept ought to be found in the tool effect in its strict sense, rather than in those more complex cases where the instrumental function is attributed to an object on the basis of simple temporal relations despite the existence of a kinematic discontinuity.

Indeed, in actual experience, the characteristic function of the tool as an intermediary in the action of the agent reveals itself in an intuitive way, and this experience does not require any supplementation since it already carries its significance within itself.

Although it has a "sense" that is immanent in what is perceived here and now and is therefore concrete, it corresponds precisely to the content of the abstract concept of an instrument; everything suggests that this intuitive significance is the basis of the concept.

Finally, would it be too outrageous to suppose that the tool effect also marks the starting point for the intentional use of tools at the very dawn of humanity? One needs to imagine that this phenomenon could eventually occur in the course of "instinctive" activities, or even pure reflexes, producing, as a result of fortuitous circumstances, a mechanical effect by means of an intermediary. Would it be surprising, then, if the corresponding direct experience had repercussions on behavior that were much more immediate than the perception of coincidences between discontinuous events? The numerous observations that have been gathered on the way the higher animals learn how to use tools clearly argue in favor of this assumption. Furthermore, as I have said elsewhere, the research on the behavior and beliefs of primitive peoples leads us to consider "the many centuries that must have passed before our earliest ancestors were able to derive from recurrent sequences the knowledge of connections that to us, as civilized people, now seem almost obvious" (Michotte, 1941, p. 328).

References

Michotte, A. (1944). La causalité physique est-elle une donnée phénoménale? [Is Physical Causality a Phenomenal datum?] *Tijdschrift voor Philosophie, 3,* 290–328.

Michotte, A. (1948). La préfiguration dans les données sensorielles de notre conception spontanée du monde physique. [The prefiguration within sensory data of our spontaneous conception of the physical world.] *Proceedings and Papers of the Twelfth Congress of Psychology at Edinburgh (pp. 20–22).* Edinburgh: Oliver and Boyd.

Michotte, A. (1963). *The perception of causality.* (T.R. Miles & E. Miles Trans.) London: Methuen.

THE EMOTIONS REGARDED AS FUNCTIONAL CONNECTIONS[1]

Albert Michotte

I would like to take the opportunity provided by this second Symposium organized by Dr. Martin L. Reymert to report on some observations relative to the psychology of the emotions. They are observations which I was able to make with my students in the course of some research on the perception of "functional connections" and on the perception of causation. (See Michotte, 1941; Sampaio, 1943; Michotte, 1946; Knops, 1947). I do not intend in this paper to make an exhaustive study of the question nor a critical discussion of the opinions of other authors, but only to put forward an idea in general outline which was suggested to me by my experimental work.

First of all, let us recall how these experiments were carried out.

By means of special technical equipment we made two (or more) little colored rectangles, 1 cm. long and 0.5 cm. wide, move along a horizontal slot 15 cm. long and 0.5 cm. wide (same width as the

---

[1]In M.L. Reymert (Ed.), *Feelings and emotions: The Mooseheart Symposium.* New York: McGraw-Hill, 1950. Pp. 114–125.

rectangles). We could stop these objects at any position on the slot or we could move them at any given moment. Moreover, we could change the direction, extent, and speed of movement at will and thus obtain an infinite variety of kinetic combinations.

As for the results, the essential data, as far as concerns us here, can be summarized as follows. Certain combinations of visual stimuli, well defined as to the initial distance between the objects, the commencement of their movement, their speed, etc., caused certain specific impressions, for example, the impression "that an object *A goes toward* an object *B*," "that *A pursues B*," "that *A joins B* and *unites itself* to it," "that *A bumps B*," "that *A chases* or *repels B*," "that *A distorts B* by exerting pressure on it," "that *A pulls B*," "that *A goes to find B* and *take it away*," "that *A pushes B* with follow up." This kind of event we call "functional connections" in order to stress the fact that one actually *sees* some change occurring in an object "in function" of another.

It is most important to remark that the production of these phenomena is essentially dependent on the *system* of stimulation and that every notable modification of this system brings about a change in the nature of the connection (principle of concomitant variations). So when object *A* is halted after reaching object *B*, and *B* moves in its turn, an impression of "throwing" can be produced; but it depends both on the relative speeds of the two movements and on the length of time the objects are in contact. The impression is very clear when the movement of *B* is slower than that of *A*; but when the relative speeds are reversed an entirely different impression arises. In the same way, a contact of a few hundredths of a second is sufficient to destroy the impression.

Here is another example: the impressions of "approaching" and "departing" occur only when the distance between the two objects is within certain limits, which we call the "radius of action" and which vary with the speed of the moving object or objects. Beyond this distance the two objects cease to be connected.

The characteristic impressions with which we are dealing must therefore be considered as *Gestalten*, as specific kinetic structures corresponding to the action of a group of successive stimuli on the eye. In other words, we are dealing in this case with primitive phenomena and not at all with "meanings" which under the influence of acquired experience could be attached to simple impressions of motions merely juxtaposed in space and time.

This opinion is confirmed by many other facts which it is pointless to set down in these pages, and which one can find set forth in detail elsewhere (Michotte, 1946).

While we were doing these experiments we noticed a rather peculiar fact which at first we considered simply rather curious, but which was repeated so often and with such insistence that it became a factor of some importance to us, and one worthy of serious discussion. Our subjects did not content themselves with merely describing in an objective fashion what they saw in the apparatus, saying, for example, that they saw "*A* pushing *B* forward," but they often had an obvious tendency to complete these indications by comparisons with human or animal actions, comparisons which implied emotional states, attitudes, tendencies attributed to the objects. The letters *A* and *B* did not then signify the little rectangles as such, but took on the value of names of persons, and the experiments gave rise to interpretations of this nature: "It is as though *B* was afraid when *A* approached, and ran off"; or "*A* joins *B*, then they fall out, have a quarrel, and *B* goes off by himself"; or again "It is like a cat coming up to a mouse and suddenly springing on it and carrying it off."

This kind of behavior frequently occurred in a quite spontaneous way, and in any case the least suggestion was usually all that was needed to elicit such a response.

Why was this? Why this tendency to translate the phenomena into terms of human or animal conduct? This was a problem.[2]

It is evident that our knowledge of the emotional states and tendencies of other people is based necessarily on their perceptible reactions, that is to say their words, facial expressions, gestures, or even a simple movement of their eyes. Moreover, these manifestations do not usually remain confined to the individual in whom they are produced, as would be an expression of joy or sorrow whose cause was unknown to the onlooker. Rather they seem to be connected to something, some animal or person. The person who is annoyed because he has tripped on a stone gives the stone a kick; if someone meets a friend he shakes his hand or grasps his arm. And on the other hand, these reactions are often followed or accompanied by other reactions on the part of the objects; the stone is sent flying, the friend returns the gesture of affection.

In all these cases, then, the observer is faced with a scene or an event in which two objects (two people or one person and a thing) take part, each moved in relation to the other. Such situations correspond in principle to the scheme of our experiments, and it is thus quite

[2]By alternately lengthening and shortening the sides of a small rectangle, it is possible to give an extraordinary vivid impression of vital, immanent movement in the object; it then takes on an appearance analogous to that of a living animal, a caterpillar, for example. This "artificial animal" can replace one of the rectangles in the experiments described, and then the interpretations in an emotional sense come even more naturally. We did not deal with this type of experiment in the present work, precisely in order to avoid as much as possible anything in the appearance of the object that would favor such interpretations. (See Michotte, 1946).

understandable that they may eventually evoke the idea of human behavior.

However, the fact is nonetheless strange if we consider that the movements used in our experiments consisted generally of simple translocations of inert objects, while human conduct expresses itself especially, it would seem, by language, by the play of facial expression, and by an infinity of extra-ordinarily complicated gestures. And further, even if we admit the possibility of such an evocation, it still remains to be seen why it is *in fact* produced with such frequency.

This calls for a few comments. Let us remember first of all that emotions and tendencies can be divided roughly into two groups, according to whether they present an *integrative* or *segregative* relationship to the person who experiences them with the thing, person, or event which is their object.

Sympathy, friendship, and love belong evidently to the integrative class. In their most perfect form do they not result in identification, union, possession? On the other hand, antipathy, disgust, hate, and fear are obviously of the segregative type. One feels poles apart from such and such a person, a certain thing is repulsive to us. We fear the presence or approach of such an individual or event.

Again, the motor reactions corresponding to the first group usually result in an approach, which may manifest itself in a simple glance, or by the fact of positioning oneself close to another, or by establishing a contact more or less pronounced, more or less prolonged – a grasp of the hand, a kiss, an embrace. It appears also in the fact that one carries on one's person the objects to which one is particularly attached, refusing to leave them. This happens often with children who will not leave their favorite toys, even taking them to bed with them.

The characteristic reactions of the segregative emotions naturally present the opposite attributes. We move away from the person we do not like. We remove, sometimes violently, the objects which displease us, sometimes even breaking them.

Now these truths are just common sense, and it would no doubt be pointless to mention them except for the fact that they make us see one thing which is important from our point of view, namely, that *the physical reactions which correspond to the emotions fulfill in fact the conditions of stimulation which are necessary to produce in an observer the kinetic structures of the kind that we have studied.* Thus the "affectual" reactions will have the effect of producing in the observer the impression that one individual is "going toward" another (once the distance between them comes within the radius of action), and they will induce the formation of new perceptual unities presenting various degrees of integration as a result of the juxtaposition, contact, or association of movements (law of common fate). Similarly, the physical reactions of the segregative emotions will give rise to definite impressions of departure, repulsion, etc.

Let us add that some of the kinetic structures we observed showed a simply indifferent reaction, as when an object moved close to another without its motion being modified in relation to that of the other (for instance, when an object simply appeared to pass in front of or behind another). And this again can find an obvious application to certain types of human relations.

It must nevertheless be remarked that the integration and segregation produced in the perceptual field are extremely equivocal when considered in isolation, in the abstract. It is clear, for example, that global unities are not found exclusively in the emotional field; nor, in this domain of the emotions, are they limited to the external manifestations of friendship and love. They can occur in quite contrary situations, as by the contact of a hand-to-hand struggle or by biting which are the manifestations of anger or hate. Similarly, segregation can correspond equally to anger and to disgust or fear. Yet the emotional interpretations given by the subjects were much more specific and, moreover, were in general agreement with each other.

That is because integration and segregation take on different characteristics according to the different conditions in which they appear. Everyone will admit that the kinetic structure corresponding to an embrace is quite different from that of a struggle, and this also was the result in our experiments. A "contact," for example, varies considerably according to the nature of the preceding or following phase.

In a general way, speed plays an important part in this respect. Rapid movement gives the impression of "violence" as opposed to the "gentleness" of slow movement. A sudden slackening of speed or a momentary pause in movement gives it a mark of "hesitation." Sudden and repeated variations of direction, or even merely of speed, give the impression of "nervousness" or "agitation," etc.

Here is a general outline, rather condensed, which gives some details on this point. The main combinations are shown.

I. Object *A* alone moves and joins *B*.

A. The contact thus established is static.

When the movement is rapid, the impression is that there is a violent clash and that the two objects become welded together.

When the movement is slow, one gets the impression that *A* goes gently to join *B* and unites itself to it.

B. The contact is of short duration.

When the movement is rapid, the impression is that *A* strikes *B*.

When the movement is slow the impression is that *A* simply touches *B*.

II. Object *B* begins to move after being reached by *A*, while *A* stops.

A. The contact is of short duration.

When *A*'s movement is more rapid than *B*'s, the impression is that *A*'s contact throws *B* forward. This can be interpreted in the sense of a reaction of anger.

When *B*'s movement is the more rapid the impression is that the contact releases the departure of *B*. The movement of *B* appears as autonomous and when quick enough often gives the impression of "flight." This flight is considered as motivated by *A*'s touch and interpreted in the sense of a reaction of fear. This is further accentuated when *B* starts to move before contact and reacts at the mere approach of *A*.

B. The contact is of sufficient duration to allow the two objects to form a global unity.

The impression produced is often interpreted in the sense of a momentary agreement between two accomplices who meet, but which gives place to a disagreement followed by separation.

III. Object *B* begins to move after being touched by *A*, and the two continue to move at the same speed and in the same direction in juxtaposition.

A. There is no pause at the moment of contact.

The impression is that *A* draws, carries off *B*, takes it with it. When the movement is slow and uniform, the association is "gentle," "friendly." Rapid movement, on the other hand, gives an impression of violence; and if there is rapid acceleration after contact following on a fairly slow approach, there is an impression that one carries off the other by brute force; this further takes on the character of a veritable kidnapping when the direction of movement is reversed at the moment of contact. The interpretations to which this can give rise are obvious.

B. There is a momentary pause after contact.

When the two objects then begin to move off again, the impression is one of "going together," the unity being naturally accentuated by the similarity of their kinetic properties (law of common fate). And when this group of two objects disappears behind a screen, it not infrequently suggests a story—a lovers' rendezvous, or two accomplices going into hiding together.

This outline, though far from exhaustive, is sufficient to show to what degree the totality of stimuli and their combinations specify the kinetic structures to which they give rise; and it is easy to see how one can thus form little "scenarios," little stories without words, which are very easy to interpret. Further, I think it would be very interesting, especially from the point of view of the projective technique, to go on to make systematic observations concerning the nature and frequency of the interpretations of such scenarios, particularly among children.

I would now like to stress one or two points in all that has been said up till now. First, in order to understand fully all that has been said, one must determine more precisely the parallel which exists between certain characteristics of the subjective aspects of the emotions on the one hand, and the characteristics of the corresponding motor reactions on the other. We have spoken several times of the "system of stimuli." This is obviously formed by light rays in a certain position in time and space which strike the retina of the observer; it could be defined by stating the geometric form of the images on the retina, their positions in relation to the topography of the retina, the nature of the light rays, their degree of energy, the movements of the images, their direction, speed, and extent. In this way we could describe very exactly what happens in the eye of the observer during our experiments and also when he observes the motor reactions typical of certain emotional situations.

But it is obvious that such a chart, though no doubt very precise, would be no guide at all to what actually happens in the perceptual field of the observer. He sees a certain person approach another in a friendly way, embrace him, etc. And let me repeat, this is not just a "meaning" *attributed* to the literal, step-by-step translation of a table of stimuli; they are primitive, specific impressions which arise in the perceptual field itself. One cannot stress too much this most important point. Thus, I do not think it is superfluous to examine in further detail the example, just quoted, of a person who approaches another in a friendly way.

The impression of "approaching" is obviously caused by the lessening of the distance between the retinal images of the two objects; but the impression is really much more than a simple perception of "diminution of distance." In fact it contains elements which are absolutely alien to the world of stimulation. The movement perceived is polarized; that is to say, it is put in connection with a definite object, that which the other approaches. This polarization is a variable of the movement, distinct from direction, and only appears, as we have seen, within the limits of the radius of action (Michotte, 1946). In other words, an "objective" diminution of distance becomes an "approach" only within these limits. Further, this impression is elective, for in a complex perceptual field the lessening of distance between two objects is necessarily accompanied by an increase of distance between the moving object and others; yet the impression of "going toward *B*" is never accompanied by the simultaneous impression of "going away from" these others. This fact alone would be sufficient to bring out the difference that exists between the system of stimuli and the structural organization of the perceptual field. There seems to be some incompatibility between the simultaneous presence of impressions of "going toward" and "going away from" in the case of the same object. It is something analogous to the distinction between "figure" and "background," where contour belongs exclusively to "figure."

Further, as we said before, the character of "going toward in a *friendly* way, *gently*," and likewise the character of violence are connected with the speed. Yet gentleness and violence are obviously properties which are in qualitative opposition, while the physical differences of speed are purely quantitative.

This is only one example of the differences between the characteristics of the perceptual structure and those of the system of stimuli, but they could be shown to be present in all the cases quoted in the course of this work. And that confirms the essential conclusion—that analogy between the characteristics of the emotions felt by the agent and those of his emotional motor reactions exists only in regard to the kinetic structures aroused by those reactions in the perceptual field of the observer.

In order to drive home this conclusion still further, let us look at our example again. Let us suppose that there are three objects (three persons, for example) all in sight of each other—*A*, *B*, and *C*. *B* feels attracted by *A* and goes gently toward him, but remains indifferent to *C*. As far as the retinal images are concerned, there is a diminution of the distance between *A* and *B* and an increase in the distance between *B* and *C*. If the impressions were the literal translation of the stimuli the situation would be absolutely ambiguous—*B* approaching *A* could be a manifestation of friendship, *B* moving away from *C* could be a sign of antipathy or fear (which emotions, *ex hypothesi*, do not exist). But in point of fact, because the structural organization is determined by various factors (radius of action, etc.), only the approach and union come into the perceptual field of the observer, and the impressions he receives actually correspond to the sentiments of the agent.

In short, the principles which govern the structural organization of perceptions come into play, and the emotional reactions of the agent evoke specific kinetic structures in the observer, the characteristics of which correspond at least partially to the emotions of the former. So certain typical traits of the affective activity of the agent are reproduced in the observer by means of his perceptual activity. It is in this sense, and only in this sense, that one is justified in talking about "expressive behavior."[3]

But the perceptual reconstruction is, of course, only fragmentary. It only gives a sort of scheme of the emotional structure. The observer does not "live" exactly the same experience as the agents. But this

[3]On expressive behavior, see the admirable pages that Köhler wrote as early as 1929 on the subject (Köhler, 1929).

scheme can be completed, dressed up in a way, either by the recollection of former affectual states which the observer has experienced and which correspond to the same scheme or by the reliving of those states, which then become fused with the data of the perceptual activity and can be "projected" into the agent. This may perhaps cast some light on the difficult problem of "empathy."

One final point must detain us for a moment. We have just spoken of the possibility of evoking affectual states by means of certain structural schemes of the perceptual activity. Such evocation is evidently at the foundation of the interpretation in terms of emotions or tendencies which appeared in our experiments. The fact that this occurred is most instructive. It proves that it is the kinetic structures as such, the combinations of movements, which are above all effective; and it proves that the nature of the moving object is quite secondary *from this point of view*. How could one otherwise explain the fact that experiments with little inert rectangles could suggest the idea of emotional reactions? In fact, the surprising thing is that the nature of the object did not paralyze the evocative mechanism entirely, whereas apparently the only effect it had was to give the process an artificial aspect, which found expression in such words as "It's as if," which occurred constantly in the descriptions.

As for the kinetic structures themselves, it must be mentioned that though they varied greatly, they were extraordinarily simple compared with those which correspond to the emotional reactions of men in real life. Yet in spite of this, their power of evocation was considerable. I think the necessary conclusion is that they must be considered as constituting a *fundamental* aspect of human action as it appears to an observer. The core of the matter, so to speak, is in the integration and segregation. These processes are enriched and take on an increasingly specific character according to factors of a kinetic, spatial, and temporal order, a few examples of which we have examined. In ordinary life, the specifying factors—gestures, facial expressions, speech—are innumerable and can be differentiated by an infinity of nuances. But they are all *additional refinements* compared with the key factors, which are the simple kinetic structures. And our experiments bring out precisely this point, that phenomena of this kind are of themselves sufficient to enable us to identify and differentiate a large number of human reactions. Naturally this does not exclude all possibility of erroneous interpretation, but it is sufficient, to a large extent, to enable us to judge the relations of human behavior in a great many circumstances.

This is an important fact from a biological and social viewpoint; for the mutual reactions of two individuals (men or animals) are often the essential element in a situation in which other individuals are present, the element which determines the reactions of the latter. So an aggressive or a friendly attitude on the part of one person toward another may eventually cause a reaction on the part of an observer or observers. Furthermore, the conditions of visibility are often deficient; any detailed perception is prevented by the distance, light, or by some other reason or, in the lower animals, by an inferior degree of development of the sense organs. But even in these cases the general outline of the behavior as shown in the simple kinetic structures enables us to be fairly sure of perceiving the nature of the social situation.

Finally, in concluding the first part of this paper, let me underline the fact that all the considerations developed above bring out in a striking way this point: that the motor reactions of men and animals, *when related in certain ways with other objects,* are of great importance as *expressive behavior.* This is perhaps a point which has not generally received all the attention it deserves in the psychology of emotion, owing to too exclusive a concentration on the study of the reactions of the organism as such, without taking account of the *perception of its relations with its environment.*

In the foregoing pages, we put ourselves exclusively in the position of the observer. It now remains to say a few words on what happens in the case of the agent, the person who experiences the emotions. And I think that in this matter also our experiments will suggest some ideas.

What we have said on the subject of the integrative or segregative character of the emotions shows immediately that we are justified in taking them as functional connections on the same footing as the visual phenomena of throwing, drawing, pursuit, etc. It is evident that an emotion toward a thing, animal, or person establishes some form of liaison between the object and the subject whom it affects. Emotion is a modification of the subject *in regard to* these objects. Joy, sorrow, fear, and anger are undoubtedly states belonging to the person who experiences them, but they are states with a characteristic type of connection with their cause, a connection which differs qualitatively according to the kind of emotion experienced.

If we look at the emotions from this point of view, then, and in an abstract and very general way, they can be classed in the same group of phenomena as the visual kinetic structures.

Their similarity is even clearer when we examine the matter more concretely. It has always been noticed that certain motor reactions of the subject contributed largely in determining the subjective aspect of the emotional states; it is such an obvious fact that popular wisdom has consecrated it by introducing into the terminology reserved for the affectual life a considerable number of expressions whose primary meaning is purely spatial and motional. I have selected a few of these expressions:

> *Ceci se traduit* en particulier dans certaines formules habituelles du langage, et tout d'abord dans le mot même "d'émotion," c.a.d., "mouvement" de l'âme. Puis, il y a cette infinité d'expressions courantes telles que: j'ai été saisi, cela m'a frappé. je me suis senti *envahi* par la tristesse, je me sens *transporté* de joie, je suis *empoigné,* cela me perce le coeur, je me sens *aplati* ou *abaissé,* cela me *coupe* bras et jambes, je me sens *dilaté* d'espoir, je me sens *porté vers,* cela est *repoussant,* je suis *écrasé* par la douleur, cela est *attirant,* cela m'a *donné un choc,* etc. (Michotte, 1946, p. 270).

It must be noted that all these phrases really express kinetic structures of the type that we have studied, with this difference, that the former were visual, while these belong mainly to the realm of somesthesia. But they are very frequently rather complex and include visual elements. Here is an example:

> Ainsi, quande une personne avance brusquement le poing dans la direction du visage d'une autre et que celle-ci fait un mouvement instinctif de recul, on retrouce une situation tout à fait analogue à celle du lancement. Le poing de l'assaillant constitute l'objet *A* et le corps du "patient" l'objet *B;* les mouvements exécutés de part et d'autre se réalisent approximativement en continuité temporelle; ils ont le même direction; et la polarisation du second est évidemment inversée (Michotte, 1946, p. 271).

In this case the first step in the incident is visual; it consists in the perception of the approaching motion of the assailant's fist. This may be followed by a tactual impression of contact and of pain; and finally the recoiling motion of the person attacked is perceived under a tactual-kinesthetic form. But all of this is integrated into one global structure.

Another example would be that of manifestations of affection—beginning with the perception of a person approaching with outstretched hand, this visual phase being followed by tactual contact, and then by the complex tactual-kinesthetic impressions of a mutual embrace. The conditions in which these episodes take place are naturally such as to create again a single structure in which the two persons are integrated; and again the unity so formed will be the greater according as the surfaces in contact are greater, the pressure more accentuated, the synchronization of movements more perfect (law of common fate).

There is no doubt that, in general, everything that has been said above about the formation of visual kinetic structures of integration and segregation, with their manifold nuances, applies equally to somesthesia. Nor, on the other hand, is there any doubt that the kinetic structures established in this domain play an important part in the subjective aspect of the emotions. But here a new problem arises. If the perceptual structures as such are similar, how does it happen that when they are exclusively visual the person in whom they are found is just an *observer;* while when they are somesthetic (at least predominantly) the person in whom they are found is an *agent?* At first sight this is a real enigma; for the somesthetic structures are in principle quite as "sensory" as the visual and consequently belong by right to the domain of perception; and yet they no longer appear as the *"expression"* of an emotion (point of view of an observer), but as *constituents* of the emotion which is experienced (point of view of the agent).[4]

This is connected with the fact that they appear as reactions of the *ego;* it is *I* who repels, who embraces, who avoids, etc. For the observer the reactions which he witnesses are conveyed by an object distinct from himself; it is that person whom he sees over there who goes toward the other and shakes his hand. In the case of the agent, on the other hand, the action is not that of another person, nor is it properly speaking the action of his own body (as a thing); it is *himself* who acts in such a way toward such and such a person or thing or who feels this affective reaction for this person or thing. And this "himself" is lived in the action, in the emotion even, without any separate "support." This is true for emotion considered as a global state, but it is verified equally, needless to say, in its properly kinesthetic aspect. How is that possible? Opinions differ on this point; but in my opinion, the essential fact is that the sensory modality which intervenes in what it has been agreed to call the kinesthetic impressions is so imprecise, so lacking in "consistency," that it is overshadowed by the formal aspect of the structure, the form, which is thus in a "pure" state, so to speak, without any supporting object, and which alone is apparent. Action and passion (which intervene in the emotions) are thus experiences *sui generis* in which the "ego" is lived immediately (Michotte, 1946).

Nevertheless, it must not be forgotten that the ego is more or less extensible and includes various zones. The most superficial, no doubt, is what we call our possessions, then come the clothes we wear, and then our bodies, in which again we must distinguish between the surface and the internal organs which are nearer to the inmost ego. (And in this

[4]Of course, I do not mean to say that the somesthetic structures are the sole constituents of the emotions, in the sense of the James-Lange theory. On the contrary I hold that the emotional experience as lived by a man is much richer in content and especially that it has an extremely important intellectual aspect. But that does not imply any denial of the most important role played by somesthesia in qualifying and shading the emotions.

connection it should be noticed how the reactions of affection and love manifest themselves in a tendency toward contact on the part of these organs.) Finally, there is the inmost ego; and it is precisely this one which is lived in action and passion: it is the ego of our thoughts, of our mental attitudes, of our desires; and these latter also intervene as factors of integration when there is community of aspiration or as factors of segregation when there is divergency of opinion or sentiment.

The ego, however, constitutes only one of the poles of emotion. Since emotion is considered as a "functional connection," it must link this ego to something else. In other words, the emotions usually have an object, and it is of some importance to determine what this means. Must we, for example, envisage the question in a purely intellectualistic sense, and conceive this term "object" as being only the object of thought? I think not, at least as regards the tactual-kinesthetic aspect of emotion or even emotion as a global state which is "lived," "experienced." For if these phenomena are considered as global structures, it is clear that we must be dealing here with the integration of the object into a global form. So to return to the example quoted above, the approach of the assailant's fist takes place in such a way that the characteristic impression of causality must be produced, one must have the impression that it is the approach of the fist which *causes* the recoil. In other cases, the situation in which the emotions are activated will be such as to arouse impressions like "drawing along," "coming from," etc. All these impressions are characteristic of certain structures and they include the object, just as they do in the case of visual perceptions; they simply express the fact that we are dealing with functional connections, that is, as we have said repeatedly, with changes which are produced "in function of." And in these conditions it is not surprising that we should spontaneously attribute our emotions to certain events as to their source of cause (Michotte, 1946). That is simply the result of the nature of a certain type of structural organization, and there is no reason to suppose that it will not take place in animals as well as in men.

But no doubt the matter is more complex in man, for he is not merely a being which "feels," but also one which "thinks" and "knows," so the emotions he experiences usually have an intellectual aspect. Onto the *felt connection* is superimposed the knowledge of the *abstract relation* implied in that connection. A man "feels" himself attracted or repelled by an object, and at the same time he "is aware" of the attraction or repulsion, he "knows" it is happening. Whatever be one's opinion about the nature of thought, this is an unavoidable distinction, and one which is of some importance in practice. It is one thing to "feel" someone going away from you, relaxing his grip, and to experience a sort of wrench, more or less painful; it is quite another thing to "tell oneself," to "be aware" of this separation, for this brings a wave of recollection of the past, of foresight into the future. The present experience then ceases to be a transitory episode limited to the moment; it is inserted into the much wider framework of a whole life, and this in its turn has repercussions on the emotional state itself, irritating it or eventually deadening it, according to circumstances.

As I said at the beginning, the ideas propounded in this paper, originated in incidental observations made in the course of experiments which did not deal with the emotions. So, many of these ideas must be considered as mere suggestions, which might, I think, form a starting-off point for a more thorough critical discussion and form a basis for interesting experimental research.

References

Köhler, W. (1929). *Gestalt psychology*. New York: Liveright.

Knops, L. (1947). Contribution à l'étude de la naissance et de la permanence phénoménales dans le champ visuel. [Contribution to the study of phenomenal "coming into being" and of "permanence" in the visual field.] In *Miscellenea Psychologica Albert Michotte* (pp. 562–610). Éditions de l'Institute Supérieur de Philosophie. Louvain: Nauwelaerts.

Michotte, A. (1941). La causalité physique est-elle une donnée phénoménale? [Is physical causality a phenomenal given?] *Tijdschrift voor Philosophie, 3,* 290–328.

Michotte, A. (1946). La perception de la causalité. *Études de Psychologie, 6* (pp. 562–610). Éditions de l'Institute Supérieur de Philosophie. Louvain: Nauwelaerts.

Sampaio, A.C. (1943). *La translation des objects comme facteur de leur permanence phénoménale.* Louvain: Warny.

3
Phenomenal Permanence

PHENOMENAL PERMANENCE
George Butterworth

Introduction

Permanence refers to the experience that objects persist through space and time despite the fact that their presence in the visual field may be discontinuous. Permanence is perceived whether the interruption occurs through spatial interposition or through discontinuous observation.

As with Michotte's writing on causality, his important claim was that the configurational quality of the stimulus is what determines the experience of permanence. Thus, when one object is occluded by another, we do not perceive it as having been annihilated but as continuing to exist, although hidden. Under different spatiotemporal conditions, an object may indeed be perceived to have been annihilated, as for example when a puddle evaporates. The conditions of stimulation obtaining when the object disappears determine whether continuity of existence or annihilation is perceived.

In the first paper in this section, "On phenomenal permanence: facts and theories," Michotte describes a number of situations in which the principle plays a fundamental role. These range from basic but unconsidered interruptions of perception, such as blinking, to everyday experiences such as the illumination of a darkened room. When a room is suddenly illuminated, as with an electric light, the contents of the room are perceived to preexist their moment of illumination. There is a distinction, within the experience itself, between the creation of the illumination and the pre-existence of the objects illuminated. There is a "coming into existence" of the light and a "bringing into visibility" of the things illuminated. It is important to note that this distinction between what is perceived as permanent and what is perceived as created depends in no way on previous knowledge but entirely on the spatio-temporal conditions of illumination. Indeed, Michotte is at pains to point out that in some cases, as at a magic show, annihilation or creation may be perceived despite the fact that we know such events to be impossible. We cannot help but perceive annihilation or creation in the conjuring trick because the spatiotemporal conditions are structured in such a way as to allow no alternative.

Whereas Michotte's first paper in this section concentrates on the dynamic properties of stimulation that give rise to the experience of permanence the second paper, "Amodal completion of perceptual structures," extends the analysis to the case of static displays that nevertheless yield an impression of occlusion. For example, when a rectangle of card is laid across the "broken" parts of an incomplete triangle, the triangular shape is immediately perceived as continuing whole behind the partial occlusion. Michotte describes this phenomenon as an example of "amodal completion." In the contemporary literature on adult perception many similar phenomena have been described (e.g. Kanizsa 1979), in which complete shapes are perceived even though the contours may be only partially specified. These phenomena are obviously related to Gestalt demonstrations, such as Rubin's vase, in which the perceptual system automatically segregates figure and ground. Michotte's contribution was to assimilate the Gestalt demonstrations into the perception of permanence. The principle of permanence is involved because the ground is perceived, by amodal completion, to extend behind the figure. It is worth noting however, that he did not seem particularly concerned to distinguish between the examples of permanence that depend on the dynamic properties of sensory stimulation and the static, configurational "Gestalt" demonstrations. In fact, Michotte's claim was that the configurational quality was the important factor in both static and dynamic cases, whereas contemporary theorists stress other aspects of stimulation. Gibson took up the dynamic case and argued for perception of the events of texture accretion and deletion between surfaces, which specify spatial depth at an edge and which are fundamental to perception of interposition and the experience of permanence, (see e.g., Kaplan 1969). Johansson stressed the dynamic case but offered an organizational account similar to Michotte's in terms of vector analysis. Distinctions between static and dynamic stimuli, between specification by structuring of light in different ways by different physical events and the role of organising factors within perception all need to be taken into account to understand fully all the factors at work in the various aspects of perception of permanence.

Toward the end of the paper on "Amodal completion of perceptual structures" Michotte appeals for developmental evidence on the question of phenomenal permanence. Given his insistence that these structures are inherent within experience and do not depend on learning, evidence from naive humans could make an important contribution to the question of the origins of structure within perception. Michotte and Piaget had been in disagreement over the precise relationship in development between the perception of object permanence and the concept (or knowledge) that objects are permanent. Michotte insisted that perception of permanence in no way depends on a concept or belief in permanence (Michotte, Piéron & Piaget, 1955), whereas in Piaget's constructivist account primacy is attributed to intellectual processes in giving structure to perception. For Piaget the concept of permanence arises as the superordinate resolution of conflicting sensory information. The concept of object permanence is said by Piaget to derive from the logical inference, drawn from the conflicting evidence of vision and touch, that when objects are no longer visible, they may nevertheless continue to be experienced tactually.

During Michotte's own lifetime the only source of empirical evidence on the developmental issue was Piaget's (1954) observation on his own three infants. Piaget showed that babies fail to search for a hidden object before the age of 9 months or so. This led him to conclude that the perception of permanence must depend on acquired concepts of substance, and he proposed that the perception of permanence would not be fully elaborated until the end of infancy at about 18 months.

In recent years, however, the empirical evidence on perception of permanence has dramatically increased (Bower, 1967, 1982). There is now a great deal of evidence to suggest that even very young babies perceive amodal completion, occlusion, and spatial interposition so long as the information is presented in dynamic form (see Kellman & Spelke, 1983; Baillargeon, 1986, 1987, Granrud et al., 1984 and Butterworth, 1982, 1986). Infants younger than 6 months will also reach in the dark for an object when the illumination is turned off, as Michotte might have expected, even though they will not search for a static object hidden under a cloth (Bower, 1982, Hood and Willatts, 1986). Infants seem not to perceive static, configurational aspects of amodal completion until the second half of the first year if spatial interposition is not accompanied by movement based sensory transformations (Kellman & Spelke, 1983). Thus, one salient dimension determining perception of permanence, revealed by developmental research, concerns a shift from perception of interposition based on dynamic properties of events to static properties of configurations.

There is other evidence which supports a sequential development of aspects of permanence between the first and second 6 months of life. For example, babies younger than 6 months perceive "biodynamic motion" in Johannson "point light walker" displays. Such displays have usually been constructed by placing lights on the limb joints of a figure dressed in dark clothing. The figure is then filmed so that only the moving lights are visible when the film is projected. Adult observers have the compelling experience of seeing a human figure in natural movement, even though all that can be observed are moving points of light. The information for the interrelation in depth of the limbs seems to be derived from interposition and successive occlusion of the lights placed at the limb joints and by the subjective contours that define the vertical links between limb joints. Computer generated displays have recently been used to establish which aspects of the display may be effective with babies. The results suggest that information derived from the successive occlusion of the limb joints is effective before six months. However, perception of the subjective contours between the lights which define a moving limb does not occur until late into the second six months of life. Again, the evidence suggests that dynamic perception of occlusion is basic, whereas perception of subjective contours is a later acquisition (Bertenthal, Profitt, Spetner, & Thomas, 1985). Thus, Michotte and Piaget may have been referring to different phases of the developmental process. Michotte has received most support on the primacy of perception of permanence through dynamic occlusion, whereas Piaget receives support in the case of later development of perception of subjective contours (in Piagetian terminology these correspond to invisible displacements).

Michotte also laid the foundations of a theory of the relation between perception and cognition which has still not been adequately elaborated from a developmental point of view. He insisted that structures within perception "prefigure" structures at the level of cognition. He expressed himself as follows:

"When I speak of a prefiguring of ideas of causality, permanence and so on [in perception] I have never tried to pretend that these ideas are preformed in the sense of classical innate ideas. What I have in mind is the existence of "intrinsic signs" of certain mental structures. . . . One can perceive something slide behind another object without having to have the concept of a permanent object. Prior to any individual experience, the transformation itself is full of meaning" (Michotte, Piéron and Piaget 1955, p 57.)

In an extensive series of experiments Baillargeon (1986, 1987) has shown that very young infants "discriminate one object sliding behind another" as Michotte would have predicted. Other investigators have shown that texture deletion within dynamic displays gives 5 month old infants visual information for depth (Yonas & Granrud, 1985). In all these cases the infants are unable to search manually for a hidden object, an ability taken as the criterion for the object concept by Piaget. Thus, perception of permanence after disappearance arises in development before the child acquires the ability to reverse relations of occlusion through its own manual actions.

In conclusion, Michotte identified in the perception of phenomenal permanence a fundamental structure which has received its greatest empirical test in recent years from developmental investigations with human infants. This very active field of research again illustrates the continuing relevance of Michotte's experimental phenomenology to contemporary psychology.

References

Baillargeon, R. Representing the existence and location of hidden objects. Object permanence in six and eight month old infants. *Cognition* 1986 23 21–41.

Baillargeon, R. Object permanence in 3 1/2 and 4 1/2 month old infants. *Developmental Psychology* 1987 23 655–664.

Bertenthal, B. I., Proffitt, D. R., Spetner, N. B. and Thomas, M. A. The development of infant sensitivity to biomechanical motions. *Child Development* 1985 56 531–543.

Bower, T. G. R. The development of object permanence: some studies of existence constancy. *Perception and Psychophysics* 1967 2 411–418.

Bower, T. G. R. *Development in Infancy* 2nd edition. San Francisco Freeman 1982.

Butterworth, G. E. *Infancy and Epistemology*. Brighton, Harvester 1982.

Butterworth, G. E. Events and encounters in infant perception. *The New Psychologist: Annual Journal of the Open University Psychology Society* 1986 1–7. ISSN0264-3456.

Granrud, C. E., Yonas, A., Smith, I, Arterberry, M. E., Glicksman, M. L. and Sorkness, A. C. Infants sensitivity to accretion and deletion of texture as information for depth at an edge. *Child Development* 1984 55 1630–1636.

Hood, B. & Willats, P. (1986). Reaching in the dark to an object's remembered position: Evidence for object permanence in 5-month-old infants. *British Journal of Developmental Psychology*, 4 57-65.

Kaplan, G. A. Kinetic disruption of optical texture: the perception of depth at an edge. *Perception and Psychophysics* 1969 6 193–198.

Kanizsa, G. *Organization in vision: Essays on Gestalt Psychology* New York: Praeger, 1979.
Kellman, P. J. and Spelke, E. S. Perception of partly occluded objects in infancy. *Cognitive Psychology* 1983 15 483–524.
Michotte, A., Piéron, H. and Piaget, J. (1955). Discussion entre les trois rapporteurs. [Discussion.] *Deuxième symposium de l'association de psychologie scientifique de langue Francaise* (Louvain 1953), La Perception. (pp. 47–61). Paris: Presses Universitaires de France.
Piaget, J. *The construction of reality in the child.* New York Basic Books 1954.
Yonas, A. and Granrud, C. E. Development of visual space perception in young infants. In J. Mehler and R. Fox (eds) *Neonate Cognition Beyond the Buzzing Blooming Confusion* Hillsdale: New Jersey: Lawrence Erlbaum Associates, 1985.

ON PHENOMENAL PERMANENCE: FACTS, AND THEORIES[1]

Albert Michotte

The problem of the permanence of objects is one of that set of puzzles that deeply interested the empiricist philosophers in the 18th century and the associationists in the 19th century, as well as other thinkers of breadth such as Bergson, yet whose repercussions among "scientific" psychologists have been weak. However, it is only very recently that systematic work has been performed on this topic. Among the most important studies are the well-known observations of Piaget and his students from the genetic point of view and some experimental work of Metzger, Ternus and Lindemann. Detailed examples can be found in Sampaio (1943) and Knops (1947).

What is the reason for this neglect? Is it perhaps because this problem is located more in the field of epistemology and is therefore considered little susceptible to experimentation? Or, is it because the laws of constancy are considered to represent the principal contribution that the psychology of perception can bring to its solution?

To what extent is permanence a problem of perception? What is meant by "phenomenal permanence?" When occupied with questions of this sort, the distinction that has been made between acquired knowledge and appearances cannot be sufficiently emphasized (Michotte, 1948).

Thus, concerning problems of permanence and nonpermanence, the

[1]First published in Acta Psychologica, 1950 (7) 293–322 and reprinted in: Causalité, Permanence et Réalité Phénoménales. Ed. A. Michotte, Publications Universitaires, 2 Place Cardinal Mercier, Louvain, 1962, 246–371.

Translated here by George Butterworth and Alan Costall.

elaboration of the complex data of experience naturally leads us to know or "believe" that certain objects exist, even before we see them (or that they continue to exist after we have stopped seeing them), as well as that other objects only have an ephemeral existence whose duration coincides with their perception. Consider the following simple example:

Everyone has seen, during conjuring sessions, the conjurer make objects suddenly appear or disappear, when one knows that they were not created or destroyed at that moment. Nevertheless, it is unquestionable that one sometimes has the clear visual impression of their creation or disappearance.

The creation and disappearance of these objects are of course only illusions, but there is nonetheless a psychological problem here, which, in the last analysis, reduces to a perceptual problem; for the production of these phenomena depends upon a certain type of "evolution" of visual stimuli whose analysis belongs to the psychology of perception.

As for apparent permanence, matters are less simple, and in certain cases it even seems inconceivable that permanence can present itself directly in the data of experience. The comparison of this problem with that of the constancies is very instructive in this respect.

The topic of constancy refers, of course, to the fact that certain properties of objects, such as their color, size, or shape, do not change in a perceptible way, even though they produce considerable differences in the corresponding visual stimulation as a result of illumination in the case of color, of distance in the case of size, and the spatial orientation of the object in relation to the observer for shape constancy.

Constancy is of central importance in the case of permanence, since, thanks to the influence of the relevant laws, the real nature of objects remains apparently unchanged over time; but permanence goes further still. Indeed, one continually encounters situations in which an object remains identical, "of itself," even though we perceive changes in its properties, such as the reddening of a bar of iron in the fire, the expansion of a balloon or the flattening of a cushion. The identity of an object can even resist partial or total disappearance from the sensory field. Here it is necessary to give some thought to what this "thing" is that persists despite everything and that is not identified with its visible properties. Is it possible that this "thing" is given in experience? Or does permanence only arise as a mental construction (as substance or the permanent possibility of sensation) belonging essentially to the realm of thought?

It was in just this way that philosophers envisaged the question, and for this reason they primarily occupied themselves with determining the origin of the belief. They thought the belief was based on and justified by certain clues in experience: recognition, tied associations, needs etc.;

without doubt all these occur. Is it entirely certain, however, that this permanence, which is resistant to alteration or disappearance of the object, is only a matter of knowledge or belief and that it does not exist except on the plane of thought?

However improbable that this may seem *a priori,* it appears that the data of experience are infinitely richer from this point of view and more far reaching than has been thought. Indeed, numerous facts demonstrate that this type of permanence is manifested in different forms in the phenomenal domain itself, and the purpose of the present study is to indicate and discuss a certain number of them. Before moving off this point, let us bring some clarity into the discussion by recalling briefly the varieties of permanence and nonpermanence one can envisage. This will permit a precise terminology, from the outset.

Three fundamental types of permanence can be distinguished:

1. *"Prior Permanence"* (permanence of precedence or antecedent permanence) is characterized by the object or one of its parts appearing to have existed prior to its perception. (It is this that is produced when, for example, an object appears suddenly from concealment by an object that hides it from view).
2. The opposite case, *"permanence of posterity,"* is that in which an object or one of its parts continues to exist, even if it ceases to be visible (because for example, another object conceals it).
3. There is also *"continuous permanence"* where an object seems to remain itself, to maintain its fundamental identity, during the whole time it is present despite apparent changes it may undergo.

As for nonpermanence, it is necessary to distinguish three parallel cases:

1. *Creation,* when an object appears "born", rises into view.
2. *Annihilation,* when an object that is present disappears, leaving no trace.
3. *Substitution,* when an object seems suddenly replaced by another.

It follows that one may encounter different combinations of these types of events, for example, that creation can be followed by continuous permanence, and permanence of posterity can succeed this; or prior permanence can be combined with subsequent annihilation.

That said, we will proceed to examine systematically and scientifically a series of experiments relating to the permanence and nonpermanence of objects. The first example is of prior permanence, which is easy to demonstrate as follows:

One projects onto a screen any colored shape, such as a circle, and one suddenly changes its color, size, or shape. This experiment, among others, which we shall describe later, was carried out under conditions of monocular viewing, using an apparatus comprised of mirrors that allowed the different objects to appear successively in the same plane in space. A very rapid shutter ensured the practically instantaneous substitution of one object by the other. Under these conditions one can have the impression that the object has undergone a change while remaining "itself:" The same colored circle has become greenish, for example, or has dilated, or become oval. This observation is so commonplace, moreover, that there is no need to dwell on it.

An important point here is that this impression of change (of the same object) is only produced within certain limits, as can be experimentally verified. If the changes are greater and especially if several properties of the object are altered simultaneously, the impression becomes radically different. One sees a new object appear at the place where the first occurred. It is no longer merely a change, but substitution, instant replacement of one thing by something else.

Although change and substitution correspond to gradual differences in the system of stimulation, they are evidently qualitatively different events: The first is a manifestation of permanence and the second in contrast relates to nonpermanence.

It is naturally tempting and it seems logical to suppose that the impression of change is justified by the fact that the perceived alteration is partial and weak and that as a result aspects of the object that have not been modified constitute the "substrate" of permanence. Why, then, is it not the same when the changes are a little more marked or when they are combined, for in the present experiment the impression of substitution is produced even when many aspects of the objects remain the same? For example, it can be produced by a combined change in brightness and size while maintaining the shape, the microstructure of the surface, flatness, film characteristics of the color, etc. Logically speaking, there is no reason to affirm permanence in one case over the other. However, it is not a question of logic here, and the experiment shows precisely how permanence can occur in the form of specific phenomena such as substitution and whose production is determined by a well-defined system of stimulation.

Here is nothing but a psychological enigma, for the object is present to us, it would seem, only by virtue of these properties. So we may well ask, what signifies the identity of the object in opposition to the modification of the said properties? The question is relevant in as much as the experimental results indicate that no property in isolation, neither shape, color, nor surface structure, has the power to assure the identity of the object.

In fact, however, it is enough to consider this problem in relation to existing ideas about perception to catch a glimpse of a solution. It would be an error to consider different variables, color, shape, and so on as if they appear dissociated and independent. On the contrary, they appear as properties of a common object; they are integrated into a unit, the same whole. One knows that many of them are not equally important, that certain ones are more important, more accentuated than others, and also that they mutually influence one another. The whole is a true hierarchy, a relatively complex internal organization.

The phenomenal object is not a sum of properties (nor is its geometric form a sum of its parts) but a total structure, a Gestalt, in which a variety of variables are integrated and coordinated.

The term Gestalt does not serve to conceal a rather mysterious "entity," of course. On the contrary, it has a very precise sense from the phenomenal point of view; for quite simply, it designates the "specific schema" that characterizes the whole in terms of the constituent parts of the object. It is nothing if not obvious that every perceived object, however simple (even if it is a lone luminous point), possesses such a schema.

Considered from this point of view, the results of our experiment become clearly intelligible. The impression of change is produced when alterations in certain views of the object respect the "specific schema" of the whole: that of substitution when it is eclipsed and replaced by another schema. Permanence, therefore, is made possible, in the last analysis, as a result of the relative autonomy of the Gestalt, in relation to the variables it unites. It remains for experimental research to determine what is essential to its maintenance and to what extent it survives modifications introduced to the system of stimulation.

This stimulation is analogous to that which is well known to all concerned with the perception of form, where the global impression of form is conserved even though it appears more or less altered, as in the figures that can be seen as distorted squares or as circles. The only difference between the two cases lies in the fact that the Gestalt, which has an effect here, integrates *disparate* properties: form, color, etc.

Let us interpolate that this way of envisaging the solution of the problem enables us to reply to the question put earlier, "What is this thing that persists despite everything?" One can say at present that this thing is not uniquely an element of thought and does not reduce to the concept of substance but that it also exists on the phenomenal plane as a Gestalt. This unity, which is not solely defined by the presence of any particular variables but essentially by their integration and their ordering, is at the heart of a global structure and constitutes what we have called the "specific schema" of the object.

We will take a second example, related this time to the permanence of priority and posterity (existence prior to perceiving and after perceiving), from research already partly published (Sampaio, 1943; Knops, 1947).

The subject is shown a colored shape, a red square for example, and then a narrower white stripe appears next to it, which gets progressively larger in a perpendicular direction. If the speed and sizes are suitably chosen, the observer does not see the stripe form and then grow (as in reality) but rather a rigid stripe of fixed size, sliding out of the square, which previously hid it. This is what we have called the "screen effect."

Evidently, there is permanence of precedence (and of antecedence when one reverses the experiment), since the stripe "jumps" from behind the square that covers it. The hidden part is present, even though one does not see it. Naturally, it is indeterminate in size and, of course, this is only possible in the context where the entire display is perceived and when at least part of the object is visible (as in the classic case of the distinction of figure and ground). A similar case is the tunnel effect recently described by Wertheimer.

The experiment is successful in 100% of cases, and it is practically impossible for the subject to see the stripe get thinner or larger, even when informed of the techniques used. However, it is not difficult to be certain that this must be the case, given that the experimental conditions used here have the effect that the boundary that separates the square from the stripe is exclusively related to the square. That is to say, the boundary is perceived only as a part of the contour of the square, and the stripe has no limit of its own in this direction. Therefore the stripe seems to extend behind the square (as the ground extends behind the figure).

Moreover, the experimental conditions that disrupt the phenomena of dilation, contraction, or apparent growth of the object may be demonstrated; these include the absence of the stripe's own limit. The result is that the apparent size of the stripe must remain constant (rigid). On the other hand, it is clear that the visible length of the stripe progressively enlarges.

It is enough to reconcile these three facts to prove that they constitute the essential features of the structure "to emerge" because, in the last analysis, this reduces to the fact that "one sees it as an increase in the visible length of a rigid stripe partially covered over by a square."

Examples of the screen effect common in everyday life have been discussed before (Sampaio, 1943; Knops, 1947): the opening of a drawer or the curtains of a window, putting a hand in one's pocket, the disappearance of a car or person turning a corner, even the simple opening of the eyelids. One cannot overestimate the importance of this effect in the apparent permanence of things.

Remember for the moment that this second experiment and many others that we have performed applying the same principles fully confirm the results of the first. It again proves that permanence is manifested in the form of specific phenomena that can be expressed here by the impression "to emerge from" (or its opposite "to enter") whose production is determined by the system of stimulation available to the observer.

A third example is given by a familiar observation but one that nevertheless constitutes a real enigma after a moment's thought. The problem refers to the situation where one is in a perfectly dark room, for example in one's bedroom at night, and when one suddenly turns on the light: objects which are seen, furniture etc. seem clearly permanent, as existing even before we see them. This case is all the more interesting because it is precisely the contrast between the permanence of objects and the intermittence of their perception that has most generally intrigued those who are concerned with the problem.

In passing, one may note that another similar demonstration involving the sudden projection of an illuminated image onto a screen in a dark room, gives a result that seems absolutely different at first sight. The image seems to be created at the moment of its appearance.

These observations are so commonplace and have such an apparently obvious explanation that at first one does not realize the difficulty attached to them. Everyone will be tempted to see the obvious evidence of our knowledge of the nature of "real objects" and of "luminous images." It would then be our knowledge that was directly in play at the time, thanks to an influence it exercises over our sensory impressions. However, this opinion immediately contradicts the fact that the "reality" of an object that appears suddenly is not sufficient to guarantee its permanence, as we have seen in the case of the conjurer. It is true that one can be a little sceptical in that case and attempt to explain the illusion by the intervention of other factors: distraction, suggestion, etc.; but consider the following experiment that eliminates these factors yet nevertheless gives the same result.

The subject is shown a uniform, rather dark gray screen, of about 6 cm square and asked to fixate its center. The square is suddenly replaced by another identical one, from the point of view of its brightness and surface texture, but in the middle of this square there is a real object, a screw for example. The apparatus is adjusted in such a way that the background undergoes no perceptible change at the moment of substitution and, therefore, appears absolutely stable during the length of the observation.

The effects of this experiment are consistent: Subjects normally describe what they have seen by reporting that "the object" seems to "create itself," "come" from nothing, without implying in any way that it seems to "come out of" the gray background in the sense that one sees an object come out from behind a curtain. Here there is no trace of the screen effect, but instead the object appears as something that suddenly manifests "itself" where there was previously nothing. This experiment allows an internal dynamism of the object, an "evolution" that is plain to see. Skilled observers do not fail to notice the presence of *Gamma movements*[2] (particularly accentuated by elongated objects), the effect of which is to make the object appear to "grow" from the point of fixation. (Knops, 1947, p. 584 et seq.)

The display produces a true impression of birth and creation, in the obvious sense of the word, analogous to that which one sees when one witnesses the lighting of a fire or the blowing of a soap bubble. In both cases, there is this *"internal process"* (travail interieur) of expansion, which, incidentally, may well be essential to the character of "creation" in the visual world.

In any case, the fundamental fact, which we are going to stress for the moment, is that the presence of this type of creation, in this particular experiment, is in patent contradiction with the subject's belief that the object seen really existed somewhere or other and in reality did not emerge from nothing! Furthermore, all normal adults are sure that it is an illusion produced by some trick.

If one can produce the illusion of the creation of an object, which one knows to be permanent, it is equally possible to produce an illusion of permanence for an object, which one knows is formed at the very moment it is seen. Thus, it is easy to confer apparent permanence of precedence to projected light images by interposing the screen effect. One places a piece of cardboard in front of the lens of the projector, which intercepts the light rays and prevents the image from being formed. One then slowly pivots the projector about its axis, in such a way that the rays pass the obstacle and strike a piece of frosted glass. The image then starts to exist and is displaced, while completing itself, during the rotation of the lamp. Physically speaking, there is creation at this moment.

[2][Gamma movement occurs when an object is abruptly presented on a homogenous background. Its sudden appearance is accompanied by an expansion of the object. In the opposite case, a contraction movement is produced at the moment when an object abruptly disappears.]

One can explain all this to the subject, make the subject see the way in which the apparatus works, but if the subject then sits on the other side of the frosted glass, he or she nevertheless sees the image "jump out" from behind something that hides it, in a compelling way. To the observer, it is the image on the frosted glass itself which slides from behind a cover which hides it, and consequently it preexisted.

The conclusion is inevitable that the impression of permanence, like that of creation, is not necessarily tied to the physical nature of objects. Its presence is determined by the conditions of stimulation, equally in the case of real objects as in that of luminous images. This point having been established, we can examine more closely the example of the dark room before considering the reason for the permanence of objects in this special case.

To this end, an experiment can be carried out that calls this situation to mind. The apparatus used for this experiment is the same as for the experiment before the last one described, with the difference that the gray background is omitted in the first phase and the visual field is completely dark (as in the bedroom). In the second phase, the gray square, with the object placed at its center, suddenly appears.

Contrary to what happened before, all impression of the creation of the object is usually lost here. The object seems stabilized from the very start; moreover, there are no experiences of Gamma movement. This last statement, although purely negative, is interesting in that it shows that the "creation" of the object is not necessarily produced each time there is sudden stimulation and that its presence depends on additional factors such as Gamma movements, which result in a true "evolution" of the object.

One could try to find why Gamma movements are absent in this case, and there would be much to say on this topic, but this question is secondary to our problem here. We shall not dwell on the fact but we shall note it.

As for the positive results of the experiment they differ and one can classify them afterwards into two principal categories: A and B for convenience.

Category A

Certain subjects confine themselves to saying that "they see the object appear," and it is difficult to obtain more precise details from them. Always, if one persists, it seems from interpreting their responses, that their reports adequately capture the physical impression. For them there is a simple succession from a state in which the "object is present" to a state where there is "nothing" and the passage from one to the other is not marked by any particular characteristic.

The observer, therefore, is entirely dominated by the inert object (i.e., by an absence of evolution), in such a complete manner that the increase in luminance, which is regularly produced in all sudden illuminations of an extended field, does not exist for him; it passes unperceived. To the extent that it exists phenomenally, it is only an unimportant accessory that plays no part in the experience of the whole.

Category B

Here the picture is quite different and entirely similar to what happens in the dark room. Subjects have the impression of the sudden illumination of an object that was already there. That is to say, there is *creation of the light* and *antecedent permanence* of the object.

The well-known dissociation between the impression of illumination and of the object, therefore, is central to this example. The light itself shows a marked phenomenal autonomy and appears as one of the principal constituents of the whole experience.

From the descriptive point of view, categories A and B differ essentially in the internal structure of perception, by the hierarchy established between its constituents.

This having been established, several points need to be discussed more deeply. In the first place, why isn't there the impression of creation in the case of category A? Reformulating this question puts it in a completely different light. In effect, it amounts to asking why the object in this case does not possess its own preceding temporal limits. It follows automatically that the appearance (and the eventual disappearance) of the object is produced at a certain moment in phenomenal time and, therefore, is placed in the general temporal course of mental life; but this resolution remains extrinsic to the object and only marks the beginning of its "presence" without giving any indication of its origin or beginnings. This remains completely undetermined; the object seems neither created nor preexisting at the moment it starts to take part in our perceptual experience. The only thing one can say about this is precisely what the observers report when they reply "there was nothing there and now there is something," a banal formulation but one astonishingly exact at its root.

One may add that this phenomenal situation is very similar to that of our first example, the case of substitution. In fact, it is an error to conceive of the substitution as necessarily implying a creation followed by a phenomenal annihilation. On the contrary, it is often the case that it is also described in the following way, "there was that at that place and then suddenly there was this," a formula similar to the last one that seems to result from the typical impression of category A, which is ultimately of a pure substitution.

The case of creation is quite different. It is no longer just a question of a *start to the object's appearance* but of a *beginning of existence,* since one witnesses the formation of the object as it unfolds from nothing! The object goes through a progressive development; one sees it "becoming" what it is through evolutionary processes that can in extreme cases be reduced to Gamma movements. It is evident that in these circumstances, the object has an intrinsic temporal structure corresponding to the rhythm of its development, and the anterior limit of this evolution constitutes the object's own temporal limit. This temporal limit relates to it in the same way that, in the spatial domain, the contour of a figure belongs to it and not to the ground on which it stands.

The whole problem, therefore, centers on the apparently essential distinction between time external to the object (in which it is simply localized) and its own time, which is intrinsic and characteristic of it, and which fixes a defined limit to the time of formation of the object in terms of the object itself, not simply as a function of the unfolding of mental life.

It is the absence of apparent evolution of the object (and also of the light) that verifies that there was no impression of creation in category A. This explains in a general way why the sudden appearance of an object in our experiment does not always present itself as a phenomenal "creation." (The same thing is also true of audition. When one hears a sudden noise in a silent room, there is a simple succession from a state of absence to a state of presence, but it is different when the appearance of noise is accompanied by a progressive increase of intensity, or when one hears a melody, which by nature has its intrinsic time.)

The preceding discussion makes it easy to understand that there is an impression of creation of the light in the case of category B. This results instantaneously from the phenomenal "expansion" normal to light, which constitutes a true evolution, and from the considerable autonomy that it has in relation to the object. (The dissociation between the illumination and the object's own colors occurs equally in other experiments, where the object from the outset gives the impression of being strongly illuminated, [under our experimental conditions]. The essential fact in these cases, however, was the absence of growth characteristic of the illumination.) Another aspect of the structure of B, which we have not yet touched upon, is also important. It seems certain that in this case there is an impression of the preexistence of the object in relation to its illumination. This constitutes a new problem given that preexistence implies a certain determination, however vague, of the object's own continuity. However, these objects are stable and inert, so how can they present this appearance of extension into the past?

Comparison of categories A and B offers a clue. If apparent preexistence only appears in category B, the important characteristic is exclusively related to category B, that is, *the presence of the impression of the creation of the light.*

It must be noted that the relation of the object and its illumination cannot be reduced to a simple juxtaposition. The light affects the object, since it illuminates it. Despite the distinction of its different aspects, the global experience constitutes a very strong unity, which is well ordered and meaningful. From this point of view, there is a contrast with the slightly incoherent nature of category A.

If the constituents of the subjective experience (object and illumination) are so intimately related, however, it is not surprising that properties of one must have a certain repercussion on those of the other. This influence may be considered in the following way.

Among others, a simple explanation can be proposed that has the additional advantage of establishing a new reconciliation between the worlds of time and space. As was said, the illumination has its own anterior temporal limit, since it seems to come into being at the moment of its appearance. The object does not have this anterior temporal limit. This is reminiscent of the distinction between figure and ground. Two constituents of experience present themselves there also, one of which has a limit and the other does not. The result of their coordination in space occurs in such a way that the background appears to extend behind the figure. In other words, the background seems to exist behind the boundaries of the figure. Why should it not be the same for time, given that the stimulus conditions are parallel in the two domains?

The two events, the illumination and the appearance of the object, physically have a common temporal limit, since they are produced at the same moment of physical time. In the same way the two areas of the spatial field (that of figure and ground) have a common boundary in physical space. Phenomenally speaking, the temporal limit only relates to one of the events just as the spatial boundary only relates to one of the areas. Under these circumstances, there is no reason why the other constituent of the total experience, the object, may not appear to be prolonged beyond the temporal limits of its illumination. In consequence, the object will be given an impression of preexistence in the same way that the background gives the impression of being present behind the figure. All the evidence seems to favor this conception.

Other hypotheses may be taken equally into consideration. It does not seem impossible that the contrast between the "growth" of illumination and the stability of the object is accentuated in the structure of the whole. It would be as if the temporal progression of the light derived from an apparent regression of the object, throwing it back into the past. Moreover, this would be an indeterminate past, which is simply expressed by the impression of being "already there."

Such phenomena may be understood in the same way as those observed in the case of induced movements. When two points form a united group and one of them moves in the direction of the observer while the other stays still, under certain conditions one gets the impression that the latter is displaced in the opposite direction. Isn't this something similar? Of course, these are not mere suggestions but ones susceptible to being tested in systematic experimental procedures.

In particular one could try to make the experimental conditions less ambiguous so that they become compelling and impose the category B impression on observers. No doubt this could be done if one considerably altered the surface properties of the ground or if one considerably altered the number of objects on it. It would be better still if one replaced the instantaneous physical illumination with a progressive increase in luminous intensity, starting from zero. This would have the probable effect of accentuating the segregation of object and illumination and permit closer study of the permanence of the object. Perhaps experiments of this kind can also give rise to the impression of simultaneous creation of the object and the illumination, in the case where at the beginning the progression is sufficiently slow for there to be a stage that is unstructured and uncolored, which develops into a definite organization and coloring.

The results of the observations of category B clearly show that the difference mentioned earlier between the case of objects suddenly illuminated and luminous projections rests on a confusion. In fact, what happens at the time of projection is entirely similar to that seen at the time of illumination of objects. The only difference rests in what one considers as object and as illumination, and it is this which is misunderstood. After all, a projected image is itself illumination (i.e., luminous projection!). Suppose that the observer is in a room that is absolutely dark. The room itself will be illuminated, along with the the screen, the surroundings, the spectators etc., once the image is projected, exactly as if one had suddenly switched on the lights. Therefore, there is permanence of the room and its contents and apparent creation of the light. (It would be a mistake to believe that the appearance of the "illumination" always carried the characteristic of creation. Illumination, as well as film colors or even object colors, can themselves seem to preexist. This happens, for example, when one physically opens the door of a room and it seems from the outset to be more or less strongly illuminated.)

The confusion arises from the fact that here an image, which itself represents objects, also serves the function of illumination; and it is in this last role that it appears created, but it is not necessarily the same for the objects represented by the image. (It is not impossible to establish such experimental conditions, where a projection gives the impression of simply illuminating an image *already* painted or drawn on the screen, but this specifically shows that certain methodological tricks give rise to a perceptual structure similar to those observed in experiment 3; and it would not carry any special, theoretical significance.) It is interesting to note that one again finds a dissociation between the object's own appearance and its illumination. This can explain the apparent permanence of represented objects. One only has to think of illumination effects seen in the cinema or on opening the curtains of a room. These are good examples of segregation and separation of "systems," which isolate the image's own space from the room in which it is projected (c.f., Michotte, 1948, p. 10).

Let us move on to examine another case of permanence, this time in the realm of touch. When we touch an object or strike our foot on an unseen obstacle, or when an object, such as a ball, hits us on the back, we do not have the impression of the creation of these objects as we feel them. Similarly, every time we take a few steps in a dark room or with our eyes closed, the floor whose resistance we feel beneath our feet seems to preexist our actual experience.

It might be said that this stems from sudden contact with an object that immediately gives the impression of a solid, resistant, physical body and that it is this characteristic that determines apparent permanence. Furthermore, there is no lack of support for this kind of reasoning, especially when it is found that other categories of tactile impression present the appearance of "creation" at the time of their appearance, for example, the tickle, itching, internal pain, or even feeble impressions of contact near threshold. Thus, one might well imagine that permanence is related to the objectivity and absence of permanence to the subjectivity[3] of response to tactile/kinaesthetic stimuli.

But our discussion of visual examples introduced a certain scepticism regarding the role of aspects of experience, such as objectivity and subjectivity. It is also worth questioning whether different principles are needed to explain permanence or impermanence, according to the modality being considered.

[3][Here *objectivity* means attributing the sensory impression to an external cause, whereas *subjectivity* appears to denote attributing the impression to the tactile-kinesthetic system itself.]

It is sufficient to examine the question more closely to be sure that the distinction between objective and subjective aspects of tactile permanence does intervene in the issue but in quite a different way than one was tempted to assume at first sight.

It is clear that in the perception of contact of an external object with the skin or of the pressure that it puts on it, there is not just a question of "pure objectivity." If it were, one would simply have the impression of an object situated at a distance, in some place in three-dimensional space, as is the case with visual experience. The impression, of an object in contact with some part or other of the body, however, is quite different. The stimulation produced at the skin surface gives rise to a double impression, one objective, the thing, and the other subjective, the contact with the skin. In other words, here there is a phenomenal duplication, the same stimuli producing two distinct impressions at the same time. It is quite obvious that if the object does not appear to be created at the moment it is sensed, the impression of contact does seem ephemeral by contrast; it is suddenly created and disappears afterwards.

The impression of contact plays the same role in the experience as that of illumination in the visual experience of category B. This is more easily understood if the contact produces a progressive change in the skin. As a result, the objective conditions are of the kind which favor the "evolving" aspect of the impression of contact and what follows from that, namely, intrinsic temporal structure, own limits of creation, and disappearance.

The analysis of the examples discussed in these pages provides sufficient material to attempt a general synthesis of problems concerning phenomenal permanence and nonpermanence. Above all it is right to emphasize the fact that the question of permanence must be seen from the perspective of the psychology of time, on which it is by definition dependent. From this point of view, we have been led to emphasize the fundamental distinction between phenomenal time external to processes and their intrinsic time.

All the events constituting mental life unfold in the framework of the phenomenal time in which they are ordered, one in relation to the other. It follows that the moment of the appearance or disappearance of the object and the duration of the appearance always have their place marked in the stream of time. However, this is of secondary importance for phenomenal permanence.

It has been demonstrated that where an object appears or disappears suddenly without undergoing any internal change, impressions of creation, annihilation, preexistence, or survival are absent. The appearance of the object marks the beginning of its presence, but the phenomenal experience indicates nothing about the beginning of its existence. If the object remains stable during the whole time of its perception, its presence continues to imply that its existence is real, but this is only guaranteed for this period of time and nothing guarantees its perpetuity on one side or the other of its being present.

All this hardly touches on the real problems of permanence, for these relate to the object's "existence" itself: its origin or period of continuity in time, preexistence and survival, and maintenance of identity across the various modifications it may undergo. The result of our inquiry has shown which of these aspects of permanence may show themselves as specific data of experience in the form of characteristic phenomena deriving from well controlled stimulus conditions. These conditions were intimately related to the fact that the processes possess an intrinsic temporal structure that constitutes their own time. In the impression of "creation" or "annihilation," they correspond to the fact that the object itself seems to form or develop at the moment of its appearance or to fold in on itself when it disappears. It appears or disappears gradually, and this growth is an intrinsic process not simply incorporated in external time but having its own rhythm and consequently, its own temporal limits, which necessarily mark the beginning or end of the existence of the object.

As for permanence, we have mentioned three examples that are undoubtedly fully representative of the great majority of cases one finds in everyday life: Change, the illumination effect, and the screen effect. At this point everything indicates that they can be compared and reconciled.

The impression of change is characterized by the maintenance of the identity of the object, despite the apparent change in some of its properties. We have interpreted this phenomenon by appealing to the notion of Gestalt, the "specific schema" corresponding to the union and coordination of the collection of properties constituting the object. That being so, the possibility of permanence of the object is obviously related to the fact that the specific schema, of which it is part, is a phenomenal datum, *sui generis,* enjoying a relative autonomy in relation to the various properties it encompasses. Furthermore, this case, which has been classed up to now as one of permanence of continuity, is basically no more than a case of permanence of precedence. In fact, the change is so rapid that it always appears to be a partial evolution of the object, and it then occurs as a "growing into," and by virtue of this has its own anterior temporal limits. This change, however, is restricted to certain properties of the object, and it does not affect the specific schema itself; the anterior limit of the change is not that of the existence of the object; this limit preexists the change the object undergoes. In this case, when one speaks of permanence of continuity, it is simply from a perspective that emphasizes the fact that the object, already existing, continues to exist afterwards. Here one sees (with the exception of the case of absolute continuity, which poses little problem in reality) that the distinction between permanence of precedence and of perpetuity rests only on the difference between the points of view adopted to explain the same phenomenal data.

In the case of the illumination effect, the prior existence of the object occurs under very different conditions in that the object is not visible and does not even exist phenomenally before its illumination. Nevertheless, we consider this to be a true case of permanence because the illumination has its own prior temporal limits beyond which, by comparison, the object seems to extend into the past. This is by nature an indefinite past and corresponds to being "already there" at the moment the object is seen.

Finally, the screen effect is also given its particular characteristics by the parts of the object that are again (or already) hidden and that phenomenally exist because the border separating the screen from the covered object is exclusively related to the screen, even though its parts are not visible and necessarily remain indeterminate in size. As in the case of time, the object makes its appearance in a special way, since it appears to come sliding progressively from behind the screen. Once again there is temporal evolution, which has its own anterior limit marking the appearance of the object. There is no question of the creation of the object, however, precisely because these conditions ensure its preexistence and apparent stability (see Knops, 1947). The object itself, therefore, is not the site of any internal change; it seems perfectly stable from the outset, as do objects in the case of illumination. As a result, the temporal limit does not relate to the sliding movement but only marks the beginning of the appearance of the object itself, without affecting it.

Comparison of these three cases is extremely instructive. In effect it shows that, despite their diversity, they correspond to a schema of structural organization in perception that is similar in principle. In the three examples, a phenomenal duplication occurs since the stimulus system gives rise to two distinct categories of impression that are relatively autonomous yet intimately connected. Furthermore, in each case, one aspect of the global experience undergoes a progressive change and possesses its own prior temporal limit; these are the modifications of observed properties in the case of substitution, the "expansion" of the light in the case of illumination, and the sliding of the object in the screen effect. In contrast, the other aspect of the experience is stable—the specific schema of the object in the substitution effect, the illuminated object in the illumination effect, and the uncovered object in the screen effect.

There is the obvious parallel in these perceptual structures, which provides the key to the whole question. It is not difficult to ascertain that this type of structure is the only one that can correspond to a permanence of precedence but furthermore must necessarily present the appearance of permanence.

In fact, permanence of precedence by nature supposes a shifting of temporal *limits* given that there cannot be, by definition, preexistence unless the object already exists before an event in which it is involved starts to take place. Therefore, its temporal limit (in so far as it has one from the phenomenal point of view) cannot coincide with that of the new event. This is only possible if there is a phenomenal division, that is, if the total experience presents two distinct parts that are strongly linked, but one of which has a temporal limit that does not coincide with the beginning of existence of the other. Thus, phenomenal duplication appears to be a fundamental condition for permanence of precedence, and in the last analysis the other cases amount to the coincidence or noncoincidence of the temporal limits. In short, the permanence of objects is not only an original phenomenal datum under certain conditions but is also easily understood to stem from the principles that govern the structural organization of perception.

The range and significance of permanence is undoubtedly enlarged by knowledge acquired in life, in relation to the concept of substance and in apparently confirming our spontaneous beliefs about it. Nevertheless, one already finds in the perceptual plane, in this matter as in others (notably those of causality and reality), a true phenomenal foreshadowing of the elaboration of the data of experience by noncritical thought (in the philosophical sense of the word) as a consequence of which human behavior develops normally.

References

Knops, L. (1947). Contribution a l'étude de la "naissance" et de la "permanence" phénoménales dans le champ visuel [A contribution to the study of phenomenal "coming into being" and "permanence" within the visual field]. In *Miscellanea Psychologica Albert Michotte* (pp. 562–610). Louvain: Éditions de l'Institut Supérieur de Philosophie.

Michotte, A. (1948). Le caractère de 'réalité' des projections cinématographiques [The character of reality of cinematic projections]. *Revue Internationale de Filmologie, 1,* 249–261.

Sampaio, A. C. (1943). *La translation des objects comme facteur de leur permanence phénoménale* [The translation of objects as a factor in their phenomenal permanence]. Louvain: Warny.

AMODAL COMPLETION OF PERCEPTUAL STRUCTURES

Albert Michotte, Georges Thinès, and G. Crabbé.[1]

Introduction

Modal Completion

It is a well-known fact that when subjects are exposed to the action of a complex system of stimuli they mention in their responses certain details, certain elements contributing to the perceptual structure, which, unlike the others, do not correspond to any local stimulation but whose presence is determined by the stimulus system as a whole.

It is with facts of this kind that the phenomena of completion of perceptual structures may usefully be grouped. These completions consist in the fact that, in certain conditions, the subjects' responses describe a structure that is complete and without any break, even though the system of corresponding stimuli presents gaps. The earliest known example of this phenomenon is undoubtedly the filling of the blind spot. In this connection Koffka (1935) cites experiments carried out well before his time by Volkmann and Wittich, who presented their subjects with a cross arranged in such a way that its center was projected on to the blind spot while the ends of the arms were projected on to the sensitive parts of the retina. They established that in these cases, despite the discontinuity of the stimulation, the subjects declared that they saw a complete cross.

As Koffka points out, however, there is a major difficulty in experiments performed on the blind spot, since because of its peripheral position the images in its immediate vicinity are not always very clear.

In addition, Poppelreuter (1917) and Fuchs (1921) had the idea of trying similar experiments on hemianopic subjects.[2] These are subjects for whom half the field of the two eyes is without visual receptive function,[3] and if a subject who is hemianopic on the left side of the visual field is presented tachistoscopically with a circle and is asked to fixate the center of it, he usually says that he sees a complete circle, even though part of the retinal image is occurring in an area that has become blind. Fuchs then had the idea of presenting on its own a half figure occupying the right part of the field. The results were variable. The

---

[1]From Les complements amodaux des structures perceptives, Studia Psychologica, Louvain: Publications Universitaires 1964. Translated to English here by T.R. and E. Miles.

[2]These experiments are also quoted by Koffka.

[3]Compare H. Piéron, 1951.

completion was obtained without difficulty with a semicircle and with an eight-pointed star, but with a square and an ellipse more than half the figure needed to be exposed.

Alongside this group of facts is another, to which Gestalt psychology has of course extensively contributed. These are the cases in which the effects of local stimulation are achieved under the influence of the total stimuli operating at any given moment. Numerous examples can be found in the Handbuch,[4] and, therefore, we shall quote only one or two of particular interest from our own point of view. From all the research projects devoted to this question[5] we have selected for special attention the work of Bobbit (1942). This author succeeded in showing that when subjects were presented tachistoscopically with figures representing two parts of a triangle, they reported what they saw either as two separate figures or as a closed triangle, depending on how large a part of the total triangle perimeter was presented. The threshold values (determined by the method of limits) above which the subjects reported a single closed figure instead of two open figures varied in these experiments from 68% to 75% of the total perimeter.

The examples just quoted are representative of the more simple type of perceptual completion. It is characterized by the fact that the subjects describe "better" and simpler figures than those they were shown and that they make no mention of the gaps, as would be expected if one limited oneself to a consideration of the figure actually presented. In other words, it is as if the figure itself had undergone alterations, usually consisting of the prolongation of its lines or changes in their direction, and the filling of gaps; for no distinction is made by the subjects between the parts of the figures that were added and those that correspond to the system of stimuli. Because these additions present the same visual qualities (luminance and color) as the rest of the configuration, we shall call this type of completion "modal" completion.[6]

Other cases of modal gap-filling, however, are structurally more complicated and are interesting to mention at this point because in structure they form an intermediate group between simple gap-filling and the completions we shall later term "amodal." These are the cases of apparent transparency described first by Rosenbach (1902) and studied systematically by Glynn (1954) under strict experimental conditions. Rosenbach used colored figures of various shapes (triangles, ovals,

[4]*Handbuch der Psychologie,* Göttingen, 1964, Vol. I.

[5]The reader will find a detailed analysis of this research in M.D. Vernon (1952) pp. 50 seq., where the phenomena of completion are considered in connection with the law of pregnance.

[6]The word "modal" is used here in the sense given to it by Helmholtz to describe the special qualitative character belonging to each sensory field.

rectangles) partly hidden by a strip of opaque black paper 1 cm wide, in such a way that only their ends were visible. The subjects were required to set the figures moving to and fro, and the experimenter asked them whether the strip of paper was transparent. The majority of them replied that it was.

In Glynn's experiments, the subject was placed in front of a ground glass screen, on which was fixed a vertical strip of opaque cardboard. An appropriate device was used to back project the moving image of a long rectangle onto the ground glass; this image followed the arc of a circle so that its orientation changed as it moved. When certain conditions were satisfied with regard to luminance, relative dimensions of image and field, speed of displacement, and amplitude of movement, and when, in addition, the subjects had been prepared by suitable instructions, the majority of them (15 out of 25) reported a compelling impression that the opaque strip was transparent. They claimed, in fact, that they saw the rectangle through the strip while it was passing this point on the glass (Michotte, 1955 pp. 79–80). At this moment, at the place where the moving rectangle and the opaque strip coincided, there was clearly no stimulus from the object in movement; nevertheless, the subjects reported that they saw it in its entirety throughout its journey, with its own luminance different from that of the "transparent" strip. Here, too, then we find a gap in the system of stimulation and a filling up of this gap. Yet this gap-filling is not done by a simple addition of a missing part, but by the setting up of a structure of transparency, which necessarily involves a phenomenal duplication at the point of meeting.[7]

It should be added that the examples just quoted have intentionally been taken from the domain of vision; the research on amodal completion, which is the particular subject of this chapter has been limited, until now, to vision alone.

Amodal Completion and the Screen Effect

Static Configurations

Simple Screen Effect. From what was said in previously, it is clear that the structure of apparent transparency was not easily established in Glynn's experiments and could be obtained only when the conditions

[7]The duplication in this case consists in the fact that one sees, in the same direction, *two* distinct objects (or parts of objects) situated one behind the other, each with its own shape, luminance, and color (as happens, for example, when one sees an object through colored glass). In this connection see D. Katz (1935) and K. Koffka, (1935).

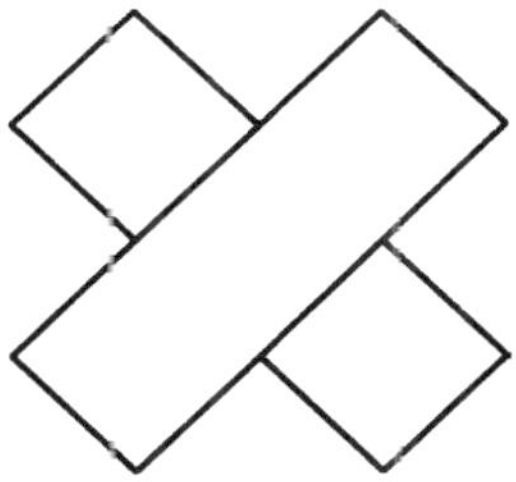

FIGURE 3.1

were controlled exactly. In contrast, another structure, which will be described later under the name tunnel effect, was very frequently mentioned by his subjects.[8] Moreover, if the rectangle was presented as coming to a halt behind the opaque strip at the moment when it penetrated it, the resultant structure was the screen effect, which is the static form of the tunnel effect. The essential feature of the screen effect is that one object covers another without appearing to alter the integrity of the latter.

Thus, one can present the subjects with two rectangles of colored paper, one red, for example, and the other yellow, with the first placed over the second to form a cross. One can even show a simple linear drawing representing only the contours of these shapes as in Figure 3.1. In both cases, the subjects describe what is shown to them as two superimposed rectangles, both complete. Geometrically speaking, of course, there is a gap in one of them, but inexperienced subjects practically never mention this, any more than they mention a complete rectangle with two irregular quadrilaterals on either side.

This phenomenon is of course not limited to rectilinear shapes, but also occurs when regular curves are partly hidden. Moreover, in certain conditions, when the nonhidden parts, for example, of a single line are not a prolongation of one another, the amodal completion can appear as a slanting line or curve that links them behind the screen.[9]

In Figure 3.1, then, we once more find a situation like those discussed in the introduction, since there is a gap in the stimulation from the rectangle underneath, but this gap is somehow inoperative, since the subjects say that they perceive two complete rectangles. There the similarity ends, however, for the way in which the gap is filled is very different in this case. There is no question of transparency, and the subjects themselves are emphatic that although they "see" two complete

---

[8]Cf. Glynn, 1954, p. 128.

[9]In the section, which deals with kinematic configurations, there will be found still more striking examples of phenomena of the same kind.

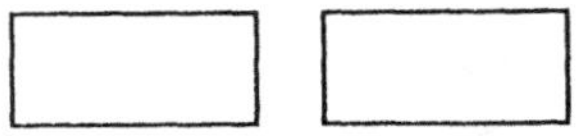

FIGURE 3.2

rectangles, it is quite clear that the one underneath is hidden at the crossing point. For this reason Michotte has proposed that completions that are "present" in this manner should be termed "amodal" to distinguish them from the previous kind.[10]

Thus the term amodal has initially a purely negative significance, since it indicates the absence of visual qualities (luminance and color) from the completion of the figure. On the other hand, it should be stressed that the impression of the unity of the whole shape and of the unbroken character of its contour is entirely compelling for the subjects; thus, there is no question of a mere inference or the projection of a mental image of the missing part. Occasionally, this does happen, as we shall see, but in such cases modal characters are present, since a visual image in the strict sense contains dim and bright parts and usually even colored ones.

In the case of continuity of color there is not so compelling an impression. It seems rather to become established secondarily, by reason of the unity of the whole shape, as an overall property of it. This point can be illustrated in the case of the rectangles, for example, by giving different colors to the exposed parts of the rectangle underneath. This then appears to be bicolored. The proof that what is involved here is a global property of the whole and not a completion restricted to the hidden area is that it is impossible to decide at what point behind the screen the color changes. In contrast the shape, direction, etc. of the figural completion can be perfectly precise at this point, so precise, indeed, that the subjects are able to draw them, as will be seen later (pp. 155-156).

Some additional information can be obtained from an analysis of the conditions necessary for establishing amodal completion.

In this connection the following experiment is particularly informative. It involves showing the subjects two rectangles separated by a gap of a few millimeters (Figure 3.2). If one then places, for example, the point of a pencil between them, a rather complex tripartite structure is formed. If, however, the pencil is moved forwards until its sides cover the edges of the rectangles on either hand, everything is immediately simplified and we see merely a long uniform rectangle with a pencil laid over it. This occurs as soon as the rectangles have no boundary of their

[10]See A. Michotte and L. Burke, 1951, pp. 179–180.

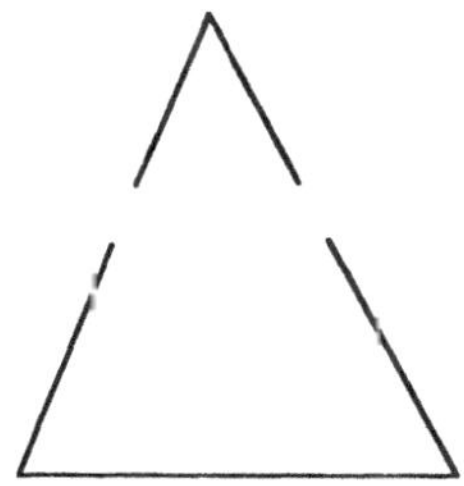

FIGURE 3.3

own on the side next to the pencil. From then on the lines of demarcation between the pencil and the drawing belong to the contour of the pencil and play no part in the structure of the drawing. This is a key character of the screen effect, as has been shown by all the research done in this field.[11] Two consequences follow: In the first place, the rectangles, having no limit of their own on the screen side, seem to be prolonged beyond the limits of the screen, and this prolongation, which clearly occurs behind the screen, implies a structuring in three dimensions. This situation is similar to the one that occurs in the well-known case of figure and ground studied in the past by Rubin.[12] It should be added that these conditions are not sufficient, in the preceding experiments, to ensure the integration of the portions of the rectangles in one total configuration; for this to happen, it is also necessary that these portions should be arranged so that the laws of structural organization (proximity, similarity, good continuation, etc.) can come into play.

Another interesting example is that of Figure 3.3. This represents a triangle whose contour is broken at two points, as a result of which it has the immediate appearance of being formed of two parts separated from each other. As soon as a screen is put over the figure so as to cover the gaps, the contour of the triangle at once appears as a single and complete whole, although objectively it remains just as "cut in two" as it was, this time by the screen. There is thus an amodal completion once again, just as there was in the preceding case and for the same reasons. The particular interest of this experiment, however, is that from the very beginning there is an integration of the two parts of the figure, since what one sees is a single triangle whose contour is in two pieces. This

[11] Cf. Sampaio, 1943, p. 21.

[12] This partial overlapping, of course, is one of the factors that causes the perceptual field to be organized in three dimensions; and it has been noticed and put to good use since earliest times for representing the distribution of objects in the third dimension. This can be observed in particular in the ancient cave paintings and carvings of more than 10 thousand years ago; there one can see animals in profile with the limbs drawn one on top of the other so as to show their relative positions in space.

FIGURE 3.5

shows that integration is not sufficient on its own in such a case to produce the completion; other conditions have to be satisfied; in this case, those conditions make the line of demarcation seem to belong to the contour of the screen.

It should be noted that amodal completion occurs not only when a figure protrudes beyond the screen on both sides, but also when the screen covers only one side of the figure. This effect occurs in particular when the figure has "pregnance," as in the case of a square, a rhombus, or a circle; in that case it seems complete and perfect when the screen covers the gap in its contour (Figure 3.5). We think it likely although we have not any exact data on the matter, that in this case the completion is often carried out by the imagination, which implies the presence of sensory qualities and, therefore, invalidates the example.

In the cases quoted cited so far, the integration of the visible parts took place in accordance with the laws of structural organization; but it seems that acquired experience can have an analogous effect. Thus, if a screen is put over the gap in (Figure 3.6) the two parts unite and are immediately seen as constituent parts of a complete face whose center is hidden. This occurs even when every effort has been made to eliminate from the drawing the elements that would permit certain factors to operate, especially that of good continuation.

The same thing occurs in other cases when the drawing protrudes on only one side of the screen, as in (Figure 3.4). If a screen is put at the point where the lines of the face stop, the face clearly continues but its shape is indeterminate. The same thing happens when we see a group of people of whom those in the front row conceal the greater part of those who occupy the next few rows; the nonhidden parts of the latter seem to be prolonged behind the people who are functioning as a screen,

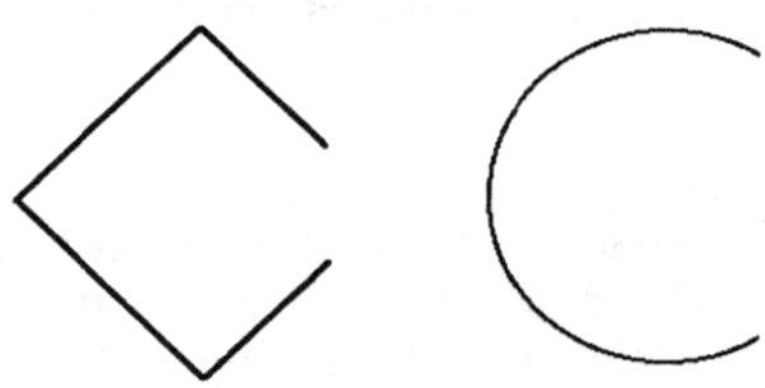

FIGURE 3.6

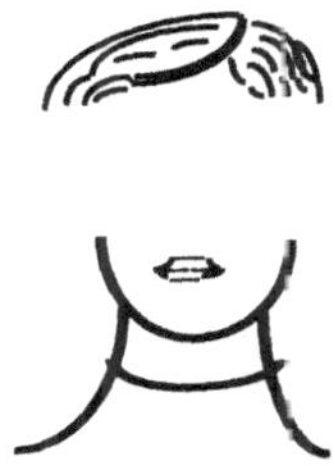

FIGURE 3.4

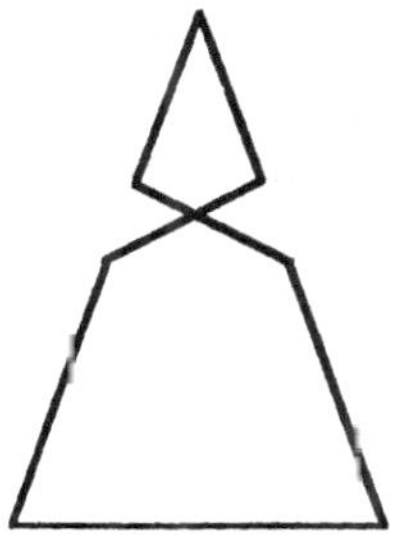

FIGURE 3.7

although these prolongations remain imprecise. Because of their influence, however, the uncovered parts are sufficient to identify the nature of the objects and so make adaptation to the environment possible.[13]

The influence of past experience on amodal completions, however, is still very limited in the sense that they remain in general vague and simple indications of the overall appearance of a certain category of object. At any rate, this is true when there is a particular well-known object whose presented parts can then evoke a fairly precise memory image; however, that is quite different from amodal completion, as has already been made clear. Moreover, it is easy to show that familiarity with the shape of a figure, even very close familiarity, cannot interfere with the laws of structural organization. For example, every time that a pencil is placed at the point in Figure 3.7 where the lines cross, the much more simple form of an isosceles triangle appears immediately. This occurs, as we ourselves have found, in spite of hundreds of repetitions during the course of many years, and would probably still occur if the experiment were repeated thousands of times.

Perception of Solids. Finally, mention should be made of a phenomenon where the screen effect again plays a part, namely the perception of

[13]This has been fully demonstrated by Metzger using a group photograph. See W. Metzger, 1953, p. 173, fig. 211.

solids.[14] A very spectacular and particularly instructive example is that of the sphere. When subjects are confronted with a hemisphere of, for example, 15 cm diameter, which is isolated in the surrounding space and fastened to a thin stem, they are unanimous in reporting that they see a ball, a complete sphere, whose surface is perfectly continuous. The edge of the presented hemisphere does not in these experimental conditions act as a limit to the hemisphere's surface; and since at this point there is no limit to this surface in the front to back direction, it necessarily seems to be continued in this direction.

It is easy to show that this is a correct account of the matter, since as soon as the stimulus system is modified in such a way that the edge of the hemisphere takes on the function of a limit, we no longer see a whole sphere but only the presented hemisphere. To achieve this result it is sufficient to place, for example, the flat of one's hand against the rear face of the hemisphere; in that case the line of demarcation between the hand and the hemisphere appears immediately as the hemisphere's own limit. If, in contrast, one simply touches the rear face, while taking care not to let one's hand jut out beyond the edge of the hemisphere, the flatness of the face is of course perceived by touch, but this does not interfere in any way with the visual perception that still remains a complete sphere. These last two points are important because they show that in this situation, once again, there is a phenomenon of a perceptual order, governed by the laws according to which the visual field is structurally organized.

The simple prolonging of the surface of the hemisphere, however, is not sufficient to account for the global structure perceived. Another factor determining the form that this takes must play a part here, namely, the exceptional pregnance of the sphere. Because the curved shape of the presented surface of the hemisphere tends to continue regularly, it must appear to close in behind the hemisphere, thus outlining the back half of the sphere, which here comprises the amodal

[14]This problem, and in particular the problem of the phenomenal presence of the invisible face of a solid, has not so far received much attention from psychologists, although there are various passages written by members of the Gestalt school, and by Köhler in particular, which could be taken in this sense. Phenomenologists, however, have been very much preoccupied with it, especially E. Husserl. This author has, of course, devoted several sections of his book to a lengthy consideration of the "perspective" character of perceptions in connection with the constructing by the intellect of the intentional object in sensory knowledge. He has stressed on many occasions that no object is ever perceived in its totality, and that from any one view only a single aspect can be seen, which necessarily excludes all the others (Abschattung). The side of an object that is visible from a particular angle hides the other sides without completely abolishing them during the momentary perception of the whole. See, for example, among other works, E. Husserl, 1950, p. 93, and M. Merleau-Ponty, 1945, particularly pp. 23 and 380.

completion without which the perception of this configuration in its totality cannot be understood.

It is also interesting to consider in detail the similarity and difference between this phenomenon and that of the screen effect studied previously. On each occasion, there is perceptual completion in an amodal form, and the intervention of this factor is made possible by the fact that the surface of the object has no limit of its own in a particular direction. The great difference, however, between the case of the sphere and cases of the screen effect is that in the latter the screen was something quite foreign to the object it hid, whereas in the case of the sphere, it is a part of the object itself, namely, the front face, which is hiding the back face. This is probably true of all cases of perception of a solid, provided the shape of the object presented is such that there is apparent continuity of its whole surface; this apparent continuity can occur even when there are changes in direction marked by the edges.

The conditions in which this apparent continuation is established, however, are not yet clearly known, and it would be very interesting to study them. In the case of surfaces with a curvature from front to back, it appears that the required condition is that the direction lines that mark off the extreme limits of the retinal image of the curve should be tangential to the curve.[15] In fact when, instead of a hemisphere, one uses small sections of a sphere, all of which have the same width of flat surface at the back but whose curvature progressively increases in radius, the direction lines are no longer tangential to the edges, and these edges are necessarily seen as the actual limits of the sections, while the apparent shape of their back surfaces remains altogether indeterminate.

Kinematic Configurations

The study of the part played by the screen effect in kinematic configurations is particularly interesting, both because it sheds fresh light on the subject of amodal completion and also because it enables us to take up the problem of the permanence, in amodal form, of objects completely hidden.

It may perhaps seem surprising that there are more details of a technical kind in this section than in those that precede and follow it. The reason is that, as far as we know, the problems described here are the only ones that have been made the subject of systematic research. Therefore, we considered that it would be of interest to present here

[15]It seems that there is no theoretical difficulty in explaining this. It goes without saying that the general conditions for the perception of this kind of shape must also be present. See particularly on this subject D.W. Smith and P.C. Smith, 1957.

some of the well-established results in this area, based on experimental work carried out with large numbers of subjects.

Covering and Uncovering. The most simple cases are those in which a moving screen progressively covers a stationary object or where a moving object progressively disappears behind a fixed screen.

The essential feature in these two cases is that, at the moment when the screen and the figure come into contact with one another, the retinal image of the figure changes shape, becoming progressively smaller. Yet in cases where the screen effect occurs, this change is not seen by the subjects. To them the figure stays unchanged until it completely disappears but a larger and larger part of its surface seems covered by the screen.[16] This may seem surprising at first, but it is easy to show that decrease in size of the retinal image need not necessarily cause an apparent decrease in size of the object. Once again it is a question of whether or not certain parts of the outline belong to the object, as was shown by Sampaio (1943). Taking up an incidental observation of Michotte's, she presented her subjects with a colored rectangular shape, *A*, 5 mm high and 25 mm long, against a white background; this was seen through a horizontal slit 5 × 180 mm cut in the apparatus. Another figure, *B*, of the same dimensions but of a different color, coming from the left, moved towards *A*, and, as soon as it joined it, progressively decreased in size, its left edge approaching the demarcation line between the two figures until *B* completely disappeared.[17]

One might expect *a priori* that the subjects would mention a gradual decrease in the size of *B*. In fact, responses of this kind are extremely rare in the appropriate conditions of speed. The subjects normally say that B "slides behind" *A*, even though both are simple colored shapes belonging in the same plane. The explanation of the phenomenon must certainly be that, at the beginning of the experiment, object *A*, which is stationary, has its own boundaries, as does object *B*, which is moving. As soon as *B* comes into contact with *A*, however, the line of demarcation that separates the two figures, being immobile, continues to be seen as part of the contour of *A* and remains foreign to *B* whose mass and rear boundary continue to move.[18] Thus, *B* does not seem to have any front

[16]It should be stressed that this phenomenon occurs in cases where the covering time is far longer than the time for which after images could last. Moreover it is hard to see how after images could play any part in cases where it is the figure that moves behind the screen.

[17]For the procedure for setting up this experiment see Michotte, 1963, pp. 27–34 (disc method).

[18]Conversely, if after the contact it is A that gradually diminishes in size as B moves forward, then B appears to cover up A.

boundary in the direction of its movement, but continues to perform this movement "behind A" while retaining its shape.

Another very interesting experiment, again by Sampaio, entirely confirms this view. It consisted in simply removing object A from the previous experiment. Object *B* then begins to move towards the right of the slit in front of an absolutely uniform background, and, at a given moment, its right hand end becomes stationary for as long as the figure decreases in size, its left hand end continuing to move at the same speed until the disappearance is complete. In these conditions, the majority of subjects assert spontaneously (and the others say the same thing after several repetitions or a mild suggestion) that *B* does not change size at all but slides through a small slit cut in the background. At this point an entirely new structure is established, in which, again, *B* has no boundary of its own in the direction of its advance, and in which the actual background ceases to be uniform, since it appears to be pierced and to take on the role of a screen. Moreover, these effects are so striking that on many occasions during this last experiment and the previous one the subjects did not believe the explanations given to them after the event and went to find out if really there was no slit or other device that whisked away the object.

A third experiment, based on the same principles, was carried out by Michotte. He presented cinematographically a succession of images. The first of these was a shape that had the "pregnant" form of a bright circle on a dark background, whereas, in the ones which followed, an increasingly large cross-section of the circle's surface was chopped off until total, or almost total, disappearance (Figure 3.8). This sequence was also presented in the opposite way, that is, with a very small segment of a circle at the start and a complete circle at the end. The abrupt change of direction in the contour, together with the immobility of the curved part in contrast with the apparent forward movement of the straight boundary, clearly favored the segregation of these two parts of the contour. This is indeed exactly the impression that is given, for in general no change in the shape of the circle is seen; but despite the

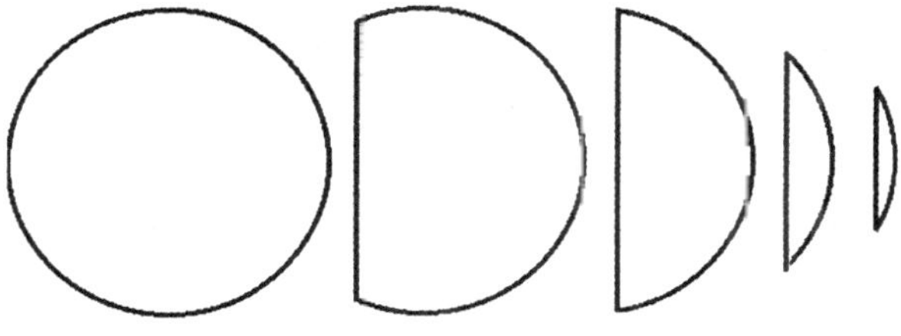

FIGURE 3.8

uniformity of the background a structure soon becomes established in which the right hand line (the chord of the curve) appears to be the limit of a screen that advanced first in one direction and then in the other; in other words, it alternately covers and uncovers the circle.

The Tunnel Effect. The tunnel effect has been well known since the classic experiments of Wertheimer (1912); but it has also been produced in a different way, particularly by Sampaio (1943), Burke (1952), Coen-Gelders (1961), and Crabbé (1963).

In Sampaio's procedure, the experimenter places in the center of the slit a small screen (e.g., 1 or 2 cm) to form a tunnel and sends across the slit a moving object (a rectangle 5 × 8 mm) at a speed of 30 to 60 cm/sec. Subjects taking part in these experiments all say that in spite of the presence of the screen, the movement is continuous and uniform and that the moving object goes behind the tunnel. It seems that there is no difference between a movement of this kind and a movement exposed throughout. In these conditions, the screen belongs to the background and has nothing to do with the movement of the object.

As can be seen, these observations made in the kinematic field are analogous to those reported earlier in connection with static configurations. In fact, two phases of movement are not hidden and are separated in space by the length of the tunnel, but there is also a gap in time corresponding to the duration for which the object is totally hidden by the screen. (We shall call this period of time the "entrance-exit" interval, or E-E.)

The continuity of the movement depends, of course, on a number of different factors. Among these, the distance between the two exposed parts of the movement (i.e., the length of the tunnel) and the duration of the E-E interval act as agents of segregation, whereas the speed of the movement acts as a factor of integration (though its action depends on the relative lengths of the exposed parts of the movement [see Coen-Celders, 1961]).

If the dimensions of the tunnel are increased to a length of 10 or even 20 cm, then in the present experimental conditions (observation distance 1.50 m) the apparent continuity of the movement can be maintained, provided the duration of the E-E interval is increased correspondingly. The increase, however, must be proportionally less than the increase in the length of the tunnel, and in all circumstances the duration of the interval needs to remain less than that which the object would have needed to go through the tunnel at the speed it maintained during the phases when it was exposed.

This finding brings to mind one of Korte's laws (Korte, 1915) in connection with the phi phenomenon, and seems to suggest some affinity between this and our tunnel effect. In other respects, however, the two phenomena are quite different, particularly because of the existence in the tunnel effect of the exposed parts of the movement, which influence the apparent speed of the moving object during the hidden phase.

In any case the continuity is much more fragile when the length of the tunnel increases; and if very long tunnels (30 to 70 cm) are used, Burke's subjects no longer mentioned continuity, whatever the speed of the moving object and the length of the E-E interval. In these conditions, the moving object seemed to enter the tunnel and be lost there after continuing for an indeterminate distance, while the exit movement seemed to start behind the tunnel. This meant that there appeared to be a gap between the end of the first phase of movement and the beginning of the second.

A final point is that changes in the E-E interval not only influence the responses that relate to the hidden part of the trajectory but they seem to affect the trajectory as a whole, in that if this interval is shortened or lengthened, the subjects often say that the total movement of the moving object is quicker or slower. This phenomenon seems important to us because it shows very clearly the complete integration that operates between the hidden part and the exposed parts of the movement.

A particularly interesting case is that in which the tunnel has approximately the same dimensions as the moving object (e.g., tunnel 5 × 10 mm, object 5 × 8 mm), for it is then possible to compare the object's halt when it is exposed all the time with what happens when it goes into the tunnel and does not come out again. In this connection, various facts must be mentioned. First, in the absence of a screen, a halt of course occurs when the moving object, instead of continually changing its position, stops at a prearranged spot. It is quite otherwise in the tunnel case, however; a halt is rarely mentioned (only 10% of the time in Crabbé's research). Her subjects, of whom half were experienced and the others new, said that the object continues its movement beyond the screen and behind the white background. This confirms the facts previously established by Sampaio.

In contrast, when in the tunnel case the moving object reemerges after a certain interval, there may be a clear impression of a halt, just as in the parallel case where an object, uncovered throughout, halts momentarily. In the latter case, however, according to the measurements of Crabbé (1963), the threshold figure at which 50% of the subjects report a halt is about 78 ms, with 90% halt responses when the time is 155 ms. In the tunnel experiment, however, the threshold value at which a halt is reported corresponds to a much longer E-E interval, since 50% halt responses occur when this is 156 ms and 90% when it is 234 ms.[19]

One can conclude from these observations that the conditions necessary for the perception of the halt of an object are different according to whether its movement is exposed all the time or whether its trajectory passes behind a tunnel. In the first case, all that is needed is that the moving object should have a fixed position somewhere that must last for a certain length of time if the halt is followed by a second phase of movement. In contrast, when there is a screen, this second phase is indispensable, and it must be separated from the first by a time interval noticeably longer than in the case where the movement is exposed the whole time. When the subjects are asked to compare their impressions of a halt in these two types of conditions, 75% say that they see no difference between them; the remaining 25% say, for the most part, that when the halt is not hidden it appears more abrupt and more violent, whereas in the other case it occurs more gently. All this seems to suggest that the perception of a halt is essentially the perception of a time limit to the movement. In any case, it is certain that the object has not been annihilated when it disappears into the tunnel; it is there, momentarily hidden, as the subjects say, or, to use our terminology, it is amodally present until its reappearance.

In the experiments on the tunnel effect described so far, the displacement of the moving object occurred in a straight line for the whole length of its course. Interesting phenomena are also seen, however, when the second path is not a direct continuation of the first. Thus, in one of his experiments Burke gave the entry path into the tunnel an angle of 155° in relation to the exit path, and this, because of the Poggendorff illusion, seemed slightly displaced vertically in relation to the entry path. (The tunnel was 75 mm long and the speed used was 30 cm/sec.). All the subjects (18 altogether, of whom the majority were new) asserted in these conditions that there was continuity of movement; but oddly enough, the shape of the trajectory behind the screen varied as a function of the E-E interval. When the interval was relatively long, this shape was altered at both entry and exit and appeared as a curve, of varying complexity, which continued on both sides of the tunnel for some distance when the trajectory was exposed. When the E-E interval became shorter, the hidden trajectory changed its shape and finally became the simple rectilinear continuation of the two exposed trajectories.

All of Burke's subjects, independently of each other, mentioned

[19]These experiments, in which the method of constant stimuli was used, were carried out on two groups of 60 subjects, one group with the tunnel present, one group without it.

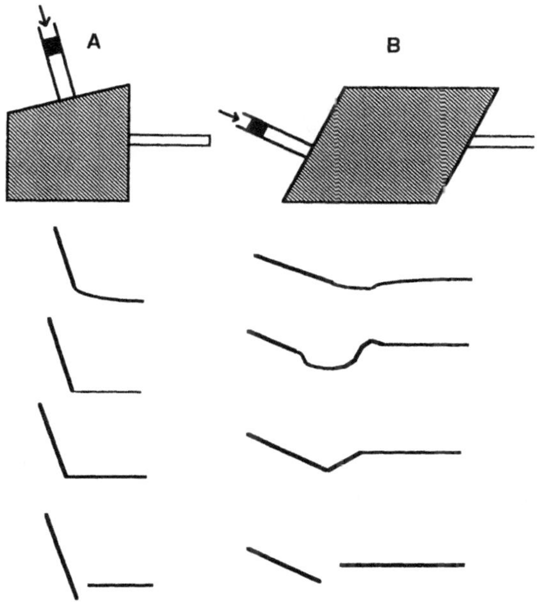

FIGURE 3.9

similar phenomena and drew what they saw. Figure 3.9 reproduces the general appearance of the trajectories as they were represented in these drawings. As the author himself points out, hardly any of the subjects included the tunnel in their drawing, as if it was of no interest! Moreover they were extremely surprised that they had been able to "see" all these variations of movement when at the end of the experiment the apparatus was explained to them. If the experiment was performed in front of them a second time, however, they had the same impression as before.[20] Similar results can be obtained if two horizontal trajectories are used which are at different vertical levels from one another, as in Figure 3.10 (difference in height 10 mm, tunnels 80 mm long). According to the length of the E-E interval the subjects reported that the trajectories bent at the entry into the tunnel so as to link up with the place of exit, either in a straight line or (if the E-E interval is longer[21]) in an S-shaped line.

[20]It may perhaps be of interest at this point to quote a remark made by a visiting subject, himself a psychologist, who said to us: "I should never have believed that there could be phenomena in the perceptual domain so divorced from the stimulus conditions."

[21]Michotte, who devised this experiment, was expecting to see the points of entry and exit joined by a straight line, and he was astounded when he saw an S-shaped curve!

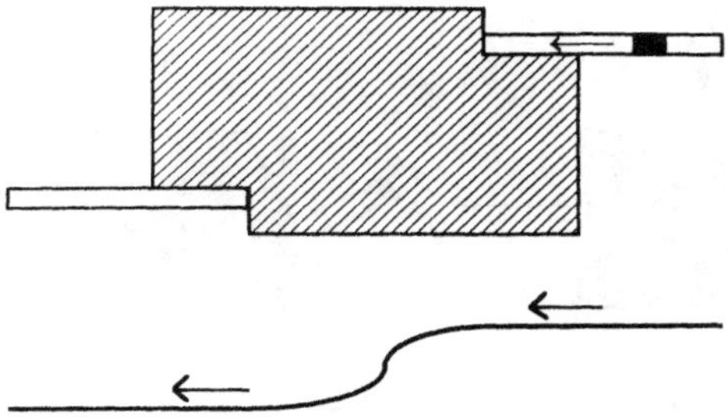

FIGURE 3.10

The significance of these last two experiments needs to be stressed. They show that when two sections of movement are completed amodally, there can be a well-defined shape and that this is linked to the conditions of stimulation by the visible parts. Moreover, they show that this completion is so integrated in the whole that it encroaches sometimes on the visible sections. Finally, they show that the subjects do not on their own initiative make any distinction between the visible parts and the invisible part of the movement.

It is perhaps worth pointing out that what we are calling "amodal completion of kinematic structures" is something quite different from the "pure phi" movement of Wertheimer.[22] Our amodal completion is clearly a phase in the total movement of the object, this phase being hidden by the screen. The responses of the subjects allow no doubt on this point.

Until now we have considered only the strictly kinematic aspects of the tunnel effect, without raising any question about the object that performs the movement. Here, too, there are a number of problems, particularly in connection with the object's identity. There is no doubt that in the case of short tunnels of 10 to 15 mm, where the speeds are uniform and of the order of 60 cm/sec or more, and where the objects are small, no more than a few millimeters long, the moving object seems to keep its identity intact throughout the length of its course.

If, however, after the subjects have given responses indicating unity of object and no halt, they are asked if they are certain on reflection that there could not have been two objects in the experiment, 42% (Crabbé's figure) reply that they are, even though naturally it was open to anyone to say that there could have been a device of some sort for substituting a second object for the first.[23] As the E-E interval increases the percentage decreases; for an E-E interval of .5 sec it is no more than 12%.

[22]See M. Wertheimer, 1925, p. 61 seq.

[23]Because of the apparatus used, this was in fact what occurred in almost all the experiments. The moving objects going into and out of the tunnel were different, although they were of the same shape, size, and color.

It should be noted, however, that the subjects often continue to mention spontaneously that there is only one object, even when the E-E interval is much longer (1 sec or more) and the continuity of the movement is broken. This is understandable since the object that comes out is similar to that which went in. Indeed it is probable that one could still obtain identity responses after days, weeks, or years, since in everyday life, after intervals as long as this, one often recognizes things that have been shut up in a cupboard or a drawer. It is impossible therefore, to determine from responses of this kind how long the object is amodally present after it has become hidden.

Moreover, in the course of her research Coen-Gelders obtained responses that unambiguously referred to two objects only in cases where the E-E interval was very brief in relation to the length of the tunnel, with the entry and exit occurring at almost the same moment.

There is also the question of what would happen if there were not complete similarity between the moving object going in and the moving object coming out. This aspect of the problem has been studied by Burke and by Coen-Gelders.

Once again we must distinguish the question of the continuity of the movement from that of the apparent identity of the object. The first question in particular received the attention of Burke. Using a tunnel 12 cm long and a speed of 36 cm/sec, he asked his subjects if the movement appeared continuous. The results were the same as those that occurred when there was no change in the object performing the movement. This seems to support the view that particular instructions can cause certain aspects of what is seen to be overlooked when the subjects give their responses.[24]

The second question is that of the influence of perception of changes in the moving object. It is surprising that quite appreciable alterations do not affect the fundamental identity of the object (Knops, 1947); the subjects in fact consider them as changes undergone by the object as it moves, not as indicating the substitution of one shape or one object for another. Thus Coen-Gelders, using the projection method, performed six series of experiments (each on a group of 20 subjects) in which she introduced striking differences in the appearance of the object at the moment of its entry into the tunnel and at the moment of its exit. Her experiments were concerned with the luminance, color, shape, direction, and structure of the objects.[25]

The experiment involving changes in luminance gave no usable

[24]In this connection one is reminded of the well-known experiments of Külpe (1904) on abstraction.

[25]The spatiotemporal conditions of the experiments were as follows: Speed, 55 cm/sec;

results because of an error in the experimental procedure. As for the others, in the conditions given in footnote 28, about 75% of responses indicated identity of the object, and some subjects did not even report any change. The change, of course, is not perceived directly while it is taking place, although it is quite easy to produce such a situation experimentally; it appears already accomplished when the object comes into view again at the exit, and, according to the subjects, happened in the tunnel. In other words, in these particular kinematic conditions, the fundamental identity of the object asserts itself in the majority of cases in spite of the changes it has undergone.

To-and-Fro Movement. Another procedure produced effects of the same type as those found in the tunnel experiments. This involves the use of a to-and-fro movement in which the point where the movement changes direction at the end of its course can be either kept visible or hidden by a screen.[26] The great difference between this experiment and that involving the tunnel effect is that the entry and exit of the moving object occur at exactly the same spot, which eliminates the segregative factor arising from the distance between the two in the tunnel effect. Research work similar to that of Crabbé[27] (except that the method of limits was used) has been carried out on this phenomenon by Renard (1963), who used 20 subjects in his experiments each of whom made observations both with and without the screen.[28]

When the durations of the object's disappearance behind the screen were short, a number of the subjects did not mention its disappearance. The object moves towards the screen; for some of the subjects the beginning of the return movement occurs before it arrives there, while for others it seems to penetrate to some extent behind the screen. This last is the impression in about 50% of the cases where the time of disappearance is zero (i.e., when there is immediate return after a complete disappearance), and it ceases completely when there is an

---

length of tunnel, 60 mm; lengths of visible paths 30 mm; duration of E-E interval 103 ms. The alterations in color were achieved by changing objects of the same luminance and size from white to red. The alteration in size was achieved by presenting a circle of 10 mm in diameter at the entrance to the tunnel and one of 37.5 mm at the exit. The alterations in shape were achieved by passing from a circle 36 mm in diameter to a square with a side of 35 mm. The alterations in structure were achieved by replacing a circle 36 mm in diameter with a quincunx made up of circles 9.5 mm in diameter.

[26]Coen-Gelders, who has studied this phenomenon in depth, called it the "piston effect."

[27]Cf. preceding section on the "tunnel effect".

[28]The track of the moving object in the experiments without screen was 58 mm long, the visible track in the experiment with the screen 46 mm and the size of the object 5 × 8 mm. The speed in both cases was 30 cm/sec.

interval of more than 130 ms. In contrast, when the duration of the disappearance was 100 ms, some mention was made of a momentary halt by the moving object behind the screen in about 10% of the cases. The frequency of these responses increased in an almost linear way until it reached 100% at one third of a second; at 200 ms it reached 50%.

The comparison between these cases and the earlier ones is interesting because it suggests the amodal presence of the moving object behind the screen. In fact the subjects consider the situation where the object goes and immediately returns after a complete disappearance as simply the limiting case of partial penetration of the object behind the screen. When the disappearance is complete the case is similar to that where the object passes through the tunnel. It is clear, however, that here, as in the tunnel case, when the time of disappearance is prolonged it is impossible to assign any upper limit to the length of time of amodal presence of the object behind the screen; for here, too, the phenomenon of recognition could possibly be playing a part.

When the screen is not present, the threshold at which 50% of the subjects perceive a halt comes at 130 ms; and it is a remarkable fact that the difference between this threshold and that obtained with the screen in position has the same absolute value and increases in the same way as the difference between the thresholds in the tunnel experiments, although the two thresholds are considerably higher in the present case. This might be explained by the change in direction, but in view of the differences in method of experimentation the exact reason is difficult to decide.

Coen-Gelders, like Renard, also tried to determine the thresholds for the halt when there was a screen, but without the subjects having the opportunity to make a comparison with cases of halt without a screen. In these conditions the lengths of time for the thresholds were much higher.

In any case the phenomenon that the subjects indicate as being a "halt" can vary within wide limits, and this provides an explanation for various points. This notion is in fact too ill defined for there to be any hope that a precise value could be given to it, especially if one tries to measure the threshold without the element of comparison provided by the halt threshold when there is no concealment. Also, the results obtained in these conditions show a wide range of variability, which is not surprising. Thus, when she worked with four extremely experienced subjects Coen-Gelders found values ranging from 60 to 200 ms for the first mention of a halt.

The Phi Phenomenon With a Hidden Starting Point. Another case that shows clearly the presence of the object behind the screen is that of the phi phenomenon when it is produced in particular conditions. If we assume from the foregoing evidence that a figure hidden by a screen remains present in some way for a certain length of time, it seems that one should be able to use this presence in producing manifestations of the phi phenomenon. This attempt has been made with success by Coen-Gelders who showed an object 5 × 12 mm moving along the slit of the apparatus over a length of 12 mm at a speed of 21 or 45 cm/sec. The figure disappeared at the conclusion of its journey behind a screen that constituted the end of the slit; then after an interval of 67 ms, a similar figure appeared at the place where the first one had started, and moved in its turn towards the screen. This display was presented cyclically, without interruption, and in these conditions the impression, which is dominant at the start, is that of a series of figures that slide successively behind the screen one after another. However, when subjects have continued to observe this succession for a sufficient length of time there is almost always a change of structure, and suddenly one sees a single figure disappearing behind the screen and then reappearing with a leap backwards.

This return movement shows all the features of the phi phenomenon. It was observed at first by chance and to the great surprise of the experimenters (Coen-Gelders and Michotte) and then confirmed not only by trained subjects but also by 14 new subjects, 13 of whom saw things develop in the same way. However, the observation has to be protracted in time, for when the same procedure was used with 14 other subjects and the experiment was presented to them 15 times there were in the end only 3 positive responses. It should be emphasized that all the subjects reported the return movement as beginning behind the screen, as if the moving object was present there, which is in line with what was found previously.

Various attempts have since been made by Renard (1960) and others to obtain exact figures as to the length of time for which this presence lasts by varying systematically the time conditions of the experiment. The results have proved contradictory to some extent, however, which suggests other intervening factors. It is worth mentioning that Crabbé performed the experiment in reverse by making a screen move towards the figure and cover it and then produced a similar figure at the place where the screen had originally been. The same leap backwards could be seen, but in this case, too, the quantitative data do not justify any firm conclusion.

Entraining By a Screen. This extremely interesting phenomenon was observed by Michotte (1963 p. 325) in the course of his research on the perception of causality. He found that when a moving object goes towards another object, covers it like a screen, and continues to move in the same direction without the hidden object reappearing, the great majority of subjects say that the screen *entrains* the figure hiding behind it (entraining effect). This fact has been observed not only by Michotte's subjects but also by those of Yela (1954), Piaget and Lambercier (1958), and Thinès (1962).

The matter has in fact been studied systematically by Yela, who sought to determine the duration over which the phenomenon continued to be perceived (radius of action). There in fact occurs a point of time, if the movement of the moving object is prolonged, when the effect disappears and when the responses indicate that this object alone is present and the object it was carrying, hidden behind it, has ceased to exist. It seems that one can justifiably regard these quantitative figures for the radius of action as representing the length of time during which the figure is still amodally present behind the screen. This is at the moment the only measure not open to objections, since the phenomenon of recognition plays no part here as it does in the case of the tunnel effect and in the case of to-and-fro movement. The time values found by Yela were a little less than half a second.

Amodal Completion Without "Cover"

In the case of the screen effect, which is what we have so far been studying, the gaps in the stimulation occurred because of the intervention of an obstacle that prevented the forming of a retinal image from one part of the object. However, gaps can also occur in the object itself when it displays empty spaces in its own structure. In these cases, too, it sometimes happens that these empty spaces are made good perceptually by amodal completions.

An example of this type of situation can be seen when a geometric shape, such as a cube (with sides of 4 or 5 cm), reduced to its outline, which is made of wire, is caused to pivot round one of its axes. The majority of the subjects react by saying that the whole cube (frame and contents) is moving, as if it were not just a mere skeleton but a receptacle filled with "something" that appears to be enclosed in the cube and is moved with it. This phenomenon is especially striking when the experiment is set up in front of a background structure visible through the mass contained in the cube. The cube then seems completely transparent and consequently has no modal character. What is involved is clearly a result of "contour," as in the well-known effect occurring in the case of plane figures that results in the segregation of the space contained within their limits from its surrounding environment, and, in particular, from the background.

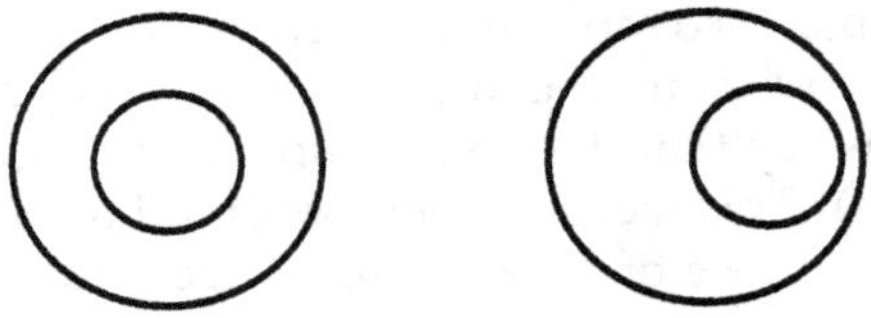

FIGURE 3.11

FIGURE 3.12

Other cases that particularly demonstrate this point can be produced by the use of a stereoscope. Among the many different ways of structuring objects, which can occur when certain linear shapes are presented stereoscopically, there are some in which a rather special kind of amodal completion occurs. This can be brought about, for instance by the stereoscopic fusion (in which the lines of sight are crossed) of the images in Figure 3.11. In these conditions, the hollow trunk of a cone (like a lamp shade) is seen, its base being on the surface of the paper and its top rising upwards. Moreover, for many subjects, the circumferences alone seem to have a modal character, whereas the space separating them appears as a stiff wall elevated in the third dimension but absolutely transparent—without any luminance or coloring—and one can see the paper through it.[29]

This phenomenon is seen even more strikingly, perhaps, in the case of Musatti's[30] stereokinetic figures, such as Figure 3.12 drawn on the surface of a disc. When this is rotated round its center, there is produced, as is well known, a striking stereoscopic effect; the subjects describe the figure as two convex saucers or shells with their concave sides facing each other. Each of them appears as a solid object, firm but hollow, whose surface is delimited by the larger of the curves and therefore comprises all the space inside this contour. Also, as a result of the stereokinetic effect, these surfaces are in different planes from that of the disc, and through the shell whose convex side appears to be turned

[29]In other cases the structure is different, and the wall appears to be of opaque white, which is a consequence of the fact that part of the background is integrated into the figure.

[30]Cf. Musatti, 1924. See also Metzger, 1953, p. 334.

towards the subject, one can see the concave side of the other one. Once again one finds rigidity and transparency.

Although in the experiments mentioned during the preceding sections the amodal completions were merely of a spatial or spatiotemporal order,[31] the last experiments just mentioned introduce us to a new property in certain completions, namely, their apparent firmness or rigidity, which at first sight seems rather unexpected. However, the matter becomes clearer when one realizes that these are not properties of completions as such, in isolation—an idea that would make no sense since, by definition, completion implies a modal frame to complete. They can belong only to the total structure; and in fact, in the examples we have given, what appear rigid is indeed the object itself in its entirety, with its walls or its surface and their limits. As for transparency, it is in no sense emptiness; it is merely the amodal character of the completions showing itself in this way because of the particular structured properties into which they are integrated. In all this, too, contour again plays a fundamental role.

A final point may be mentioned briefly. It is perhaps possible, if one extends the notion of amodal completion, to apply it to the interpretation of the way in which a perceptual field is structured—so called "empty space," separation of objects in space, distance separating them, etc. Unfortunately, we know of no systematic research on this subject from the point of view taken in this chapter.[32]

Conclusions

From the above account a number of facts have emerged. By way of conclusion, it may be helpful to recapitulate briefly the main ones. This will make possible a better overall view and a more accurate assessment of their significance.

When part of a visually perceived object is hidden by a screen, the perceptual structure of this object can in certain conditions still be complete; but the part corresponding to the screen possesses in that case only a purely formal character It is deprived of every sensory quality in the strict sense, such as luminance or color and is thus an amodal completion. This amodal completion is so intimately integrated with the uncovered parts of the object that the overall shape appears as an

[31]It is not impossible, so it seems, that similar questions might arise in the sphere of temporal structures.

[32]A large amount of research, however, has been carried out on problems connected with the perception of apparent distance in the third dimension; among the most recent may be mentioned in particular that carried out at Cornell University by J.J. Gibson and by O. Smith and P. Smith.

entirely continuous whole (which implies secondarily the continuity of color).

A second case, somewhat similar to the preceding one, is that of the perception of certain solids, of which the most characteristic example is that of the sphere. What is in fact perceived is the complete spherical form of an object, although only the half of the sphere turned towards the subject can be seen. The rear half of the sphere, although hidden by the other half which forms a screen, is nevertheless present in amodal form.

The same kind of completion also occurs in the case of objects in movement when one part of their trajectory is hidden by the interposing of a screen (tunnel). In optimal conditions, the movement nevertheless appears continuous. Moreover when the orientation of the uncovered parts of the trajectory is different at the two ends of the tunnel, the hidden part can take diverse forms, consisting, for example, of curves of different degrees of complexity, which vary systematically as a function not only of the orientation in each case but also of the speed of the movement. What is more, these formal properties of the completion can bring about apparent changes in the uncovered parts of the two trajectories that it links.

It is also the case that, in the absence of a screen, there can be amodal completion of certain structures corresponding to stimulus systems that contain gaps. Thus, it can happen that these gaps are not perceived as such but as completely transparent parts of the perceived object, yet having the same solidity as the object itself.

Again, when an object is gradually covered by a screen and at a given moment becomes totally hidden, this object does not immediately cease to be present. For a considerable period it can be integrated, as if it were still exposed, with certain complex structures such as entraining by screen or the phi phenomenon from a concealed starting point.

Having demonstrated that amodal completions occur in very diverse perceptual structures, we must next undertake the equally important task of identifying the factors that give rise to them.

Now it is certain that they do not appear in any capricious or arbitrary manner. In the great majority of cases their presence in perceptual structures is directly determined by the action of the stimulus system upon the subject just as is the case with the nonhidden parts of these structures. In other words, their presence is governed by the laws of organization of the perceptual field, for example those that determine whether a limit belongs to one or the other of two adjacent surfaces, that is, the laws that control integration and segregation, namely similarity, proximity, good continuation, closure, etc.

The fact that this is the case demonstrates, we believe, the perceptual character of amodal completions—a point, moreover, which the subjects continually emphasize—and excludes any attempt at an explanation based on inferences or on the intervention of mental images.

However, a qualification needs to be made at this point, namely, that there are numerous cases where our familiarity with certain categories of objects can bring about the forming of a completion when they are partly covered. In these cases, however, it seems that the completions remain vague and indeterminate.

It would be difficult to exaggerate the importance of these perceptual completions. To convince ourselves of this we need only cast a critical eye about us, at the furniture in a room, for example, or at the traffic in a street. It is astonishing how rare it is to find examples of objects where the side facing the observer is completely uncovered. Nearly all of them have parts hidden by other objects (screens), and despite this the shapes we see are neither interrupted nor breeched. Indeed it is clear that the world as it appears to us is not made up of fragments of objects but of things with a complete shape presented to us in this way despite the partial and temporary concealment that happens to them. This is to a great extent due to the formation of amodal completions, which are thus seen to be an essential factor in the phenomenal permanence of things and consequently also in the adequate adaptation of the behavior of humans and animals to the environment in which they live. Moreover detailed examination of completions in ordinary life situations shows that they are not just products of the laboratory but for most of the time are determined by the laws of structural organization that govern perception.

Everything that has been described and discussed in this book arises from observations and studies made solely with human adults; and it is highly desirable that they should be supplemented by genetic research[33] and also by research in animal psychology, for there are many observations and many well-known research findings that show that animals, when placed in situations involving the partial or total concealment of an object, often display reactions in remarkable agreement with the verbal responses given by human beings.

References

Bobbit, J. M. (1942). An experimental study of the phenomenon of closure as a threshold function. *Journal of Experimental Psychology, 30,* 273–294.

[33]In this connection it will be remembered that many years previously Piaget made some remarkable contributions to problems in related areas; although they were made from a somewhat different point of view, they are full of valuable observations. See, for example, Piaget (1955).

Burke, L. (1952). On the tunnel effect. *Quarterly Journal of Experimental Psychology, 4,* 121–138.

Coen-Gelders, A. (1961). *Le role du donnée amodal dans la perception de l'identité et de la pluralité phénoménales.* [The role of amodal data in the perception of phenomenal identity and plurality.] Unpublished doctoral dissertation, University of Louvain, Louvain.

Crabbé, G. (1963). Research conducted at the Experimental Psychology Laboratory, University of Louvain. Unpublished.

Fuchs, W. (1921). Untersuchungen über das Sehen der Hemianopiker und Hemiamblyopiker. II: Die totalisierende Gestaltauffassung. [An examination of the vision of the hemianopic and hemiamblyopic]. *Zeitschrift für Psychologie, 86,* 1–143.

Glynn, A. J. (1954). Apparent transparency and the tunnel effect. *Quarterly Journal of Experimental Psychology, 6,* 125–139.

Husserl, E. (1950). *Ideen I.* [Ideas.] The Hague: Nijhoff.

Katz, D. (1935). *The world of colour.* London: Kegan Paul, Trench, Trubner & Co.

Knops, L. (1947). Contribution à l'étude de la "naissance" et de la "permanence" phénoménales dans le champ visuel. [A contribution to the study of phenomenal "coming into being" and "permanence" within the visual field.] *Quarterly Journal of Experimental Psychology, 6,* 125–139.

Koffka, K. (1935). *Principles of gestalt psychology.* New York: Harcourt, Brace, & Co.

Korte, A. (1915). Kinematoskopische Untersuchungen. [A study of stroboscopic moment.] *Zeitschrift für Psychologie, 72,* 193–206.

Külpe, O. (1904). Versuche über Abstraktion. [A study of abstraction.] *Bericht. über den 1st Kongress für. experimentelle. Psychologie, Giessen.* Pp. 56–68.

Merleau-Ponty, M. (1945). *Phenomenologie de la perception.* [The phenomenology of perception.] Paris: Gallimard.

Metzger, W. (1953). *Gesetze des Sehens.* [The laws of vision.] Frankfurt-Main: Waldemar Kramer.

Michotte, A. (1963). *The perception of causality.* (T. R. & E. Miles, trans.) London: Methuen. [English translation of Michotte, 1946.]

Michotte, A. (1955). Perception and cognition. *Actes du 14ème Congrès Internationale de Psychologie, Montréal 1954, Acta Psychologica, 11,* 70–91.

Michotte, A. & Burke, L. (1951). Une nouvelle énigme de la psychologie de la perception: le 'donnée amodal' dans l'experience sensorielle. [A new enigma in the psychology of perception: amodal data in sensory experience.] *Actes du 13ème Congrès Internationale de Psychologie, Stockholm.* pp. 179–180.

Musatti, C. (1924). Sui fenomeni stereocinetici. [On sterokinetic phenomena.] *Archives of Italian Psychology, 3, 105–120.*

Piaget, J. (1955). *The child's construction of reality.* (M. Cook, Trans.) London: Routledge & Kegan Paul.

Piaget, J. & Lambercier, M. (1958). La causalité perceptive visuelle chez l'enfant et chez l'adulte. [Visually perceived causality in the child and the adult.] *Archives de Psychologie, Genève, 36,* 77–201.

Piéron, H. (1951). *Vocabulaire de la psychologie.* [The vocabulary of psychology.] Paris: Presses Universitaires de France.

Poppelreuter, W. (1917). *Die psychologischen Schädigungen durch Kopfschuss im Kriege 1914–1916.* [Psychological impairment through missile wounds to the head.] Leipzig: Voss.

Renard, L. (1960). *Étude expérimentale du mouvement phi amodal.* [On amodal phi movement.] Research carried out at the Experimental Psychology Laboratory, University of Louvain, Louvain. Unpublished.

Renard, L. (1963). Research carried out at the Experimental Psychology Laboratory, University of Louvain, Louvain. Unpublished.

Rosenbach, O. (1902). Zur Lehre von den Urteilstauschungen. [Study of judgment errors/illusions.] *Zeitschrift für Psychologie, 29,* 434–448.

Sampaio, A. C. (1943). *La translation des objects comme facteur de leur permanence phénoménale.* [The translation of objects as a factor in their phenomenal permanence.] Louvain: Warny.

Smith, D. W. & Smith, P. C. (1957). Interaction of the effects of cues involved in judgments of curvature. *American Journal of Psychology, 70,* 361–367.

Thinès, G. (1962). *Contribution à la théorie de la causalité perceptive: Nouvelles recherches sur l'effect entrainement.* [Contribution to the theory of perceived causality: new research on the entraining effect.] Louvain: Studia Psychologica, Publications Universitaires de Louvain.

Vernon, M. D. (1952). *A further study of visual perception.* Cambridge University Press.

Wertheimer, M. (1912). Experimentelle Studien über das Sehen von Bewegung. [An experimental study of the visual perception of movement.] *Zeitschrift für Psychologie, 61,* 161–265.

Wertheimer, M. (1925). Experimentelle Studien über das Sehen von Bewegung. [An experimental study of the visual perception of movement.] *Drei Abhandlungen zur Gestalttheorie.* Erlangen: Weltkreis.

Yela, M. (1954). La nature du 'rayon d'action' dans l'impression de causalité mécanique. [The nature of the 'radius of action' in the impression of mechanical causality.] *Journal de Psychologie Normale et Pathologique, 51,* 330–348.

4
Phenomenal Reality

PHENOMENAL REALITY
Alan Costall

Pictures have a curious place in the psychology and epistemology of perception. They have been fundamental to the theory of vision, not only as a result of the familiar analogy between the eye and the camera but also because of a more implicit and pervasive assumption, "the spectator theory of perception," where mere *looking* is held as the paradigm of normal perception. Yet the very centrality of pictures in traditional theory has itself ensured their neglect as a specific topic of study, for they have simply been taken for granted. Thus, although pictures are frequently used in experimental research as convenient substitutes for the real topic of inquiry (as in studies of object or face recognition), research *on* pictures has been sporadic and fragmentary, and conducted primarily by critics of the traditional "image-based" approach to perception (e.g. Kennedy, 1974). The two volumes edited by Margaret Hagen, published several years ago, still remain the only substantial overview of this field of research (Hagen, 1980, 1981).

It is a mark of the fragmented nature of picture perception research that Michotte's own work on this topic is hardly known among English speaking psychologists. It was an interesting surprise for me to discover Michotte's writings on pictures when I embarked on the present project of translating his work. His distinctive approach to the problem of pictures concerns the question of phenomenal reality. As he explained, he came to consider the question of pictorial representation as a result of observations made during his studies of causality. Although the participants in those studies were aware that the displays involved mere patches of colour, they insisted that the causal collisions seemed real:

> I had been struck by the fact that the subjects had the impression that the impact between the objects was real (in the physical sense) rather than just a mere representation of such a collision. Yet, of course, they were aware of the technique employed and therefore knew that it only involved an optical illusion. This observation aroused my curiosity, and so I attempted to investigate the apparent reality of perceptual data by experimental means. I felt that a good method would be to compare systematically cases that involve apparent reality and those that do not. The most obvious case is that of a volume represented in a perspective picture compared with the corresponding solid object itself. . . . (Michotte, 1954, p. 213.)

Thus, as in his other studies, Michotte's approach involved the method of comparison—in this case, the contrast between those situations that are experienced as compellingly real and others that seem unreal or imaginary. His purpose was to ascertain what *perceptually* distinguishes the real from the unreal (see also Metzger, 1963, pp. 35–37; Köhler, 1947, p. 18; Richer, 1979).

Michotte's reason for concentrating on the perception of perspective pictures was their highly qualified reality. On the one hand, of course, we experience depth in such pictures; indeed, as Michotte showed, observers have little difficulty in setting a comparison object (an adjustable, wire figure) to match a three-dimensional object represented in a picture. Yet the depth is not experienced as real; we are not, for example, tempted to put our hands into the picture and touch the depicted objects. Why is this? The apparent reality of the image, Michotte argued, is limited by a perceptual conflict between the flatness of the picture's surface and the depth of the depicted object; indeed, he attempted to show that the reality of the image could be varied in a continous way by manipulating the factors giving rise to this conflict:

> The loss of the character of 'reality' in ordinary pictures arises from a conflict between organisational factors structuring perception. This conflict occurs because the lines of the figure tend to produce an illusion of real volume, but other factors tend to make us see these lines simply as traces attached to the flat surface of the picture, and hence as 'belonging' phenomenally to that surface. Clearly, these tendencies are incompatible, and the conflict is resolved by a stable compromise in which the three-dimensionality of the picture is retained but the volume it represents loses

all appearance of reality. Thus the special 'iconic' quality of pictures. (Michotte, 1957/1962a, p. 515.) (Further discussions of this issue can be found in Pirenne [1970], Polanyi [1970], Kennedy & Ostry [1976] though these authors make no reference to Michotte's important contribution.)

The first paper included in this section, "The psychological enigma of perspective in outline pictures", discusses the various factors that serve either to increase or decrease the character of reality in the pictorial image. To account for the unreal character of the depicted volume, Michotte drew upon David Katz's concept of "phenomenal duplication" (as he had also done, previously, in the development of his theory of ampliation for the case of phenomenal causality). The two, conflicting aspects of the picture, the flatness of its surface and the depth of the depicted object, both occur at the level of perception itself, but do not give rise to an unstable, unresolvable experience (as in the case of reversible figures). The image, as a recent writer has put it, is "two-faced but, unlike Janus, both its faces are presented at once (Sesonske, 1973, p. 401)". They are combined in a unitary way, so that we are aware of both the flatness and the depth, the latter thereby being rendered unreal for us.

The second paper included in this section, "The real and the unreal in the image," is concerned with the same problems raised in the first paper, but provides a more extensive discussion, using many more examples of different kinds of representations (sculptures, drawings, replicas). A basic purpose of this paper is to demarcate truly perceptual from more strictly "conceptual" factors involved in our experience of a representation as a representation. For example, we may come to treat a forgery of a valuable antique as a representation of the real article, not because there is anything intrinsically anomalous about it, but rather because of what we have learned about its provenance.

The third paper in this section, "The character of 'reality' of cinematographic projections" presents a remarkably insightful account of a familiar situation, the experience of watching a film. The central issue concerns the deep involvement we can feel in the events of the film even though we seldom entirely lose sense of the fact that we are indeed watching a film. Michotte notes those aspects of the film, over and above those of the static image, that engender a heightened sense of its reality and those that counteract the effect. In a brilliant development of his discussion, he makes a further comparison with the case of the theater. Here, unlike the film, we are in the presence of real people, and yet even so, they serve to represent the characters they portray and their actions are still not entirely real for us; we would be appalled, for example, if we felt we were witnessing actual violence and murder. In this way, Michotte teases out the various factors that constitute the cinematic situation. Although this classic paper is often cited in the literature on film theory, it is largely unknown to English-speaking psychologists. In fact, the topic of film is itself neglected within perceptual psychology, and the available reviews of the psychology of film, such as Hochberg and Brooks (1978), and Hochberg (1987), make no reference to Michotte nor to the important phenomenological issues he considers (cf. the earlier studies by Arnheim, 1933/1983; Münsterberg, 1916/1970).

The question of what it is about our experience that makes it our own is central to theory of intentionality of Thomas Aquinas (see Kenny, 1984, pp. 93–95). Michotte never went further than to acknowledge a possible, general influence of his own Catholicism and the Thomist Institute in which he worked, but this very question is the topic of the final paper we have included. It concerns the extreme sense of involvement we can experience while watching a film. Sometimes the actions represented in the film not only seem real to us but actually come to be experienced as our own. Michotte's discussion is more tentative here than in the previous papers, but it once more demonstrates his sensitivity to what is remarkable in the commonplace and reveals especially clearly his commitment to the psychodynamic perspective. It is interesting to note that the French psychiatrist Pierre Janet was in contact with Michotte about a possible analogy between the factors that govern the integration of the objects in a causal collision and those involved in the dissociation that occurs for paranoid patients from the projection of their own experience onto others (Janet, 1942).

Michotte's discussions of the reality of the image have not been superseded. They have a richness of detail and insight concerning our normal experience of pictures that many more specialized and technically impressive studies fail to provide. Like Gibson, Michotte was acutely aware that picture perception, far from being an easy explanation of perception, constitutes a fundamental problem, and one that has implications far beyond the problem of pictures as such:

> It relates to much more general problems of interest not only to psychologists but also to psychiatrists, and it even touches upon the most subtle questions within philosophy, such as the origin of the concept of reality. (Michotte, 1962b)

References

Arnheim, R. (1983). *Film as art.* London: Faber & Faber. (Original work published 1933)

Hagen, M. A. (1980). *The perception of pictures: vol. 1: Alberti's window.* New York:

Academic Press.

Hagen, M. A. (1981). *The perception of pictures, volume 2: Durer's devices.* New York: Academic Press.

Hochberg, J. (1987). Representation of motion and space in video and cinematic displays. In K. R. Boff, L. Kaufman, J. P. Thomas (Eds.), *Handbook of perception and human performance, Vol. 1: Sensory processes and perception.* New York: Wiley

Hochberg, J. & Brooks, V. (1978). The perception of motion pictures. In E. C. Carterette & M. P. Friedman (Eds.), *Handbook of perception* (Vol. 10, pp. 259–304). New York: Academic Press.

Janet, P. (1942, January 14). Letter to Albert Michotte, Sanatorium Vert-Lapin, Avon-Fontainebleu, Seine et Marne.

Kennedy, J. M. (1974). *A psychology of picture perception.* San Fransisco: Jossey-Bass.

Kennedy, J. M. & Ostry, D. J. (1976). Approaches to picture perception: Perceptual experience and ecological optics. *Canadian Journal of Psychology 30,* 90–98.

Kenny, A. (1984). Aquinas: Intentionality. In T. Honderich (Ed.), *Philosophy through its past.* Harmondsworth: Penguin.

Köhler, W. (1947). *Gestalt psychology.* New York: Liveright.

Metzger, W. (1963). *Psychologie.* Darmstadt: Dr. Dietrich Steinkopff.

Michotte, A. (1954). Autobiographie de M. le Professeur A. Michotte van den Berck. [Autobiography.] *Psychologica Belgica, 1,* 190–217.

Michotte, A. (1962a). Les variations de réalité apparente de la troisième dimension dans les perception visuelles. [Variations in the apparent reality of the third dimension in visual perception.] In A. Michotte, *Causalité, permanence et réalité phénoménales.* (pp. 512–522). Louvain: Publications Universitaires, 1962. (First published 1957.)

Michotte, A. (1962b). L'énigme psychologique de la perspective dans le dessin linéaire. [The psychological enigma of perspective in line drawings.] In A. Michotte, *Causalité, permanence et réalité phénoménales.* (pp. 454–471). Louvain: Publications Universitaires. (First published 1948.)

Münsterberg, H. (1916). *The film: A psychological study.* New York: Dover, 1970. (First published 1916.)

Pirenne, M. H. (1970). *Optics, painting and photography.* Cambridge: Cambridge University Press.

Polanyi, M. (1970). What is a painting? *British Journal of Aesthetics, 10,* 225–236.

Richer, P. (1979). The concepts of subjectivity and objectivity in Gestalt psychology. *Journal of Phenomenological Psychology, 10(1),* 35–55.

Sesonske, A. (1973). Cinema space. In D. Carr & E. S. Casey (Eds.), *Explorations in phenomenology.* (pp. 399–409). The Hague: Martinus Nijhoff.

THE PSYCHOLOGICAL ENIGMA OF PERSPECTIVE IN OUTLINE PICTURES[1]

Albert Michotte

The representation of volume by a flat image, such as a painting, drawing, or photograph, is so common today that it seems the most natural thing in the world, and we hardly stop to think about the strange problems it poses. The evidence of our senses usually lulls our curiosity, and, without thinking, we simply treat representations as an inevitable fact of life.

Yet it is strange that an impression of volume can be produced by mere lines on a sheet of paper, appropriate shading by means of light and dark strokes of paint, or the technique used by the impressionists or "luminists." Furthermore, a moment's reflection makes us appreciate the real contradiction underlying the fact that, although the image itself is flat, we are able to see volume in it; for there can be no question that we do *see* the depicted object as extended in depth, that there is the appearance of relief in a perspective picture. This is by no means a mere interpretation of the image, as is the case when we try to make sense of the contour line in a map, for example.

This fact is of central importance, and so it is worthwhile to emphasize and clarify its significance by means of an example, a figure that can give rise either to the impression of a flat shape or to that of a volume. When naive observers (i.e., those unaware of this issue of the third dimension) are shown Figure 4.1A, they generally see only a pattern, an elongated hexagon decorated with some straight lines, or else a surface composed of simple shapes like triangles, diamonds, and trapezoids, a kind of flat shield with geometrical designs as shown in Figure 4.1B. However, it is also easy to see this same figure in perspective, and see it as a compressed parallelepiped, as indicated in Figure 4.1C.

Under these conditions, the internal structure of what we perceive is totally different. The triangles, diamonds, and trapeziums no longer exist for the observer: Instead the observer sees four rectangular shapes and two square shapes. Furthermore, this new way of seeing the object is clearly incompatible with its insertion on a flat plane, given that all these surfaces are formed from shared parts of the actual picture and that they cannot maintain their integrity or be distinguished from one another on the basis of appearing to be localized in front of one another. Moreover, it is clear that the angles of the square section of the parallelepiped can in no way seem to be standing upright if they are

[1]Translated by Alan Costall from "L'énigme psychologique de la perspective dans le dessin linéaire" *Bulletin de l'Académie royale de Belgique*, 1948, 5e Série, Tome 34, 268–288.

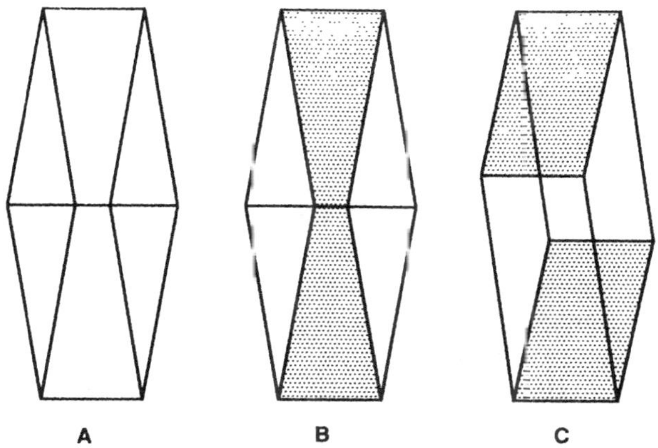

FIGURE 4.1

seen as lying on the surface of the paper. Analogous effects can also occur when one looks for some time at a reversible perspective figure, such as a reversible cube. The object seems to change its orientation every now and then, and the changes possess an undeniable "sensory" character.

Pictorial perspective, therefore, is a great puzzle. Psychologists have investigated this issue ever since the study of depth perception entered its truly experimental phase, especially after Wheatstone's discovery of the stereoscope in 1838. A rather general consensus soon emerged concerning the appropriate explanation of the phenomenon. In accord with the dominant ideas in the psychology of the time, the effect was interpreted in terms of the influence of past experience: Since seeing substantial objects extended in space is so habitual, we imagine all represented objects as extended in depth if they lend themselves to this perception in any way. According to this view, the perception of perspective pictures is a hybrid process involving certain aspects that are "sensory" in the strict sense of the word, whereas others, such as the distance and the apparent depths of the objects, are supposed to be constructed by our imagination and are then combined with the former.

At first, this explanation seems simple, coherent, and basically sound. However, in the early part of this century the first work of the Gestalt school provoked a profound reassessment of psychological conceptions of perception (see Guillaume, 1937). Indeed, the Gestaltists showed that simple explanations of perception, in terms of training and perceptual habits, had been particularly misused and that such theories in fact ran into such serious difficulties that they needed to be restricted, as well as completely revised.

Initially, the Gestaltists were concerned with the perception of two-dimensional forms and movement. Later, however, Kopferman (1930) tackled the problem we are addressing in the present paper, and he arrived at some quite revolutionary conclusions about the conditions under which flat images give rise to the impression of volume.

We tend to assume that a flat picture must give us the impression of depth as long as it corresponds to the exact perspective of a real object, but this is not true. Certain forms, which can be considered as correct perspective representations, geometrically speaking, never give us the impression of the third dimension (Figure 4.2) (see Metzger, 1936).

It is easy to see the irregular quadrilateral in Figure 4.2D as a square or rectangle viewed from the side, or the cross with the inclined transversals as a cross with perpendicular arms. But it is impossible to see the square as a quadrilateral at a slant, or the straight cross as as a cross with inclined arms viewed somewhat to the side, although, geometrically, this should be possible. In the same way, Figure 4.2B gives the impression of a rod or tube with circular cross-section, whereas Figure 4.2A gives no impression of a rod with eliptical cross-section, even though it could represent this. When the latter is seen in depth, it usually appears as a segment of a ring extending backwards with circular ends facing the observer.

How can we explain these effects? In the light of a good deal of supporting evidence, the Gestaltists proposed that these effects involve a law of perceptual stimulation, the law of "Prägnanz." This law was strongly emphasized by Wertheimer, who explained it in the following way. When a complex system of stimulation can give rise to different perceptual forms (as is usually the case), one of these forms is usually preferred, which is most simple, the best balanced, the most symmetrical, the best centered, or the one in which the continuity of the contours is best preserved (Wertheimer, 1925).

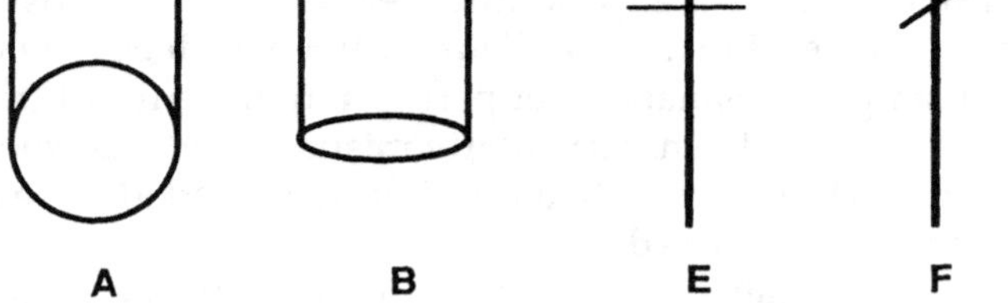

FIGURE 4.2

Sometimes a form imposes itself with a really inevitable insistence, like the square or rectangular cross in Figure 4.2. In other cases, however, the precedence is less marked, and then one is concerned with ambiguous forms like the oblique cross or the quadrilateral, or the example of Figure 4.1A. Then what we perceive can be influenced by the effects of what we have previously perceived, or by adaptation, or even the mental attitude of the observer.

The Gestaltists considered the principle of "Prägnanz" as the counterpart in the domain of perception to the dynamic laws, which in the physical domain govern the establishment of certain forms in preference to others, such as a drop of liquid or a soap bubble formed through the action of molecular forces. These same laws govern the reactions occurring in the brain under the influence of sensory stimulation, and "Prägnanz" is simply its manifestation at the mental level.

The role of "Prägnanz" is also evident in the case of more complex perceptual forms. Kopferman has presented several examples, such as those given in Figure 4.3. Figure 4.3A appears spontaneously as a flat shape, whereas Figure 4.3B appears as an object extended in depth. The first possesses two axes of symmetry and the vertical lines are continuous; in contrast, the second, where certain parts of the figure are shifted, no longer has an axis of symmetry on the surface of the paper, and some of the verticals are split in half and displaced. As a result, this figure is extremely complicated and irregular if seen as flat, whereas its structure is infinitely simpler if seen in depth.

On the basis of prototypes, which were gradually modified, Kopferman has constructed a series of figures in which the forms present progressively fewer and fewer main axes of symmetry and continuous

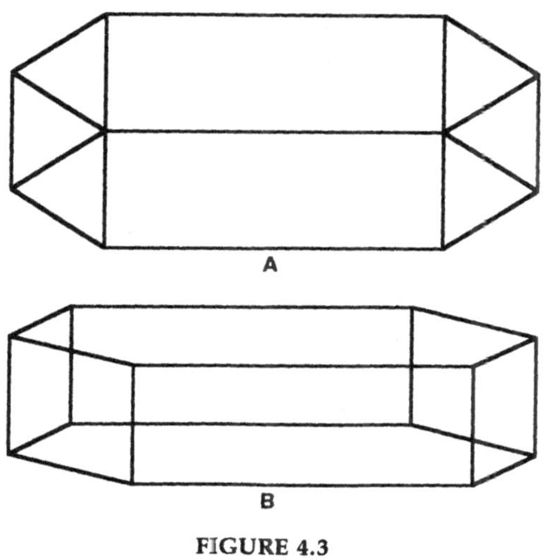

FIGURE 4.3

lines, and it has been found that the tendency or ease of seeing them in depth varies in relation with these geometrical properties.

A similar effect occurs in the perception of movement (e.g., Metzger, 1934). For example, when an observer is shown two objects (in fact, two shadows) performing periodic to-and-fro movements in relation to each other, one often has the impression that the two objects remain a constant distance apart and are turning in depth in a continuous motion around a center of rotation situated between them. Once again, of course, this uninterrupted circular movement is again much simpler than the to-and-fro motion involving periodic stopping and changing of direction. The same principle holds for the case of stroboscopic movement; it is possible to show that the apparent motion of objects organized in depth, arising from the use of different shaped objects, has a less complex structure than that of the movement occurring on the surface of the display.

In short, a three-dimensional structure is spontaneously established if it corresponds to a form that is simpler and more symmetrical than an organization on the plane (i.e., the law of "Prägnanz"). The effect is not determined by past experience, or by acquired knowledge, and these factors only intervene as a kind of accessory influence in certain cases. (Their role can be demonstrated by appropriate methods, but there is no need to consider them here.) The law of "Prägnanz" has been successfully applied to the explanation of other aspects of the perception of relief and distance in pictures, such as the recognition of different surfaces and the important effects of light and shadow.

What we have been considering so far, though essential, is just a preliminary move towards understanding the paradox of linear perspective. We must now try to specify the differences (and similarities) that exist between the impressions of volume given by perspective pictures and by real, substantial objects. This task, of course, if it is to be performed exhaustively, will ultimately require extensive research. Here we must confine ourselves to essential details. Therefore, we will restrict our attention to two particularly relevant cases.

If, in an experiment, one asks people to try to pass a rod, such as a pencil, through a parallelepiped made out of metal wires, they obviously do it without any objection; but if one then asks them to perform the same task in relation to a perspective picture, their behavior changes completely, and, in so far as they understand the instructions, they make no attempt to stick the rod into the volume, although they can nevertheless *see* it. This is of great theoretical significance, but so commonplace that it is sufficient to note it just for the moment.

Now consider a second study, which is a bit more complicated and has only recently been completed. Using a parallelepiped made out of metal wire as a model, we asked observers to adjust a second parallelepiped so that the two objects appeared to be of the same size. (This second object was constructed in the same way as the first but could be varied in length by means of a special device.) The position of the two objects remained fixed over a series of successive adjustments, and the subject's head was held in a fixed position so as to ensure a constant viewpoint. We also used models of different dimensions so as to avoid stereotyped responses.

Although there was a small systematic error, which varied with the distance between the two objects, the results revealed an approximate match between the standard and the variable parallelepiped, in accordance with size constancy. We then substituted a picture of the model parallelepiped, but this was constructed so that it was an exact perspective projection of the metal object used in the first condition, as observed from the position of the subject. (This is only possible with any accuracy in the case of monocular vision, since obviously the retinal images formed by the real object are different for the two eyes—the distance of the object from the point of observation being about 90 cm. When we have performed experiments with binocular viewing conditions, the perspective was based upon the position of the "cyclopean eye.") When the picture was used as the model, the subject was instructed to adjust the variable parallelepiped to the same depth as that of the object represented in the picture.

This experiment was highly informative for a variety of reasons. First, it showed that the adjustment task was generally quite easy. The main difficulty we encountered was that the square section of the object usually appeared to be a shade larger in the picture than for the actual object, and this slightly distorted the overall judgment of the volume. Nevertheless, the comparisons of depth were certainly as direct and immediate for the picture as for the object itself, and the judgments of the former were by no means based on any extrinsic criteria.

Second, there was a relatively appreciable error of underestimation. The parallelepiped judged equal to that represented in the picture was on average (over seven subjects and all of the experimental conditions) about 30% shorter than that which served as the model in constructing the perspective image. The value of 30% was that obtained for binocular vision. As would be expected, it was slightly less for monocular vision, yet it still reached a value of 20%. Therefore, there was a significant apparent compression of the object despite the precision of the perspective. (Interestingly, since the apparent depth of a depicted object varies with the viewing position of the observer, it is possible to obtain the paradoxical result that the depth is distorted when one views the picture from the proper station point, and yet be undistorted when the picture is viewed from the wrong position. The apparent flattening of the object could possibly be corrected by means of shading.)

Our most important finding, however, concerns the precision with which the depth was reproduced, that is, the consistency of the variations made over a series of successive adjustments. The precision was rather similar and high, for both the real model and the perspective image. For the real object, the coefficient of variation was 3.2%; for the perspective picture, it was 4% for binocular vision, and 4.2% for monocular vision.

This study shows, therefore, that it is easy to make a match between the real depth of a substantial object (the adjustable, metal parallelepiped) and the apparent depth produced by the perspective picture. Furthermore, the depth of the real model and that seen in the picture show practically the same degree of perceptual constancy over a long series of successive comparisons. Finally, when one considers the behavior of the subject, that is, the actions performed during the task, one must say that they are of the same kind; the subject, even if a little more hesitant in relation to the picture than to the metal model, nevertheless tackles the adjustment with the usual motor actions and mental operations and with a similar outcome. One must conclude therefore that the property of the object that determines the response of the subject is the same in the two cases.

If the volume perceived is the same, however, why is there a difference in behavior in the earlier test involving the penetration of the object with a rod? Obviously, it must be because the type of action performed is quite different in the two experiments. The adjustment experiment involves a comparison made "at a distance" and does not involve direct contact with the model, whereas the penetration study entails a reaction of manipulation, that is, the potential for actually handling the object, passing something through it, or grasping it, and this reveals a radical difference in the subject's behavior in relation to the real object and the picture. The latter type of response is no longer determined solely by the extent of the volume perceived, but by some additional factor that we are convinced must concern the reality or unreality of the volume as it appears to the observer. One must conclude that, in terms of perception, the object represented by the perspective picture differs from the actual object solely in terms of the *lack of apparent reality of the material of which it is formed.*

At first, this thesis is a little perplexing, since we tend spontaneously to assume that the fact that an object is extended in depth or, at least, intergrated within a three-dimensional space, is the distinguishing mark of its material reality in the visual domain; some have even wished to treat them as identical. It is striking how most psychologists studying pictorial representation have avoided making any reference to "reality." Thus, when they try to specify the difference between the impressions obtained with a stereoscope and those produced by a perspective picture, they talk of the greater "vividness" of the third dimension, or a "more accentuated three-dimensional effect," of an appearance of "solidity," or of "naturalness," of a greater impression of "relief", and so on. Some, however, like Hering (1879) and Jaensch (1911), and more recently Metzger (1941, p. 35) have referred to the opposition between "the real" and "the unreal," or else (less precisely, in our view) the opposition between intuitive "reality" and "appearance." Basically, it seems that the past discussion of this problem has been dominated by a fundamental confusion. No doubt under the influence of prejudices of psychological and philosophical schools, these authors either have failed to see, or else failed to explain clearly, that three-dimensionality and reality are different properties of our perceptions and must be considered as *independent dimensions* of our visual experience.

However, the suspicions surrounding the term reality can only be dispelled once we have taken care to clarify the exact sense we intend by the terms we are employing. By *reality* we mean an empirical characteristic, the potential for being manipulated. By *three-dimensionality* we mean another empirical characteristic, the capacity for being matched to the volume of a substantial object.

Perhaps the objection will be made that the criterion of manipulation, though perfectly worthwhile in the psychology of behavior, remains ambiguous in relation to phenomenology. There can be no question that our actions occur generally as a function of what we believe to be reality, especially in relation to the external aspects of things, which we know to be often misleading. We know, for example, that objects seen in a mirror are not really behind it, and, despite the perceptual evidence, we behave appropriately; it is like this every time we find ourselves in a "situation" that we recognize as illusory.

It is, therefore, essential when we are gathering psychological data to keep in mind the distinction between the belief in reality and the impression or character of reality and to recognize that the criterion of manipulation is incapable, by itself, of distinguishing between the two cases. However, our everyday experience hardly leaves us in any doubt about the question of perspective pictures; it is quite clear that what is involved, in this case, is not merely a *belief* but also an intuitive character of unreality. However, to substantiate this point it is necessary to complement the manipulation criterion by an additional test, which we will explain shortly.

Having discussed some properties of perspective images, the new problem arises of why the apparent reality of the volume of a substantial object is absent in the case of a picture, even though the retinal images of the object and its image can be practically identical, as was the case in some of our adjustment experiments under monocular viewing conditions.

One explanation, which can be traced far back, for example to Hering (1879), and which has since been developed, notably by Koffka (1935), attributes the special aspect of perspective pictures to the fact that they are connected or belong in some way to the surface upon which they are traced. Therefore, we should consider how perception is affected when the lines of the picture are separated from the surface that supports them. This can be achieved by methods that have been known for a long time. The use of a stereoscope would seem to be the most promising, but the problem here is that the introduction of binocular vision complicates matters, and so it is better to use a technique compatible with monocular vision.

Any perspective picture, when viewed with one eye from some distance, can give an impression of depth significantly more real than that obtained under binocular viewing conditions. But other devices are much more effective. For example, it is possible to construct a picture on a perfectly transparent support or even produce it in wire and place these items in front of a uniform background from which they are separated and on which they can be seen in profile. When observed monocularly some meters away, and sometimes even binocularly, the volume seems perfectly real. It is also possible to project the shadow of an object, such as a wire cube, on a screen. When the image is viewed from a small distance, it yields an impression analogous to that of a picture. If, however, one then rotates the cube, the movements of the shadow become "detached" from the screen, and the cube takes on a heightened character of reality. Incidentally, the effect of movement is one of the factors that accounts for the aspect of "reality" normally possessed by objects portrayed in films, produced physically by the effect of a rather complicated pattern of shadows.

We have mainly examined and developed a third method that has been extremely effective despite its simplicity. It involves the use of a very elongated perspective image such as that shown in Figure 4.4, which is viewed monocularly from a very oblique angle (the angle between the line of regard and the surface of the image being about only 15°).

Under these conditions, one sees an object shaped more or less like a cube or parallelepiped (depending on the viewing position), and this sometimes has a disconcerting character of reality, which is as good as that produced by the best processes of stereoscopy.

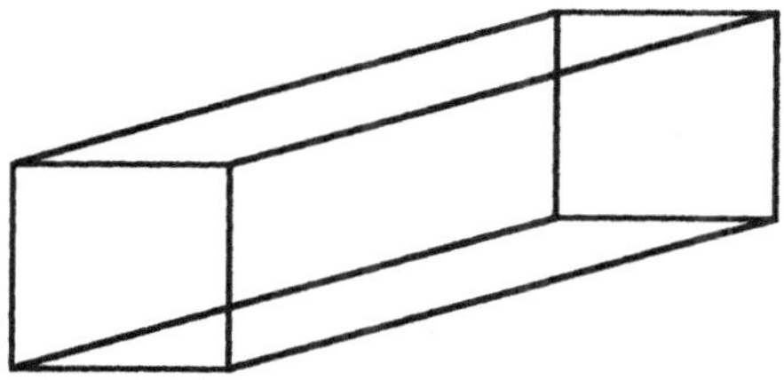

FIGURE 4.4. This figure should be viewed monocularly from the end marked B, with the eye placed almost in the same plane as the paper, and at the distance of distinct vision (The original figure was 70 cm wide.)

This effect has already been described, in another form, by C. Ladd-Franklin, 1887, and used as a method for determining the horopter. However, she noted that converging lines drawn on a sheet of paper can give the impression of vertical lines standing upright from the surface of the paper when it is placed horizontally and viewed monocularly at a glancing angle, and the point of convergence coincides with the position of the subject's eye. This observation is rarely cited, especially in recent papers, and its great importance has not been appreciated. The theoretical account presented by Ladd-Franklin, which was in terms of the orientation of the lines in relation to retinal topography and the determining role of past experience, can hardly be defended today. It is easy to show that the effect is based on the opposition between the direction of the frontal projection of the depicted lines and the orientation of the surface of the paper.

When the stimulation is such that the lines can seem almost perpendicular to the surface, they become detached and take on the appearance of needles sticking out of the paper. When, in contrast, the orientation of the surface and the direction of the projection of the lines are compatible, they appear simply as traces on the paper. What is involved here, therefore, is a special case of perceptual organization concerning the lines and the surface that constitutes their frame of reference. This effect also depends on the form of the figure. Although the character of substantiality occurs spontaneously when isolated lines or perspective images are used, it no longer occurs for other structures such as Figure 4.5, which is only the external contour of the perspective image of Figure 4.4. Even though certain aspects of this phenomenon are still under investigation, it is possible to confirm that its explanation lies within the realm of Gestalt psychology.

The object seems to be connected by one of its faces to the paper,

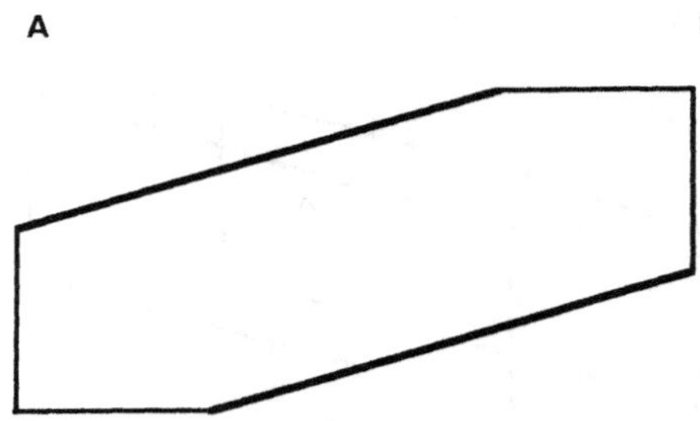

FIGURE 4.5. This figure should be viewed in the same way as the previous one. (The original figure was 70 cm wide.)

which serves as its support, but the others seem to be entirely free and projected into space. At the same time, the lines lose their character as traces on a surface and take on an independent existence.

The effect of reality of the volume can be so intense that if one suggests to the observer to attempt the manipulation test and pass a rod through the object, the observer does not hesitate to try and is extremely astonished to find that the rod hits the paper and slides along its surface above the object! The manipulation test is quite clear, for the observer knows perfectly well that the perceived object is unreal yet he acts as if in the presence of a tangible object. The impression of reality is so powerful at the time that it is able to overpower any effect of the observer's belief in the unreality of the object. (Similar observations are easily made during 3-D film shows. When the spectators have the impression of a ball thrown in their direction, they spontaneously duck so as to avoid it, even though they appreciate that it is only an illusion.)

This experiment is also interesting for another reason, since it allows us to vary the apparent reality of the object in gradual stages. In fact, as the angle of regard is progressively changed, by turning the picture around some convenient axis, one finds that the object becomes detached from its support only little by little, and there is a continuous series of stages between the two extreme cases. The impression of reality of the volume increases as a direct function of the extent to which the object appears to become free of the supporting picture surface.

Thus, the character of reality can occur in various degrees. Phenomenally, the real and the unreal are not contrasted as contradictories in an all-or-none fashion, therefore, but as limits of a continuous series.

This conclusion itself is by no means novel (see, e.g., Jaensch, 1911), p. 467 et seq), but our experiment has served to show that gradual variations in reality correspond to progressive variations in the stimulation, which are both well-defined and controllable.

The fact that concomitant variation is possible here, analogous to the case of movement perception, shape, and color, could be taken to imply an empirical and direct dependence. This study, therefore, supports the remarkable idea that the character of reality should be considered as a primitive and original dimension of phenomena, in the same way as the properties previously mentioned.

Under everyday conditions, for normal people, these impressions produced by stimulation of the sense organs generally possess a clear character of reality, and the case of depth perception in pictures is perhaps the only, or one of the only, examples where this characteristic is reduced to a minimum. It is quite different, however, in certain mental illnesses where the sense of the real is lost; in contrast, in the case of hallucination, what is imagined gives rise to reactions analogous to those caused by the presence of real objects. Unfortunately, it seems difficult to establish to what degree these anomalies are based on the belief or the impression of reality (or unreality), and one might suspect that it will not be possible to decide this on the basis of studies of such cases. This very fact adds to the theoretical interest of the study of perspective pictures, from the viewpoint of general psychology, since it is possible here to perform systematic experiments on the real and the unreal within the phenomenal domain.

On the basis of the three experiments we have described, we can draw the following, fundamental conclusion: In the absence of conflicting factors, a flat, perspective form, isolated from its support, produces not only an impression of three-dimensionality, but also that of the reality of the perceived volume. Consequently, when the represented object seems unreal, it is because of certain factors that tend to bind it to the plane of the paper on which it is drawn. These factors include the effect of binocular vision, the similarity of the microstructure of the traces and the surface of the paper (e.g., their roughness), the absence of depth in the traces, and so on.

(Thus, in the last experiment referred to, the effect of reality is destroyed once one opens both eyes, and then one only sees a picture "drawn on the paper." Moreover, if the form of the retinal image formed under oblique, monocular viewing conditions is accurately determined and drawn on a sheet of paper placed in the frontal plane, as in Figure 4.6, it is perceived simply as a picture.)

As Koffka (1935) has noted, we are concerned here with a situation of perceptual conflict between different organizational factors. Some tend to make us see an object extended in space, whereas others tend to restrict the object to a plane. (According to Koffka, the conflict merely produces a less "strong" or less "vivid" effect of three-dimensionality.)

Conflicts of this kind often occur in perception, and the effects depend on the power of the competing factors. Sometimes they lead to total disorganization, and what we perceive has a chaotic aspect. In

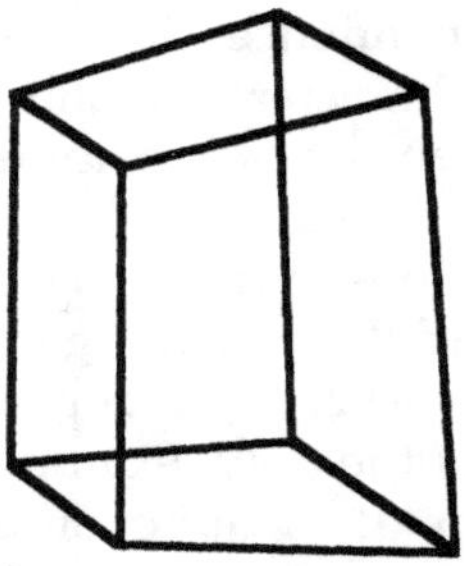

FIGURE 4.6

other cases, fluctuations occur between different possible organizations. Often, however, the conflict is resolved by a compromise, but this never occurs without something being lost. Some characteristic of the phenomenal organization is destroyed or is at least profoundly changed. (see Michotte, 1963, for numerous examples.)

In the present case, the effect of the conflict is not restricted simply to making the picture "less three-dimensional," as claimed by Koffka; for, in addition to the flattening of the apparent depth of the object previously noted, it is primarily the character of reality that is impaired. Its destruction seems to be the essential condition for the resolution of the conflict. Although the integration of a real volume on a flat surface would be contradictory, in fact only the surface and the traces on it are real, whereas the volume loses all reality.

In conclusion, I would like to stress, once again, that the psychological study of perspective pictures far exceeds the particular issues pertaining to the enigma of pictorial representation as such. It relates to much more general problems of interest, not only to psychologists but also psychiatrists, and it even touches on the most subtle questions within philosophy, such as the origin of the concept of reality.

References

Guillaume, P. (1937). *La psychologie de la forme* [Gestalt psychology]. Paris: Flammarion.

Hering, E. (1879). Der Raumsinn und die Bewegungen des Auges [Space perception and eye movements]. In L. Hermann (Ed.), *Handbuch der Physiologie* (Vol. 3, Part 1, pp. 343–601). Leipzig: Vogel.

Jaensch, E. R. (1911). Über die Wahrnehmung des Raumes [On space perception]. *Zeitschrift für Psychologie. Erg.*, (pp. 467 et seq.) Bd. 1, Leipzig.

Koffka, K. (1935). *Principles of gestalt psychology.* New York: Harcourt.

Kopferman, H. (1930). Psychologische Untersuchungen über die Wirkung zweidimensionaler Darstellungen körperlicher Gebilde [A psychological

study of the three-dimensional appearance of physical displays]. *Psychologische Forschung, 13,* 293–364.
Ladd-Franklin, C. (1887). A method for the experimental determination of the horopter. *American Journal of Psychology, 1,* 99–11.
Metzger, W. (1934). Beobachtungen über phänomenale Identität [An observation on phenomenal identity]. *Psychologische Forschung, 19,* 1–16.
Metzger, W. (1936). *Gesetze de sehens* [The laws of vision]. Frankfurt: Kramer.
Metzger, W. (1941). *Psychologie* [Psychology]. Leipzig: Steinkopf.
Michotte, A. (1963). *The perception of causality.* London: Methuen.
Wertheimer, M. (1925). *Drei Abhandlungen über Gestalttheorie* [Three essays on Gestalt theory]. Erlangen: Weltkreis.

THE REAL AND THE UNREAL IN THE IMAGE[1]
Albert Michotte

The function of an image is to represent something other than itself, and this obviously precludes the actual presence of the represented object at the same location as that of the image. The unique and marvelous psychological capacity for representation occurs in the use of all symbols and, therefore, is at the source of all human progress.

Images stand apart from other symbols, however, since they entail a resemblance to the thing represented, and indeed it is no mere accident that they are in fact the source from which all other symbols have eventually developed, whatever their degree of abstraction and transformation.[2] Although it would be pointless to list the limitless variety of images, we should note that they can be classified in a number of ways: in terms of the role they play in our behavior, their detail, the degree of their resemblance to the objects they represent, or the nature of the objects represented. The present study will concentrate on the special case of portrait images, that is, images representing definite things or people. What we have to say on this topic will nevertheless be applicable to other cases as well, particularly to images with anonymous

---

[1]Translated by Alan Costall from "Le réel et l'irréel dans l'image", *Bulletin de la classe des Lettres de l'Académie royale de Belgique,* 5ème Série, 1960, *46,* 330–344. (Reprinted in Michotte et al., Causalité, Permanence et Realité Phenomènales. Louvain: Publications Universitaires, 1962. pp. 523–540.)

[2]As a result, objects currently called "images" lack the specific characteristic of images and should be considered as pure symbols when they represent spiritual entities, as is the case of certain religious images. On the other hand, the distinction between images and conventional symbols, which is clear in extreme cases, is sometimes difficult to apply in relation to schematic pictures, such as architectural plans and all kinds of diagrams, especially those representing events occurring over time. For this reason, it is useful in our view to clarify the concept of the image by reference to manifest (or latent) resemblance.

and collective significance representing nonindividualized objects, or even images representing objects that do not actually exist, for example, plans for construction projects.

To avoid any misunderstanding, it is important to stress that our topic concerns the realm of perception and, therefore, will be treated from a psychological point of view, or, more precisely, from the perspective of "experience." Consequently, the word "real," which will occur very often in this paper, will always refer to what is commonly called the "physical world," that is, the world of creatures and things, including our own bodies, which we see and can touch, manipulate, and employ in our activities. As far as the concept of the "unreal" is concerned, this will initially be treated in a purely negative fashion, though one of the aims of this study is to provide it with a new, positive meaning.

Let us begin, then, by considering a very simple case, that of two objects similar in every appearance, such as two jewels, two medals, two items of silver, or two vases. We eventually confirm that they are similar, and then, usually, matters are left to rest. However, in certain circumstances, we sometimes discover that one of the objects is of some antique value, whereas the other is just a copy. Then everything changes. The new information, which is external to the objects themselves, gives them a totally different significance, as is revealed usually in a considerable difference in market value.

This example is of central importance to our inquiry because it shows that in such cases there is neither a copy nor an original for those who merely see, but only for those who both look and *know*. It, therefore, serves as a pure case in which the difference between the copy and the original is not a function of their structure as such but exists only at the level of thought and as a result of a context external to the objects themselves.

However, the psychological implications are important. When an object comes to represent another, we think of the latter when we see the first object. One might even say that we see the original itself in the portrait, since, as the result of a mental operation to be discussed later, all the perceived properties of the copy, such as its shapes and colors, are attributed in our thought to the original. In other words, the original is *present*, though in a fictitious or unreal way, in the copy. This is quite different, of course, from just jogging our memory, in the way that the sight of somebody reminds us of someone similar.

The mental operation, referred to here, necessarily comes into effect every time a sensory structure becomes representative. Consequently, the concept of a portrait, and of the image more generally, is essentially functional. To be precise, there is no such thing as an image in itself; an object is an image only in so far as it is representative for someone. It is only by an extension of the use of this term, no doubt justified by the practical requirements of language, that we currently designate as images the objects, statues or engravings that perform or favor this representational function. For similar reasons, physicists use the word "image" for the objective point-to-point correspondence between certain arrangements that occur in the fields of optics or electricity.

Our example of a complete correspondence between the image and the represented object is quite rare; usually there is only a partial similarity between them, and the relative degree of their similarities and difference can vary quite considerably. Sometimes, the image seems, at first sight, to replicate entirely the external appearance of the model, as is the case for the wax figures on view in the Musée Grevin at Paris or Madame Tussaud's in London. It requires very close inspection to notice that the material from which they are made totally conflicts with their form. On the other hand, in the case of bronze or marble statues, the discrepancy between the form and the material is obvious, and this is even more marked, of course, in the case of busts or statuettes.

In addition, there is the immense field of photographs, drawings, and other kinds of pictures, in which the image is created by projection of a three-dimensional object onto a surface, in some cases preserving the original colors and size. This is a very special case of great theoretical importance, which we must return to later.

Some representations are a good deal more abstract, and the resemblance is restricted to a contour or a schematic form, such as simple outline drawings, silhouettes, and certain cartoons based on just a few lines.

Lastly, we should include those cases in which the similarities are no longer purely static but serve to reproduce some of the actions of the original, such as the representation of the behavior and gestures of people on film or television, or even by means of shadow shows, the impersonation of another's speech or behavior, and finally the highly complex case of theatrical representation.

These varied examples do have certain features in common. First of all, the similarity between the image and the model is, in some respects, obviously limited; and this gives rise to their manifestly artificial character. In general, this artificial character is immediately apparent once the combination of properties present in the image fails to conform to what our everyday experience has taught us about their physical nature. However, we are so used to seeing statues, photographs, and all kinds of pictures that we are no longer amazed by this discrepancy. Nevertheless, we are still astonished when images have an exceptional appearance, as in the case of gigantic ancient statues or those fantastic natural shapes that occur, for example, when tree roots become deformed so as to resemble animals or even human heads.

Another typical feature of images is that the similarities to their models are primarily restricted to their "formal" properties. The term "form" is used here in the technical sense given to it by Gestalt psychologists and denotes not merely geometrical shape but, more generally, the specific impression of an entire configuration, characteristic of complex sensory structures. In addition to the precisely global aspect, this comprises surface properties, such as the veinings on certain stones or the impression of roughness, graininess, or smoothness in the case of visual perception, rhythmic or melodic structures in audition, or tactile-kinaesthetic structures, either rhythmic or not, corresponding to the movements of our limbs, and so on.

Such forms possess several psychological properties that are highly relevant to our present study, but the most important concerns their considerable functional autonomy. This functional autonomy is especially evident in the remarkable way in which similar configurations, created by means of quite different materials, seem not only to resemble one another, but to be really identical. Musical transposition is a classic example; one continues to hear the same melody whatever the key in which it is played, or the sound of the instrument employed. Similarly, objects differing in color and size can possess the same visual form. This is not simply playing with words, but a psychological fact. It is as though forms were endowed with an independent existence, with a remarkable capacity of being realized in a variety of ways, rather as in the realm of abstract thought, the same general concept can be applied to any number of individual cases.

Furthermore, significance is generally attached to the form of the perceived thing as a whole; thus, it is more apt to say, when describing the impression made by a particular statue, that one sees a bronze horse rather than that one sees a mass of bronze shaped in the form of a horse. Consequently, whenever a form becomes meaningful, it is by virtue of its context; this context includes not only the entire perceptual field but even the knowledge acquired through past experience of the object represented.

We have learned through experience that the form of the human body is almost always of a certain order of size and that it is only the external aspect of an organism composed of flesh and blood. We also know that this form corresponds to the disposition of the internal organs of the body and its activities and that, therefore, it is intrinsically linked to the structure and functioning of the organism in question; this is not the case, of course, for wax or plaster statues.

In the case of a portrait of a relative or friend, we associate their typical mannerisms with the features of the face or their more general appearance, and where the representation of inanimate objects is involved, the form is associated with their function. In all these cases, then, the form has become strongly associated in past experience to the other properties of the represented object; indeed, mainly because of its intimate relation to the functions of the object, the form has become, psychologically speaking, one of its essential properties. As such, the form is an integral part of the object; it belongs to it entirely. As a result, despite its artificial character, the image seems to draw our thoughts directly to the model itself; we see the form of the object in the image. The intermediary role of the image dissolves for the observer, exactly as when listening to speech or reading text, the sounds or geometrical forms of the words become subsidiary, and we have the impression of directly hearing or reading the ideas expressed. We are aware of an immediate contact with the signified itself rather than with the signifier.

This implies a true duplication in the psychological domain, since if the perceived form leads us to think of the model itself, this very same form is also seen as embodied in the material of the image, be it stone, bronze, lines, or colors.

Such a duplication is enhanced, of course, by the relative autonomy of forms, as well as by the blend within the image of features both similar to, and different from, the model. One might say, therefore, that by virtue of their structure, images constitute a medium ideally suited for the function of representation. Nevertheless, as was just indicated, the fundamental basis for such duplication must, in the final analysis, be sought elsewhere, in a functional dualism. In fact, the structural properties of the image function at two psychological levels: At the sensory level, they constitute the visual field; and at the cognitive level, they contribute, in combination with the context, to the contents of thought.

The same form can specify two things at once: the model that the image leads us to think of and the image itself, which is before our eyes. However, we are not aware of the image, which is actually present, but of the absent model. As a result, the model exists for the observer, though in an unreal way, in the real image.

A particularly striking example of such duplication to which I would like to draw your attention is the duplication of space and time that occurs in theatrical representation. The space of the scene seems to be the space in which the represented events are actually taking, or have taken, place, and yet it is also continuous with the space of the theatre itself. Similarly for time also, instants, intervals, and successions for the spectators belong primarily to the events they are watching, but they are left nevertheless in their own present. A further peculiar phenomenon that vividly confirms the unreal character of the representation concerns the way in which an interval, which really lasts usually a matter of minutes or seconds, comes by this process of transposition to have the apparent significance of days, months, or even years.

In addition to all that has already been said on the subject of the "fictitious" presence of the model in its image, we should add that this presence can be rendered still more vivid by the influence of the process of projection, the importance of which can hardly be overestimated. As you know, in projection the formation of perceptual structures, as well as their meaning and emotional significance, is controlled by the observer's past experience, drives, needs, and individual interests. Under the influence of such subjective factors, a simple patch of color of irregular shape can become loaded with extreme emotional content. Both in the perception of others and in that of portraits, especially when the latter represent people who are known to us and to whom we are emotionally attached, the process of projection leads us to attribute unconsciously our own feelings to them. We believe that these feelings belong to the portrait itself, and we have the paradoxical impression that we ourselves feel what another is experiencing or has experienced in the past. In a portrait, a little of the past is nearly always revived; and the more vivid it is, the more intense are the emotions we seem to see in the image. This quality makes some portraits extremely moving to view.

Nothing demonstrates this presence of the model in the image, and its unreal character, more clearly than the kinds of behavior images can evoke. Such behavior differs from that elicited by something really present, yet it is closely related, as many others have noted. This is evident, in a very striking way, in the almost religious respect afforded to family portraits and pictures of highly regarded individuals, as well as in the practice of sympathetic magic, belief in which still persists even in so-called civilized societies.

A few words should now be said about two categories of image that both possess very special properties. The first category includes pictures, photographs, and drawings produced by projecting three-dimensional space and objects onto a plane surface. As you may recall, on a similar occasion 12 years ago, I discussed the puzzle set by such representations (Michotte, 1948a, 1948b). Since then, further research has thrown light on the central claim that we *see* volume and space in all perspective drawings. I stress the word see because what is involved here is not a process of inference or interpretation, nor, as is naively claimed, the expansion somehow of a flat sensory image into depth by the imagination. We are concerned here with the immediate perception of volume and depth.

This is easily shown, once it is remembered that a three-dimensional form has a perceptual structure quite different from that of a flat image corresponding to the same lines. Not only are their parts different, but they are also differently arranged, as inspection of any linear perspective figure, such as Figure 4.7 soon reveals.

Once a three-dimensional structure is established in Figure 4.7 (which can happen in two ways, since the figure is reversible), one notices that the perceived parallelepiped consists of six rectangular or square faces, whereas a plane image would involve the juxtaposition of two triangles and four trapeziums enclosing a central quadrilateral. Furthermore, the upper face (or the front face) of the parallelepiped appears to be transparent, through which the far edge, back, and one side of the object can be seen. This, of course, is only possible if the object does extend into the third dimension because the transparent face must stand in front of what is seen through it.

Finally, it should be noted that a new effect of duplication occurs here, as the regions of the drawing that seem to be transparent appear simultaneously to form part of two distinct planes. This kind of duplication is quite different to that discussed previously; the former involved two psychological levels, whereas here it occurs within the level of perception itself. It is a phenomenal duplication, as is often encountered in the field of perception, in which the same stimulation gives rise to the simultaneous appearance of two distinct impressions.

The appearance of depth in a drawing can also be produced, as you know, by the influence of factors other than linear perspective. In particular, the partial overlapping of one object by another is, historically speaking, the most ancient method of representing the extension of space in depth; indeed it was used in paintings and drawings as long ago as the quaternary period. In the example shown in Figure 4.8, you surely see a shaded strip overlaying a hatched one, both objects appearing to be in different planes. In addition, relief is also portrayed

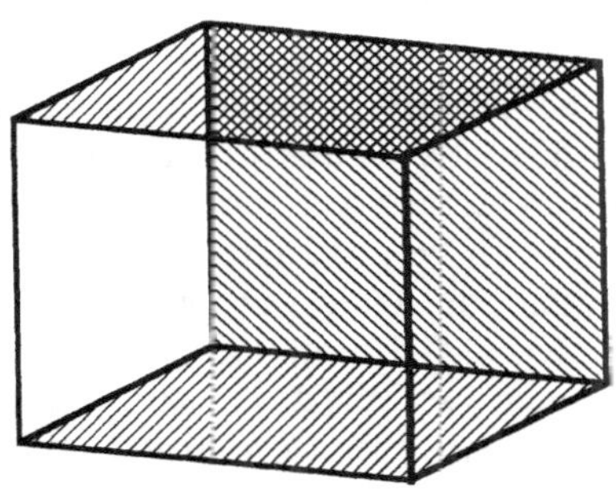

FIGURE 4.7

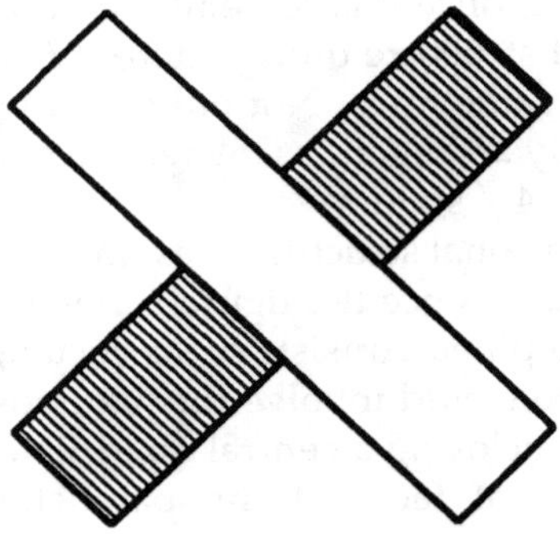

FIGURE 4.8

by the play of shadows and light, the impression of distance can be given by aerial perspective, and so on.

All these factors combine to emphasize the three-dimensional character of the represented object; and yet, under normal conditions of viewing, paintings and drawings always remain surfaces. Why then should this be so? By what mystery can the volumes arise psychologically from their surfaces? What role is played by the innate and past experience in this process? Although these questions are fascinating, we can only mention them here. What matters for our immediate concern is that we are apparently faced with a real contradiction, and we must consider whether this can be avoided. I myself tried to do just this when I formulated the hypothesis that the three-dimensional depth perceived in a painting possesses an intrinsic character of unreality, that is, it is directly seen to be illusory.

This calls for some explanation. In my opinion, a variety of considerations and a good deal of research force us to conclude that any perceptual structure possesses among its characteristic features not only its qualities, intensity, duration, extent, etc. but also a special property of "reality" or "unreality," which can vary in degree as do the other sensory dimensions. This can be shown experimentally. Given an appropriate display, it is actually possible to give the observer a totally convincing impression of real volume, even though the display itself is perfectly flat. Also, by systematically manipulating the conditions of viewing, this impression can be gradually changed until eventually the very different appearance of a simple perspective representation is produced (Phemister, 1951; Michotte, 1957).

Apart from the evidence just cited, it is only possible to specify the phenomenal character of reality or unreality in terms of its effects. In view of this, I suggest that it only because of the presence of this character of reality that we are convinced just by looking at a substantial object that we could physically act on it. Thus, when we look at a drawing of a parallelepiped, we immediately realize that we could take the paper in our hands and touch the lines of the drawing itself; yet, under normal viewing conditions at least, we are all just as convinced that it would be impossible to place something within the depth of the drawn parellelepiped or crush it flat. It is in this latter respect that the character of unreality reveals itself.

Before finally dealing with the notion of unreality, which we encountered at the outset of this paper, at least a few words should be devoted to a last category of images, mental images, which can also function in an extremely effective way. In perspective pictures, the volumes and distances, but not the lines and contours, seem unreal; whereas in mental images, everything has an unreal character when we are awake. These creations of our imagination allow us, even in the absence of sensory stimulation, to see again people or things we have known or to hear their voices. Like sensory impressions, these images are composed of lights, colors, and sounds; but their structures are generally quite fragmentary, lack sensory detail, and are weak and quite unstable. Nevertheless, in some cases, namely in so-called eidetic images, they approach much closer to true perception in being stable, detailed, and intense while still retaining their character as images.

In other cases, however, as in dreams and actual hallucinations, the objects represented by the images have an absolutely real character. Furthermore, about 10 years ago it was discovered that such hallucinations could even be induced in the state of wakefulness by local electrical stimulation of the cerebral cortex during surgical operations on the brain.

Needless to say, all these facts help to confirm the existence of a character of "apparent reality or unreality" and so justify this distinction, which I believe is not only well founded, but truly essential in the field of perception.

In our review of the various categories of portrait, we have encountered some very different kinds. From the borderline case of the representation of a real object by another real object that is physically similar, we finally arrived at the opposite extreme, to the case of the representation of a real object by a mental image, itself bearing a character of total unreality. Between these limits lie the huge majority of portraits that we see in everyday life: plastic representations in the form of statues, paintings, photographs, and drawings.

What can we conclude from this review? First of all, the very diversity of the different kinds of portraits shows that the function of representation is not confined to a particular class of object. This is especially remarkable once we recall that a particular object or individual can be represented by a close copy, a mere outline, an actual object, or a mental image. In view of this, the character of reality or unreality would seem to be irrelevant, or only incidental, which only goes to show that the term "unreal" as used here in fact covers some quite different notions.

As we noted at the beginning, the function of representation is primarily intellectual in nature, entailing the cognitive capacities of both selective abstraction and identification. These are essential for us to appreciate that certain formal properties of the portrait in front of us are those of the absent model and, therefore, to *see* the model in the image without confusing the two.

Matters are more complicated when the portrait is a painting or a perspective drawing. Then, in addition to the unreal presence of the model in our thought, the image itself has an entire perceptual structure that is distinguished by a special phenomenal character, which we have termed "unreality." This unitary perceptual structure arises from the combination of those features of the image that correspond to its three-dimensional appearance and its other sensory properties.

Besides the unreal presence of the object in our thought, therefore, there is a further kind of unreality at the phenomenal level, within the field of sensory structures themselves. Both play a part in most of the images we encounter in everyday life. If, for the sake of simplification, we try to assimilate one of these to the other, we are then faced with the stark fact that although the characteristic combination of the real and the unreal in a perspective picture is determined by the conditions of sensory stimulation, the representative function as such seems to be largely independent of them.

Let me end, then, on a rather provocative note concerning the phenomenal character of the unreal. From an epistemological point of view, *all* perceptual structures must be considered as appearances, indicating something beyond their sensory aspect. Nevertheless, only those perceptual structures that manifest themselves as *appearances* truly convey their *real* function.

References

Michotte, A. (1948a). L'énigme psychologique de la perspective dans le dessin linéaire [The psychological enigma of perspective in line drawings]. *Bulletin des Lettres de l'Académie Royale de Belgique* (5e Série), *34,* 268–288.

Michotte, A. (1948b). Le caractère de "réalité" des projections cinématographiques [The character of "reality" in cinematic projections]. *Revue Internationale de Filmologie, 1,* 249–261.

Michotte, A. (1957). Les variations de réalité apparent de la troisième dimension dans les perceptions visuelles [Variations in the apparent reality of the third

dimension in visual perception]. *Archivo di Psicología Neurologia e Psychiatría, 18,* 200–213.
Phemister, M. R. (1951). An experimental contribution to the problem of apparent reality. *Quarterly Journal of Experimental Psychology, 3,* 1–18.

THE CHARACTER OF "REALITY" OF CINEMATOGRAPHIC PROJECTIONS[1]

Albert Michotte

There can be no doubt that a motion picture provides, for most people and for the greater part of its presentation, a very vivid impression of the reality of the things and events perceived on the screen. This impression greatly exceeds that achieved in any of the other plastic arts.[2] Film, therefore, poses a very interesting problem for psychologists, for it is equally obvious that neither adults nor children react in the same way to the events that we see in the cinema as we would to their counterparts in everyday life. In real life, such violence or tragedy, for example, would provoke active intervention, flight, or screams; yet these never occur in the cinema. In fact, the reactions of the audience hardly ever go beyond the level of emotion.

There is "reality" and "reality," therefore, and it is advisable to be clear about which sense we are giving to this term. We will be using it in a special way in the psychological context. That is to say, the topic of this study will not be concerned in any way with its ontological or epistemological meaning, which is the province of philosophy; it will also differ from the notion of reality often used by scientists to distinguish the physical world from "appearances" (colors, shapes, movements) studied in the psychology of perception.[3]

As psychologists, however, we must be careful to remember that what is given in our experience is always elaborated and integrated in our thought. Human beings not only perceive but also engage in physics and especially metaphysics, and this has consequences for how we behave, which the psychologist cannot disregard. At the outset, there-

[1]Translated by A.P.Costall from "Le caractère de 'réalité' des projections cinématographiques." *Revue internationale de Filmologie,* 1948, *1,* 249–261.

[2]Animated films are, of course, a different matter.

[3]We will not examine the extremely interesting question here of the relation between aesthetics and the apparent reality represented in film. To what extent is it desirable, from an aesthetic point of view, to emphasize this impression or to remain within the realm of the unreal? Does this depend on the particular conditions or subject of the film? These questions are an aspect of the general problem of realism in the arts, which we cannot pursue here.

fore, we are forced to stress the distinction between the psychological fact of *belief* in the reality of an object or event and the intuitive character of reality it may possess. Certainly there is a rather general correspondence between the two, but experience soon teaches us to distinguish them and reveals that they can often be in conflict. The cinema itself offers a typical example. Movement is evident on the screen, and as Wertheimer showed long ago, it is impossible to discriminate between the real movement of an object (such as a point of light) and stroboscopic movement, the basis of cinema.[4] The perceived movement is "real," and yet we know that nothing other than a rapid succession of static images occurs on the screen. There is a contradiction, therefore, between apparent reality and the knowledge we have acquired about the technique of cinematographic projection: between apparent reality and what we will consider naively as the realm of "things in themselves." This kind of conflict, common enough in everyday life, is resolved by the introduction of the concept of illusion, or appearance, which exactly recognizes the divorce between what we know or believe to be reality "in itself" and what "seems" real. Furthermore, there is the crucial fact that apparent reality (that of movement in the case of the cinema) is in no way weakened or altered by "the knowledge that it is an illusion."

This distinction is important for the psychologist because, where it applies, the course of our activities is in general determined more readily by the reality that is the basis of our beliefs than by the reality that is intuitively evident. Needless to say, the case of cinema is again typical in this connection, for our general attitude towards the film is that of a conviction of unreality, despite the apparent reality of the events represented, and this may partly explain the difference in our behavior towards film, which I mentioned a moment ago. It would be a mistake, however, to suppose that the whole question has been settled. On the contrary, the psychological connection between the belief and the impression of reality has given rise to some extremely tricky problems in both the cinema and the theater, which are little understood. One can

---

[4]Perhaps stroboscopic movement is most simply demonstrated by successively projecting two points of light on a screen a certain distance apart. When the rate of alternation is slow, what we see corresponds to the objective state of affairs; that is, the first point first appears and then disappears at a definite position, followed by the second at another location and so on. But as the rate is increased, a stage occurs when we see just a single point moving back and forth from the two positions. Contrary to a popular misconception, the impression of movement is not the result of the persistence of vision. The latter serves mainly to eliminate the flickering of the images. The movement itself should be considered as a perceptual form, which is spontaneously established when the appropriate configuration of stimulation occurs; according to Wertheimer, this corresponds to a kind of short-circuit between the regions of the nervous system subject to excitation.

hardly doubt, for example, that our belief in the unreality of the perceived objects does not continually hold (as it might), yet nor is it ultimately stifled by the impression of reality. The reactions of spectators of a stereoscopic film, when they are made to see a balloon floating in the cinema, for example, provides the proof. It is equally the case, however, that at certain times the appearance of reality is absolute in ordinary cinema. There are certainly many variations, and it is important to know what determines them.

The distinction that concerns us (between impression and belief) applies equally to the question of the representative function of cinematographic images. Indeed, supposing that film did give us the impression of seeing real people in the flesh, as in the theater, it would still be the case that these people often serve as substitutes for other characters, such as the historical figures Caesar or Napoleon. So once again the problem returns because we do not confuse the actor, although seeming entirely real, with the person represented, and it is the latter who is truly the real thing, the object of the thoughts and concern of the spectator! We ought to ask, therefore, to what degree this new distinction, derived from logical considerations, is realized psychologically in the course of the film (as in the course of a theatrical presentation). Is the awareness of the duality of the characters diminished, and is there, at certain moments at least, a total fusion of the two objects, a complete identification of the "symbol" and the "referent" so that one encounters a single reality? We must wait for experimental research to provide an answer to this question.

It should be noted that the word "unreal" is used rather often in everyday language to refer to impressions that are more or less "strange." For example, we describe a scene as having "something unreal" about it, when its colors or composition differ rather profoundly from what we have become used to seeing. In this case, the notion of unreality becomes tied to that of deviation from our past experience and expresses the feeling of novelty, of the unexpected, and of astonishment, whereas the word "real" corresponds in this context to the opposite feeling of déjà vu, of familiarity. This use of the term clearly runs counter to strict usage, but it helps us appreciate an aspect of the question that is of very great interest from the psychological point of view; for these subjective reactions can tend to establish an atmosphere of artificiality, which, as we shall see, plays an essential role in what we might call the "cinematographic situation."

These considerations give us a glimpse of the tremendous complexity of the problems that the psychologist must face when embarking on the study of the "reality of the cinema" and makes us realize the need to restrict the present study to a particular aspect of the question. We will confine ourselves, therefore, to examining the degree to which the laws known to govern perception can explain the existence of an impression of reality and in what respect this impression differs from that which we obtain from real objects and events. To this end, we will provide a brief and extremely superficial review of the principal approaches to the cinematographic image in relation to the psychology of perception.

Before doing so, it is necessary to emphasize the well-known fact that our sole contact with external objects is by means of light rays passing from objects to our eyes and that, therefore, the ultimate differences between the perception of film and that of real scenes must be determined in the last analysis by the way in which these rays are combined. It is necessary to take into account the superposition of rays corresponding to color impressions, as well as their distribution in space and time, which determines form and movement.

An important discrepancy occurs in the pattern of stimulation both at the beginning and end of the film, as well as at the outset of each sequence. The changes of scene that arise in everyday life correspond in general to the action of a psychological mechanism, which is so curious that it has been studied in some detail under the name of the screen effect (this of course has nothing to do with the projection screen). The effect is evident when something obstructing vision is removed, such as a curtain or door, or by its convolution when either we go out of a room or someone else comes in, or even more simply, by changing our direction of gaze or by opening our eyes as we awake. In all of these cases, there is either a displacement of the screen (curtain, door, eyelids, etc.) or of the object originally concealed, or both, each complementing the other. As a result, there is a sliding of the line of common demarcation, which separates their retinal images, and the image of the uncovered object progressively increases by the successive addition of new portions. One might expect, therefore, to obtain the impression of an object that begins to exist as soon as it becomes visible and that grows larger in a process of continuous creation and, conversely, is progressively annihilated when it is covered again. In fact, this does not happen at all. Objects seem to be permanent: They exist before they appear and persist after their disappearance, the screen merely serving to render them visible or invisible. Examples of apparent creation in the visual domain, such as the bursting of a flame from a match or the formation of bubbles at the surface of boiling water, are extremely rare.

Contrary to a long-standing assumption, the screen effect is not based ultimately on acquired experience. It seems that it must be explained in terms of the fact that the common boundary between the screen and the object belongs phenomenally to the screen alone, in accord with the laws that govern the spontaneous organization of the visual field. As a result, the partially concealed object does not have a boundary of its own at the edge of the screen; it does not seem terminated, or curtailed, in the direction of the screen but appears to extend behind it, as Rubin demonstrated long ago in his famous study of figure and ground. Thus, for example, the side of a curtain appears as the limit of the curtain itself, whereas the scene viewed through the window seems to extend beyond the region we can actually see. In this way, the screen effect ensures the continued existence of things, their phenomenal permanence, and acquired experience only serves to confirm this primitive impression *(donnée primitive)*.

Matters are quite different in the cinema, however, at least concerning the image as a whole. The image appears and disappears in its entirety and is not simply "disclosed." Indeed, what happens in "fades" and "links" is not a successive projection of different parts of the field but specifically an increase or decrease in the intensity of the whole image, a phenomenal "creation" and "annihilation," and in our view this represents a true anomaly compared to the normal conditions of perception. In addition, there is the further anomaly of the abrupt (more or less instantaneous) transition from one scene to an entirely different one: from an interior, for instance, to a road or the country, without any displacement of the spectator.

The screen effect not only occurs in the case of one object obscuring another but also holds for the limits of our field of view. No matter how indefinite the objects seen in peripheral vision, this indeterminacy never seems to be a property of the perceived objects themselves; indeed, we always have the impression of space extending beyond what we actually see. Once again, the situation is quite different in the cinema. Not only does the image cover a very restricted region of our field of view, but it is currently much smaller than the screen itself. In these conditions, the boundary of the image should normally belong to itself, and so the part of space it encloses should appear closed and strictly curtailed, like a photograph mounted on a piece of cardboard. This represents yet another strange perceptual characteristic of film.

It should not be difficult, however, to reduce this problem by surrounding the image with a frame so as to give the impression that it extends beond the projected region. A similar result is obtained by using passe-partout on photographs, and it is possible to appreciate the point of the previous discussion by noting the disruptive effect of removing a picture from its frame once the edges of the image become visible. One might suppose that providing a frame should give the observer the impression of looking at the scene through a window or an opening in the wall of the room. This does not happen, however, because it would require the formation of a much more profound segregation between the surface of the image and the three-dimensional space perceived in the image than in fact occurs. The field would have to be specially structured in such a way that this space was constantly localized in complete depth behind the screen, but, in our opinion at least, this never happens as a general rule.

Let us now turn to the question of the image as such and consider first of all what comprises the sensory stimulation from which the perceived object is constructed. A moment's reflection should reveal a rather strange fact. What is projected on the screen consists, of course, only of patches of light, the dark regions having to be considered, from a physical point of view, as a sort of negative corresponding to those regions of the object that do not stimulate the retina. Exactly the opposite occurs in the visual field; the things we see are in effect composed for the most part by the dark areas of the image, by the shadows; the more opaque they are the more substantial seem the objects. In contrast, the great expanses of uniform light generally correspond to a skylike, insubstantial background, from which the objects are separated.

The shadows themselves, therefore, do not possess their characteristic appearance as "film colors" superimposed on a supporting surface to which they do not belong. They seem like the actual color of the objects ("surface colours"). This is the result of several organizational factors though primarily because, as research has shown, the contours are clearly defined rather than taking the form of a penumbra becoming gradually brighter towards the edges. In addition, there is the influence of the integration of the shadow areas into a definite form and in particular the fact that these constitute substantial objects.

Nevertheless, we should not forget that the shadows combine with the light regions and work with them to create the substantiality of the objects. In fact, the light regions frequently introduce a further complication. They often have the quality attributed to colors of luminosity, analogous to that of incandescent objects. This can occur in a particularly striking way with the exaggerated reflections from silk and velvet and also from faces with the result that they lose all their naturalness.

The absence of chromatic colors in black-and-white films is not terribly troublesome because we are used to it and also because color has only a slight effect on the perceptual organization of form and spatiality. Nevertheless, it is an additional factor contributing to the sense of artificiality. The introduction of color has improved this situation, but only partially since there is often a considerable discrepancy between the colors perceived on the screen (which often are luminous as well) and the actual colors we see in everyday life.

Having considered the composition of images, it is appropriate to consider the form and size of the objects they represent. This question is especially interesting because movement plays a fundamental role in this domain. As is well known, the perception of shape and size is dominated by the fact that an object largely retains its apparent size and shape when observed from different points of view or from different distances (the laws of constancy).[5] As a result, when we approach or move away from an object, we do not usually see it grow or shrink as we should if our impressions were totally determined by the size of the retinal image. The apparent distance has an effect and assures that the dimensions of the object are maintained. But it also follows, of course, that any deficiency in the perception of distance or change of distance ought to lead to a breakdown of constancy, and this frequently occurs in the cinema. The perception of the third dimension is indeed often rather deficient there; and, as a result, in many cases, notably in tracking, instead of seeing objects simply approach or recede from us, they seem to dilate or contract, often to an extremely disturbing degree. The introduction of 3-D cinema could undoubtedly lead to a considerable improvement in this respect.

In the case of tracking and panning, it is often possible to observe another no less striking anomaly, where things, which by their nature ought to be immobile, such as houses, fences, trees, and furniture, themselves seem to move. This kind of illusion, which is sometimes also encountered in everyday life, poses difficult and very complex problems; but it seems that they primarily produce a modification in the normal system of spatial reference on which is further superimposed the effects of certain experiential factors.

Generally, any object (including our own body) that is enclosed by another is referred to the latter, so that when any change occurs in their relative positions, it is the enclosed object that seems to be moving, even if it is stationary and only the framework moves (given that additional factors do not intervene to impose a different perceptual structure). Thus, when the retinal images of the objects we move around (furniture, trees, etc.,) undergo deformations and slippage as the result of our movements, the objects, nevertheless, seem to remain stable. We have the impression that we ourselves are moving, which, in this case, corresponds to the real state of affairs. Certain experiments have shown,

[5]We should note that constancy is much less marked for perspective images. Thus, for example, the further the viewing distance from the correct viewing point, the greater the apparent depth of the represented space. This is very marked, especially when we view photographs taken with a 6cm × 9cm format camera or less from the distance of distinct vision. In the same way, the third dimension is usually greatly exaggerated for the spectators at the back of the cinema. Often we obtain the absurd impression of interiors, rooms, and halls, etc. looking as large as cathedrals.

however, that the same effect can be produced if the observer's body is kept stationary and instead one rotates the entire chamber into which he is placed (a mock room, for example); the walls and the furniture appear immobile, whereas the subject has the impression that he himself is undergoing rotation. Again, therefore, there is apparent immobility of the framework and apparent movement of the object to which it is referred.

The same should occur if the cinematographic projection filled the entire visual field of the spectator.[6] In fact, however, the image occupies only a small part of the field and the space it represents does not form the system of reference for the spectators. Such conditions give rise in fact to a segregation of spaces. In one, the actors move and "live," whereas, the other belongs to the spectators. This schism is analogous to that which occurs in the theater between the set and the auditorium, but it is, in general, certainly more profound in the cinema. This amounts to a juxtaposition of two different worlds, which in turn arises from the system of visual stimulation. Nevertheless, it would be rash to claim that, in certain cases of extreme concentration upon the image, the person in the audience cannot enter into the world depicted on the screen, though this might perhaps be tending towards the pathological. Furthermore, for the same reasons of structural organization, the changes in position of the objects in relation to the spatial limitations of the image normally ought to provoke the impression, previously referred to, of unnatural movement of certain of the objects.

All of these aspects of the cinematographic image examined so far hardly favor the formation of the impression of reality mentioned at the outset of this paper. If anything, they ought to accentuate the peculiar character of the objects represented. These include the mode of appearance and disappearance of the depicted objects, the limited field of view that they cover, their color, their dilations and contractions, the apparent motion of normally stationary objects, the peculiarities, and the contradictions with all that we have learned from everyday experience. Indeed, if we were to stop at this point, we would be tempted to conclude that the cinema is the most artificial of art forms and that it must be infinitely less realistic than a simple photograph or even a line drawing! In our view, this is an issue of extreme theoretical importance,

[6]One cannot be too precise about this since it is not possible to predict the extent to which past experience will have an effect and the artificial character of film would disrupt the influence of other organizational factors. Nevertheless, it should be possible to attempt this (i.e., the presentation of film filling the complete visual field) without encountering great technical difficulties.

as we shall soon explain, and that is why we have emphasized it so insistently; but it is now time for an examination of further properties of the cinematographic image, which will reveal that our choice of title for this paper (i.e., its reference to the reality of the image) was not stirred by a love of paradox!

Cinematographic projections usually display perspective images, and so it is first necessary to provide a precise account of the perceptual characteristics of such images as seen in still projections or in the form of paintings and drawings. The type of perceptions they give rise to are really extraordinary; in effect, they almost miraculously reconcile the impression of volume and that of a surface. We undoubtedly *see* volume in these images: We experience depth in the picture just as we do height and width, and indeed the depth is indistinguishable from that of a solid object. It is easy in fact to obtain matches between them, and our own recent research has shown that adjustment of the variable depth of a solid object to that of a model can be done with the same precision in practice, whether the model consists of a perspective drawing or is an actual object of the same shape. It follows that the property on which the adjustments are based must be identical in the two cases and, therefore, that the reason for the specific character of three-dimensionality of perspective drawings is the same as that for the objects they represent.

It is no less true, however, that there is a world of difference in their appearance and in the kind of behavior they can produce. A second variable must be operating, therefore, which, in our opinion, is their degree of reality. The volume of solid objects seems "real," whereas that which is represented in drawings seems "unreal."[7]

Research confirms that this absence of apparent reality of the volume in the case of pictures is connected with the action of organizational factors in perception that tend to confine the figure to the surface. Indeed, if one tries in some way to separate the lines comprising the object from the surface that supports them, the volume of the depicted object immediately takes on a vivid appearance of reality, which can sometimes be totally convincing. This can be achieved in different ways, though one which is especially interesting in our view involves setting the lines constituting the object in motion relative to one another. The opposition between the movement of the figure and the immobility of the screen then acts as a factor to segregate them and frees the object

[7]For more complete details see: A. Michotte, L'énigme psychologique de la perspective dans le dessin linéaire. *Bulletin de l'Académie Royale de Belgique,* 5e série, 1948, *34,* 268–288. We have cited this particular research since it completes the present study in a number of ways and also includes the main references on this topic.

from the surface with which it had been integrated. It becomes substantial to some extent and takes on an independent existence: It becomes a substantial object.

This can be demonstrated by a very simple experiment first performed long ago (there is a reference to it in the early work of von Recklinghausen dating back to 1859). The shadow of a solid object made from metal wire, such as a parallelepiped or a cube, is projected onto a screen. Observed from a small distance, the shadow gives the impression of a simple perspective drawing traced on the screen; but rotation of the object is sufficient for the shadow to become real to such a degree that, under certain viewing conditions, it would be impossible to distinguish the moving shadow from the metal object itself.

This is a crucial experiment since, in effect, it precisely replicates what occurs in the cinema. The movements, gestures, and changes in the facial expression of the characters; and even the simple translation of inanimate objects should evidently produce a similar result, though even more effectively because of the complexity of the images, the complex play of their highlights and shadows, and to some extent perhaps the effects of past experience. Here once more we have an entirely remarkable phenomenon linked, on the one hand, to the particular structure of perspective images and, on the other, to the laws of organization that determine the segregation of the object in relation to the surface.

An identical effect can also be obtained in the case of immobile objects by means of motion parallax when the camera is displaced during shooting. Furthermore, it is easy to confirm this fact by abruptly stopping the running of the film during projection. The relief seems to suddenly subside, lose its reality, and become the unreal volume of a simple, flat, perspective image.

Movement as such is also an important aspect of reality. If, in effect, the volume of an object can lose its appearance of reality in the image, this is not so for phenomenal movement; the latter always has a character of reality, whether it involves the displacement of material objects or of elements of an image or a figure, as in Wertheimer's famous experiment. The same peculiarity occurs in the case of actions and all functional relations in general. When we consider these in terms of their perceptual conditions, they clearly amount to more or less complex combinations of movements. Yet, as we have shown over the last years, these complexes of stimulation give rise to specific impressions, which are quite characteristic, such as the various aspects of mechanical causality: launching, pushing, pulling, and carrying. Other systems of movement give the impression of impact, approach, separation, flight, pursuit, or even active search. All these dynamic impressions seem real no matter what artificial device is used to produce them. Furthermore, it is not impossible that their intrinsic reality, as movements, serve to enhance considerably the character of reality of the things, which are the sources of these activities or bases of these movements.[8]

This in no way implies, of course, that the movements or activities cannot eventually take on a representative value. For example, in a planetarium, the represented movements of the stars are not for us just a copy of the actual movements. Similarly, when we use film to depict the accelerated growth of a plant, this is not only an image of the process. In both cases, a real movement represents another real movement, for the image function as such does not necessarily lead to the loss of reality of the symbol, either for a process, such as movement, or for an object, such as a flag.

Finally, we ought to consider one last aspect of the problem. Film evokes numerous powerful emotional reactions in the audience, and these obviously have an inherent character of reality. Fear, pleasure, humor, sympathy, dislike, and even disgust or enthusiasm stemming from a specific action or character are really experienced; this is hardly surprising, of course, considering the close connection between our emotions and our motor reactions. These emotions are intimately linked to the visual display, especially it seems to its apparent reality, since generally it is not the image of the character that evokes our admiration or sympathy, but rather what we take from the character's appearance and manner to be the actual personality. In addition, as is well known to psychologists and students of aesthetics, there is empathy: We project our own emotions onto the characters we see on the screen. This must surely create an effect on us in turn, a circular process of reciprocal interaction, more powerful than it might seem at first sight, which will strongly reinforce the reality of the characters, as well as the objects among which they move.

We thus arrive at quite a different conclusion from that of the earlier part of this study: The experience of film would seem to be a unique conjunction of reality and artifice. On the one hand, the perceptual reality of the things and activities take on an almost sensory actuality, yet, on the other hand, film has a number of anomalous features that contradict our everyday experience. In our opinion, this conflict, which

[8]It would be useful to make a psychological comparison between ordinary cinematographic films and animated cartoons in this respect, since the apparent reality of the represented objects is certainly diminished if not absent in the second case. Is it, as we believe, mainly because of differences in aspects of perspective (the exaggerations of contours in the cartoon, limitations in shading and lighting, and so on), is it that the conviction of unreality becomes dominant, or else is it that there is a greater degree of psychological distance (to be considered later)? We can only raise the issue.

occurs to such an unusual degree, typifies the cinematographic situation.

There remains the task of specifying the exact nature of this conflict. The contradiction is very different from that, mentioned at the beginning, which sometimes occurs between what we sense and what we know and which lies at the basis of the concept of illusion. Nor is the conflict between different factors within perceptual organization itself, which would serve to modify the internal structure of perception. Instead, it is based on an opposition between a well-defined perceptual organization—real actions performed by real beings—and what has been acquired through experience, the latter, however, hardly amounting to simple knowing. Our experience does in fact consist of material accumulated throughout our own lives and by a wealth of fleeting experiences, the subconscious traces of which nevertheless determine our attitude to any emerging perceptual states. These traces determine when we will react with surprise, and when we will experience strangeness, anomaly, or uneasiness, as when there is a stark discrepancy between what we perceive and what we are accustomed to. All these pertain to the realm of affect and subjectivity rather than to consciousness strictly speaking and occur in the absence of the actual conscious recollection of past experiences.

This conflict has a special effect on our attitude to, or personal involvement with, the show and does not influence the internal characteristics of the latter. This becomes manifest, it seems to us, by an impression of distance, where distance is to be understood in a psychological rather than uniquely spatial or temporal sense; for we certainly do not have the impression of seeing things far away (in terms of meters or kilometers), nor of witnessing an event from the past. It is quite the opposite: The characters act here and now; it is just that our contact with them lacks the immediacy of real life.

Reference to psychological distance has already been made by Pierre Janet in relation to mental disorder and by K. Lewin in relation to the motivation of normal people; this notion is therefore not new to psychologists or psychiatrists. It is difficult to define, nevertheless, for like most subtle distinctions in the realm of psychology it is impossible to describe, and the best we can do is make appeal to comparisons.

Psychological distance occurs more clearly at the social level. We can feel very distant from someone beside us, and yet very close to someone far way. We may hear a familiar voice over the telephone or on the radio as if a friend were really present, though as a result of certain distortions in quality or changes in pitch, the voice lacks naturalness and the sense of immediate contact proves artificial. Finally, we should note the separation of spaces mentioned earlier that makes the spectator feel outside the world in which the characters in the film exist; this should play an important role in the creation of psychological distance.

To summarize, we believe that the cinematographic situation can be characterized as giving the impression of actually perceiving real entities and events, but this involves a more or less distorted reality belonging (psychologically speaking) to a world not entirely our own but to one which seems somewhat distant. Here, no doubt, lies one of the primary reasons for the difference between our reactions to film from that towards real life.

In the course of this study, we have cited a number of facts, and proposed many hypotheses of certainly varied importance. This is inevitable in a field where almost everything remains to be discovered, but we should not forget that provisional hypotheses, no matter how they ultimately fare, are still useful to progress as long as they stimulate research and define a new direction of investigation.

THE EMOTIONAL INVOLVEMENT OF THE SPECTATOR IN THE ACTION REPRESENTED IN A FILM: TOWARD A THEORY[1]

Albert Michotte

The term "involvement" used in the title of this paper refers to the phenomenon of empathy. This occurs when we observe what someone else is doing, and we ourselves live it, in some sense, rather than just understand it at an intellectual level, or classify it into some category or other.

These phenomena frequently occur not only in everyday life but also when we are at the theater or even reading a novel. However, they seem to be particularly striking when we are watching films as a result of the conditions under which they occur.

Clearly, what we are concerned with here is an aspect of the more general question in psychology of "projection;" but we need to be careful here, since the term "projection," which is so common nowadays, is used in so many different senses by different writers. It can refer to the "objectivication" of our sensory impressions, to the influence of our personal motives on the structure or meaning of perception, or even to the interpretation of a series of images. In psychoanalysis, it mainly

[1]Translated by Alan Costall from "La participation émotionelle du spectateur à l'action représentée à l'écran", *Revue Internationale de Filmologie,* 1953, 4, 87–96.

has to do with defense mechanisms, and so on. Thus, this general term is in need of better definition, as is the more restricted term "empathy." Any discussion of this topic, therefore, needs to be precise about its exact subject matter.

As is well known, the emotions are intimately linked to our motor reactions. This surely implies that we should search for a definition of "involvement" or "participation" in terms of motor reactions, especially since the field of motor behavior (motricité) provides such clear and striking examples.

When we are watching any activity—be it dancing; acrobatics; or competitive sports, such as tennis or football—we are capable of reacting in very different ways to what we see. Consider the following examples.

1. Sometimes, if infrequently, what we observe remains separate from our own motor reactions. This occurs most often if, while we are looking at some activity, we ourselves are engaged in a different activity involving quite different movements. Perceptually, there is a complete segregation between the visual impressions corresponding to the activity being observed, and the tactile-kinesthetic impressions relating to our own movements.

2. In other cases, our own movements accord with those we are viewing, and they seem to be controlled by them. For example, we may notice ourselves automatically tapping our foot or hand in time with the rhythm of the perceived movements. This can happen even when there is still a segregation between the two movements, in the sense that we are aware that our own movements are perfectly distinct from the ones we are viewing and they are merely synchronized with them (i.e., there is a parallelism between two different events).

3. Sometimes the similarity between the movements of our own body and those of the person we are watching becomes more extensive, even to the extent that the spectator overtly imitates what he can see (see, for example, Figure 22 in Boring, Langfeld, & Weld, 1948). Usually, however, the reactions of the observer are more restrained—incipient movements perhaps—but they are generalized and influence the entire motor system. In such cases, it is common for an actual fusion to occur between the visual data corresponding to the movements of the performer and the proprioceptive and tactile-kinaesthetic data relating to the spectator's own movements. This can reach the point where there is just a single movement, so that it is almost as if we were watching one of our own limbs moving.

Nevertheless, the fusion that occurs is restricted to the motor effects and does not extend to the people themselves. The actor remains as that individual perceived on the screen, distinct from oneself—the spectator seated in the cinema; the first is present in the form of visual impressions, the second in the form of tactile-kinesthetic impressions. One might describe the situation as "*feeling* what the *other is doing*." In other words, while I remain myself, I have the impression of feeling what is happening internally in the other person. To put it more abstractly, there is a single action, which is present in two forms (a visual and a proprioceptive one) but which "belongs" phenomenally to two different people.

4. Finally, in extreme cases, the identification extends to the people themselves. As Lipps has put it, there is then only a single self (moi), which is "empathized" or "projected" onto an external object. ("In der vollen positiven Einfühlung existiert für mich zunächst nur ein eiziges Ich, nämlich dies eingefühlte oder objectivierte, in ein äusseres Objekt projizierte eigene Ich." [1906, p. 202]) The actor then ceases to appear as a distinct personality, and the spectator is no longer someone seated in his chair; to use a popular though highly appropriate expression one "enters the skin" of the actor. There is just a single person, oneself in the body of the actor, and, naturally, also a single action, as in the preceding case.

In the first two cases, the spectator simply remains an external observer, and our reason for mentioning them was to stress just how different the very strange phenomena of "involvement" covered by the last two cases really are. There can be no question that they occur, yet it is difficult to understand how this can be, and so they pose a very interesting problem for psychology.

The research on the perception of purely visual motion and of movement combinations should throw some light on this issue, for such studies involve phenomena that can be easily controlled by experimental manipulation, and they also present clear analogies to the phenomena we have just been describing.

1. When two or more objects are moving within the visual field but at different speeds or directions, there is a complete segregation of their movements. (This is the case of simple simultaneity.)

2. When two or more objects in the field of vision begin to move at the same speed in parallel with one another, they still remain segregated, if they are sufficiently far apart, and especially if they move in relation to different frames of reference. They simply impose a global, unitary structure of parallelism, as a consequence of their kinetic and temporal similarities (i.e., parallelism of movement).

3. If the objects are closer together, and begin to move together at the same speed in the same direction, within the same frame of reference, then observers unanimously report that they see a single movement performed by the group of objects. This result is extremely interesting since it shows that the difference in their paths of motion (which are parallel but not identical) is not sufficient to ensure that they each possess their own exclusive motion. Each object no longer has its own movement; instead, the movement belongs to the group, and each object participates in the movement of the group (i.e., collective possession of a single movement).

4. Finally, if two objects, which are separated by some distance, eventually meet during the course of their movement and then immediately begin to move together in the same direction, they soon fuse into a single, global unit that depends on their form (e.g., two squares of different colors). One then simply sees a complex object (a two-colored rectangle) that possesses its own motion.

These effects can be easily produced by relatively simple techniques, and it is then possible to obtain one effect or another quite systematically and progressively in accord with the well-known laws of perceptual organization (proximity, similarity, common fate, etc.). Analogous effects can also be produced in relation to the tactile-kinesthetic perception of the movement of our limbs.

The above results allow us to draw the following conclusions:

1. A movement physically performed by an object does not necessarily belong to that object at the phenomenal level.
2. The movements of several objects can fuse into a movement of a unitary whole and belong collectively to all of them.
3. When juxtaposed objects are moving together in the same fashion, they can eventually fuse together so that they become a single, complex object.
4. I should add that further experiments have shown that the movement performed by one object can, under certain conditions, appear to belong to another object, as in the perception of causality, for example (Michotte, 1963).

The relevance of these results to the phenomenon of motor empathy should be perfectly clear; however, there are also differences between motor empathy and these purely visual structures. First of all, in the case of motor empathy, the movements performed by the "actor-object" are visually perceived, whereas those of the "spectator-object" are perceived in an exclusively tactile-kinesthetic form, since, of course, the spectator does not usually look at his own body during the performance. In fact, this is only a minor complication, which can easily be set aside, for it is clear that the difference in the sensory modalities of movements possessing analogous kinetic structures hardly prevents their phenomenal fusion. However, there are some more serious problems, which we must consider.

The two objects, and hence their movements, are generally separated by a considerable distance. Now, as is well known, distance is a powerful segregating factor, and one might well be surprised that the movement of the spectator in the cinema could be identified with that of the actor on the screen. It is necessary to remember, however, that the effect of distance can be largely offset by the influence of other integrating factors, such as temporal contiguity, common fate, and so on. "Launching at a distance," in the perception of causality, is a particular example of this.

We should also bear in mind that the psychological or apparent distance, rather than the physical separation, is important and it may be that, phenomenally, the separation between the actor and the screen is not so great. The distance is much less in the case of "visual contact" across an "empty" space where there are no obstructing objects, as in the darkness of the cinema. Just think of the immediate "visual contact" that can occur when two people look at one another, which virtually amounts to touching.

Granted this, it is possible to accept without too much hesitation, perhaps, that the movements of the spectator could appear to be identified with those of the actor, in accordance with the principles of similarity of structure and also common fate. Therefore one can understand how it can be that the spectator has the impression that "he feels what the other person is doing".

However, once we consider the case of complete identification, where the ego of the spectator becomes confused with that of the actor, we encounter new difficulties. This is not simply a case of fusion at the level of groups of movements in different modalities and with different characteristics, but the apparent incorporation of "oneself" to another person. This seems to defy common sense.

Before considering this issue, it will be useful to examine the effects of *emotional* empathy and the closely connected empathy of feelings, mental attitudes, judgments, and thoughts, etc., that is to say, all those kinds of events that seem to be intimately linked to our own deepest self. This is the self that is "me" in the full sense of the word and that we consider as naturally distinct from our body.

In relation to emotional empathy, it is not difficult to find cases that parallel those already described in relation to movement. At the theater or cinema, the "hero" or "heroine" is the main focus of empathetic projection. For some reason, such as their physical appearance or the expression of emotions they share with the spectator, these people stand apart from the supporting actors whose actions serve to create the context or "situation" in which the heroes find themselves.

The relation of empathy between the spectator and the heroes can take different forms:

1. The relation can be completely destroyed when the emotions, etc., manifested by the hero are clearly different from those elicited in the spectator by the "situation," for example, anger as opposed to amusement.

2. There can also be a mere parallelism. For example, suppose that the hero is being criticized by somebody for certain shortcomings, and these criticisms also apply to the spectator's own behavior. These criticisms might come to affect the spectator personally, quite independently of the rather similar behavior of the hero. This kind of thing also happens in everyday life, and we use such expressions as "sharing someone else's joy" or "participating in their grief."

3. It can also be the case, however, that the internal reactions of the spectator and the expressive behavior of the actor become totally fused, even though the individuals themselves remain perfectly distinct. The clearest example is the classic one of language comprehension. The listener hears the sounds uttered by the speaker (expressive movements), and these sounds provoke in the listener the meaning he has learned to give them. Yet he has the impression of directly perceiving the thoughts of the speaker in the words themselves. The same thing also occurs in relation to affect, when the spectator perceives in the actor's face the expression of the spectator's own feelings, or, conversely, he has the impression of experiencing the emotion expressed by the actor.

4. Finally, there are the cases of identification of the spectator's personality with that of the hero. These are experienced so often and have been so frequently described that there is no need for us to stress them here. It is these cases, clearly, which pose the essential problem; for the preceding ones do not give rise to any difficulties that have not already been encountered in relation to motor reactions, and perhaps these too can be explained in terms of the principles of organization that govern integration and segregation within our experience.

At first sight, it does seem inconceivable that our "self" could be experienced as that of the character we are observing on the screen or on the stage and that we could identify ourselves with him. Here lies the great puzzle, and we can only begin to solve it by exactly specifying the relevant details. First of all, we must define what we mean by the "self" in this connection.

We are all convinced of the existence of our own "self"—a self that is substantial, real, and the ultimate source and basis of our actions, feelings, and wishes, etc. Yet this notion is not based on the presence of anything within our own experience that we could call a "self-object;" this would be contradictory, for if it were an object it could not be "me." It is for this reason that our own body, which we are able to perceive by touch and by sight as an object, is not confused with the self. My body is mine without it being "me" in the full sense of the word.

What is more, the self can—and does—only appear to us in the form of actual activities: It does not appear to us as a thing but only as processes, the source of which are not present as such. Nevertheless, under normal conditions, we localize these processes within our own body, and they seem to be connected to it in some fashion.

As for the movements performed by our body, in terms of vision and external touch, these belong to our body in the same way that any movement seems to belong to the object that "carries" it. In addition, the internal aspect of these movements presents a special character of subjectivity, which Claparède has called the character of "me-ness" (*moiité*). Furthermore, our movements are one of the most important aspects of our phenomenal body, and, although these movements are, by nature, processes, they are our body in action.

It follows, therefore, that in the case of the complete identification of the spectator with the actor, all of these processes must then belong phenomenally to the visual-actor-object alone. If this is so, then the spectator must necessarily have the impression of acting within the "actor" and that the actor's body has become his own, since he "feels" the movements of the body he is watching, and, feeling these movements, he feels his own body in action. Similarly, the gestures of the actor become, for the spectator, the expression and outer aspect of his own emotions and feelings. Thus, the spectator "becomes" the actor, or, you could say, the visual aspect of the actor becomes the external aspect of the spectator's own personality.

But how can this happen? It has already been established that the correspondence between the movements of the actor and the rather similar movements induced in the spectator, or else the correspondence between the expressions of emotions by the actor and the emotions experienced by the spectator, tend to provoke the fusion of these processes in accord with principles outlined earlier. Furthermore, because the movements and gestures of the visual actor-object naturally seem to belong to him, it is conceivable that this relation of belonginginess will extend to all processes where fusion involving movement and expression has occurred.

Everything would be rather easy to explain if the processes occurring in the spectator were not united, at the same time, to the spectator's own bodily self (*moi-corporel*), for this would seem by nature to counter this new relation of belonging. Indeed, the spectator receives sensory messages that *should* inform about the position of the spectator's own body (the position sense), as well as contact with the chair. Furthermore, visual information is available with *should* allow the spectator to identify his or her own location with respect to the surroundings. In addition, the spectator knows what his or her own face and general appearance are like from mirrors, and one would think that the spectator *ought* to take into account the fact that everything experienced is tied to his or her own face, rather than the actor's, which is usually quite different. Finally, the fact that the actor is present on the screen only as an image *ought* to give his personality a quite different degree of reality than everything that characterizes the body of the spectator, and so on.

In order for the internal processes of the spectator to belong exclusively to the actor, it is necessary for those processes to be freed from all the factors (determinations) to which they are naturally united. In other words, these factors must be rendered ineffective, or at least temporarily nonexistent on the phenomenal plane. (According to our argument, it is this which distinguishes complete identification from identication limited to the processes.) Since identification does in fact occur, one must conclude that this can happen, although it may seem most strange; however, this only happens under specific conditions.

One very important condition is the intense and exclusive concentration of the spectator on what is happening on the screen, and particularly on the "heroes." As a rule, this gives rise to practically complete segregation between the "world of the screen" and that of the cinema itself, and this can be so extreme that the latter disappears completely beyond the spectator's perceptual horizon (i.e., the well-known phenomenon of "negative abstraction").

In addition, the research on the perception of motion and movement combinations consistently demonstrates the primacy of dynamic over static aspects of experience. This is clearly shown in those cases where the kinetic impression remains unchanged despite profound modifications of the moving objects themselves, such as their color, shape, or size. Thus, in the present case, this means that the impressions of movement and the affective processes of the spectator should become primary and overshadow or even displace the impressions of position, etc. Similarly, the gestures of the actor dominate the physical aspects of his own individuality.

Finally, we must not forget the frequently emphasized fact that the entire situation in which the spectator finds himself serve, by their very nature, to induce the appearance of mental states, which can sometimes verge on the abnormal. All the conditions favor mental dissociation and hence complete identification. These conditions include the darkness of the cinema; the brightness of the screen; the fluctuations in retinal stimulation; the attitude of sustained concentration, fatigue, and so on.

In this paper, I have reviewed a number of facts, and suggested many hypotheses—perhaps too many! Nevertheless, maybe this attempt to establish some relation between the phenomena of empathy and some simple, well-established findings and to explain these phenomena in terms of the laws of perceptual organization has not been completely in vain. Indeed, it might suggest some experimental tests of these hypotheses—it is certainly easy to imagine how this could be done.

References

Boring, E. G., Langfeld, H. S., & Weld, H. P. (Eds.). (1948). *Foundations of psychology*. New York: Wiley.

Lipps, T. (1906). *Leitfaden der psychologie*. [Manual of psychology.] Leipzig: Engelmann.

Michotte, A. (1963). *The perception of causality*. London: Methuen.

5
Perception and Cognition

PERCEPTION AND COGNITION
Alan Costall and George Butterworth

In describing his research on the experimental phenomenology of perception, Michotte stressed the extent to which he depended on chance observations. He would often find that a display set up for one purpose would give rise to a totally unexpected effect which he would then explore with great enthusiasm. These surprise discoveries, however, did not determine his basic agenda, but rather suggested ways in which he could experimentally address the questions that had long concerned him. Thus, the progress of his research was far from haphazard. First, the main themes of his phenomenological studies were hardly disconnected; as he himself noted, they are among the most central questions of philosophy. In addition, each of his studies involved the same basic method, the determination of differences. He would establish especially favorable conditions for producing an effect, and then vary the display in various ways to determine those changes that preserve the effect, those that destroy it, and those that give rise to a new category of the effect. Thus in his research on mechanical causality, he sought to determine the basis on which the perceiver visually differentiates causality from mere succession, animate movement, and so on. This was not, however, a matter of simply specifying the relevant stimulus conditions, but rather of characterizing how, for example, causality appears to the perceiver.

Whereas the preceding chapters have been concerned with the substantive topics of Michotte's experimental phenomenology of perception, the present chapter is devoted to an important theoretical issue that unites those topics, the relation between perception and cognition. It would be a mistake to suppose that Michotte denied the importance of reflective intelligence or shared knowledge about the world. Indeed, they figure centrally in his method and argument. Because his aim was to establish that *under some circumstances* we can perceive causality, permanence, and reality, he therefore sought to determine how *seeing* causality, for instance, differs from believing or inferring its existence.

Before considering Michotte's own views in more detail, it will be helpful to consider different views of the relation between perception and cognition that have prevailed in the history of psychology. The first may be termed rationalism or intellectualism. On this view, not only are perception and cognition quite distinct, but also, perception itself is considered to have a very inferior status. Perceptual knowledge, as such, is held to be impossible since what is immediately given within perception (it is claimed) is meaningless—mere sensations, sense data, or cues. Thus, knowledge is not intrinsic to perception but derivative, and can only be achieved through the intervention of an intellectual process of interpretation, inference, or judgment. It is a sign of the prevalence of this viewpoint in modern psychology that the ambiguity of the term 'cognition' is typically unremarked. The reason is that cognition refers both to the epistemological relation between the knower and known, and to the interventions of the intellect ("cognitive processes") that are assumed essential to give meaning to raw and impoverished sensory data.

As Guillaume noted in his classic review of Gestaltism, "once we rule out the role of the intellect in organizing 'sensations', then the question of the relation between the realms of the sensory and of the intellectual must be posed once more, but in different terms" (Guillaume, 1937, p. 213). One alternative view of the relation between perception and cognition is sensationalism, which has been very influential in the history of psychology, especially in relation to evolutionary thought (see Richards, 1987). According to sensationalism, perceptual experience and intellectual functions are continuous: The contents of thought are nothing more than the associations and recombinations of sensations and images. An important implication of this continuity assumption was that the sensationalists were not inclined to treat perception as a purely mechanical relation between knower and known; rather, perception itself was regarded as "intentional," as giving access to meaning.

The revival of Thomism gave new currency, however, to a third view of the relation between perception and cognition that is distinct both from rationalism and also sensationalism. As in sensationalism, perception is treated as intentional, and hence knowing is not regarded as an exclusively intellectual function. However, the intellect is held to constitute a distinct faculty, and not one derived from a more primitive cognitive function:

> An animal with the same senses as ours perceives and deals with the same material objects as we do; but . . . cannot have intellectual thoughts about them – [the animal] cannot, for instance, have a scientific understanding of their nature. To explain our ability to do so we have to postulate a species-specific capacity for abstract thought, what Aquinas calls the agent intellect, the *intellectus agens,* which he contrasts with the receptive intellect or *intellectus possibilis.* We, because we can abstract ideas from the material conditions of the natural world, are able not just to perceive but to think about and understand the world. (Kenny, 1984, p. 89)

Michotte acknowledged the important influence of Thomism on his research work, though he never discussed this issue in any detail (see Chapter 1). The influence is very evident in his own treatment of the relation between perception and cognition. By attempting to demonstrate that *meanings* can indeed be perceived, and in a way largely autonomous of intellectual intervention, Michotte came to the following crucial conclusion: that perception is, in fact, a distinct mode of *knowing,* capable, in itself, of supporting an adaptive relation between the organism and its environment. The research claiming an essential role for inference or judgment in perception, he argued, simply failed to establish what it claimed to prove; it concentrated solely on those situations where the available stimulation is either incomplete or ambiguous, and hence where perception might well be expected to be disrupted by extraneous factors (see also Gibson, 1950, p. 210; 1979, p. 166). However, although Michotte considered that perceptual knowledge is the ultimate basis of all our knowledge of the world, he denied that perception constitutes the limit of that knowledge. The intellect is distinct from perception, and the capacity for reflective intelligence allows us to go beyond perceptual information, through elaboration and abstraction.

Historically, the debates concerning the nature of perception and its relation to cognition have become fixed upon questions of development and comparative psychology: do animals or even infants experience their worlds as coherent and meaningful? Piaget's disagreements with Michotte concerning the onset of permanence and causality in develop ment are familiar (e.g., Piaget, 1969). Piaget denied a linear continuity between perception and cognition in development. Instead, he distinguished between figurative and operative aspects of knowledge and insisted that the figurative aspects (perception, images) only acquire structure by a process of enrichment from motor and intellectual operations. In fact, Piaget itemized a number of fundamental differences between perception and cognition, which, to his mind, ruled out any possibility of a direct developmental link between them. According to Piaget, although there are some similarities or, as he put it, "partial isomorphisms," nearly all the evidence suggests that developments arising in action have organizing repercussions on perception (Piaget, 1969, p. 293). Recent research certainly seems to favor Michotte's claim for the primacy of perceptual structures in human development; for example, there is evidence that the perception of permanence occurs very early in development, much earlier than Piaget's own evidence led him to believe (see Chapter 3 of this volume; Baillargeon, 1986, and Baillargeon, Spelke, & Wasserman, 1985). It is important to note, however, that if Michotte denied a necessary role for cognition in perception, he nevertheless agreed with Piaget in the further, basic assumption that perception and intelligence are distinct mental functions with no direct developmental connection.

The autonomy of perception from the influence of prior knowledge and its intrinsically meaningful character have been the subject of several recent discussions (e.g., Fodor, 1983; Kanizsa, 1979; Rock, 1984). (Sometimes, as in Rock's treatment, the aim seems to be to rescue the intellectualist position by granting perception its own quasi- or protorational status.) In the following two papers, Michotte discusses his own views on the relation between perception and cognition. The first, "The prefiguration in sensory data of our spontaneous conception of the physical world," provides a very concise summary of Michotte's view that phenomenal causality, permanence, and reality are original properties of perception, not intellectual elaborations of sense data, and that these are "coercive"—we cannot help but perceive the world according to these principles. The second paper on "Perception and cognition" discusses these points much more extensively. Michotte argues that perception and cognition correspond to two distinct levels of adaptation to reality. Perception itself provides a limitless and continuous flow of information about our surroundings, whereas cognition allows us to go beyond this information, to integrate, categorize and explain it.

Perceptual and conceptual knowledge usually conform but they can sometimes conflict, and it was these special cases, "illusions," that intrigued Michotte. He argues that the disjunction between these two modes of knowing reveals that perception is *always* accompanied by a personal acceptance or denial, faith or doubt, in the data of experience, at least once a sufficient developmental level has been attained. Sometimes perception is overruled by disbelief, as at a magic show (see also Gibson, 1982), when knowledge of the conservation of objects runs counter to the evidence of our senses; indeed our enjoyment of the show depends upon our appreciation of the impossibility of what we see. In other cases, however, we may come to accept what we see even though this conflicts with our previous experience.

Michotte argues that the basic categories of perceptual experience (phenomenal causality, permanence, and reality), though distinct from our conceptual knowledge, are "homologous" with the fundamental concepts by which we understand the physical world. This claim amounts to more than an insistence on similarities between perceptual and conceptual knowledge. First of all, Michotte maintains that our prereflective, perceptual knowledge of the world is primary in both an evolutionary and developmental sense. The basic perceptual categories, he suggests, might explain the adaptation of animals to physical reality, in the absence of symbolism and intellectual processes, as well as the child's initial coordination with his or her surroundings. However, conceptual understanding is not merely overlaid on this more primitive, perceptual mode of knowing Michotte's important claim is that in human development the fundamental, intellectual concepts by which we understand the physical world are already "prefigured" in perceptual experience. Although the capacity for intellectual thought does not derive from perception, the basic meaning categories of perception provide the framework of reflective thought and rationality.

References

Baillargeon, R. (1986). Representing the existence and location of hidden objects: Object permanence in 6 and 8 month-old infants. *Cognition, 23,* 21–41.

Baillargeon, R., Spelke, E., & Wasserman, S. (1985). Object permanence in five month old infants. *Cognition, 20,* 191–208.

Fodor, J. (1983). *The modularity of mind.* Cambridge, MA MIT Press.

Gibson, J. J. (1950). *The perception of the visual world.* Boston: Houghton-Mifflin,.

Gibson, J. J. (1979). *The ecological approach to visual perception.* Boston: Houghton-Mifflin.

Gibson, J. J. (1982). Ecological physics, magic, and reality. Unpublished manuscript, 1979. Reprinted in E. Reed & R. Jones (Eds.), *Reasons for realism.* (pp. 217–223). Hillsdale, NJ: Lawrence Erlbaum Associates.

Guillaume, P. (1937). *La psychologie de la forme* [Gestalt psychology]. Paris: Flammarion.

Kanizsa, G. (1979). *Organization in vision: Essays on Gestalt psychology.* New York: Praeger.

Kenny, A. (1984). Aquinas: Intentionality. In T. Honderich (Ed.), *Philosophy through its past* (pp. 82–96). Harmondsworth: Penguin. Books.
Piaget, J. (1969). *The mechanisms of perception.* London: Routledge & Kegan Paul, 1969.
Richards, R. J. (1987). *Darwin and the emergence of evolutionary theories of mind and behavior.* Chicago: University of Chicago Press.
Rock, I. (1984). *Perception.* New York: Scientific American Library.

THE PREFIGURATION IN SENSORY DATA OF OUR SPONTANEOUS CONCEPTION OF THE PHYSICAL WORLD[1]

Albert Michotte

This lecture is intended as a contribution to the study of the relations between the data of sensory experience, as such, and the conceptual systems that constitute naive "physics" and "metaphysics". Its general topic is the relation between thought and visual experience.

Our research at Louvain, particularly on vision, seems to demonstrate that some specific phenomena (or, more precisely, certain phenomena that possess specific characteristics) occurring at the level of perception correspond to concepts fundamental to our spontaneous, non-critical, understanding of the physical world. These include the *reality* of things; the *persistence of their substantial identity* during change (displacement or transformation); the *continuity of their existence* despite the discontinuity of their presence in our experience; and the *actions* they perform upon one another (causality) or in relation to one another (fleeing, pursuit, etc.) (Knops, 1947; Michotte, 1941, 1946, 1948a, 1948b, 1950; Sampaio, 1943).

The appearance of these phenomena is directly linked to specific spatio-temporal combinations of stimulation acting upon the sense organs:

1. These combinations prove to be "coercive" in the sense that all normal adult observers when exposed to them reveal, through their verbal and other reactions, the presence of these phenomenal properties.

[1]Translated by A.P. Costall from "La préfiguration dans les données sensorielles de notre conception spontanée du monde physique" in *Proceedings and Papers of the 12th International Congress of Psychology*. Edinburgh: Oliver and Boyd, 1950, pp. 20–22. The text is an abstract of a paper presented to the 12th International Congress of Psychology, Edinburg, 1948. The original paper was accompanied by a film showing demonstrations relating to the recent research of the author and his colleagues.

2. Variations of the system of stimulation produce corresponding, systematic variations in the reactions of the observers. In this respect, the stimulus-response relations are analogous to those that exist for simple stimuli and their corresponding responses (e.g. colors and sounds). We can therefore assume that we are concerned here with original properties of perception rather than the secondary elaboration of sensory data on the basis of acquired knowledge. This view is supported by the following arguments.
3. Once the conditions for the appearance of the phenomena in question have been determined, it is possible to produce combinations of stimuli so that the phenomena that occur actually contradict our acquired knowledge of the physical world ("paradoxical experiences"). Other combinations, that should give rise to these impressions if they were the effect of acquired knowledge, fail to have an effect because the system of stimulation is inadequate ("negative experiences").
4. In numerous cases, it is possible to demonstrate that the phenomena in question must arise as an inevitable consequence of the effect of the laws of structural organisation in perception, given the particular system of sensory stimulation.

In view of the above four points, it follows that our basic *concepts* concerning the physical world (such as causality) are represented at the strictly sensory level by characteristic, primitive *impressions* (such as "pushing" or "launching"). Furthermore, these impressions can be regarded as constituting an *actual prefiguration* of such concepts.

We can consider prefiguration from two perspectives:

1. Phylogenetically, these impressions may arise in organisms which, as a result of their level of development in the evolutionary scale, are incapable of attaining the level of intellectual thought and symbolism necessary for concept formation in the strict sense. In this case, the impressions perhaps constitute a kind of substitute for these concepts, and allow the organism to adapt to the conditions of the physical surroundings in which it lives. This would explain the analogy between the behavior of animals and humans.
2. Ontogenetically, the same situation no doubt occurs in children below a certain level of maturation. In this case, the problem of the genetic relations that unite impressions and concepts poses itself in a particularly vivid way. Do concepts themselves derive from impressions, or through some other process?

Finally, there is a further problem, in addition to that of the developmental relations between impressions and concepts, and this concerns the question of adaptation. How does the potential for adaptation differ depending upon whether it is based on impressions or the corresponding concepts?

References

Knops, L. (1947). Contribution a l'étude de la "naissance" et de la "permanence" phénoménales dans le champ visuel [A contribution to the study of phenomenal "coming into being" and "permanence" within the visual field]. In *Miscellanea Psychologica Albert Michotte* (pp. 562–610). Louvain: Éditions de l'Institut Supérieur de Philosophie.

Michotte, A. (1941). La causalité physique est-elle une donnée phénoménale? [Is physical causality a phenomenal given?]. *Tijdschrift voor Philosophie, 3,* 290–328.

Michotte, A. (1946). *La perception de la causalité* [The perception of causality]. Louvain: Éditions de l'Institut Supérieur de Philosophie de Louvain.

Michotte, A. (1948a). Le caractère de "réalité" des projections cinématographiques [The character of "reality" in cinematic projections]. *Revue Internationale de Filmologie, 1,* 249–261.

Michotte, A. (1948b). L'énigme psychologique de la perspective dans le dessin linéaire [The psychological enigma of perspective in line drawings]. *Bulletin des Lettres de l'Académie Royale de Belgique.* (5e Série), *34,* 268–288.

Michotte, A. (1950). The emotions regarded as functional connections. In M.L. Reymert (Ed.), *Feelings and emotions. The Mooseheart Symposium* (pp. 114–126). New York: McGraw-Hill.

Sampaio, A. C. (1943). La translation des objets comme facteur de leur permanence phénoménale [The translation of objects as a factor in their phenomenal permanence]. Louvain: Éditions de l'Institut Supérieur de Philosophie de Louvain.

PERCEPTION AND COGNITION[1]

Albert Michotte

It is 25 years since I had the honor of addressing the International Congress of Psychology, at the 9th Congress held at Yale in 1929. My address then was entitled "Perception and Action" and was an attempt to shed some light on what I felt were the main questions concerning the

[1]Address presented at the 14th International Congress of Psychology (Montreal 1954), and published in the Proceedings of the Congress, *Acta Psychologica,* 1955, *11,* 70–91. English translation by A. P. Costall, G. E. Butterworth and G. Thinès. Subheadings added by the translators.

relation between these two aspects of behavior. Since then my colleagues and I have attempted to resolve some of these questions. Among other things, we have investigated the perception of apparent physical causality and phenomenal permanence [see the other papers translated in this volume]. As always, however, experiments designed to sort out one problem revealed others: The behavior of the subjects in our research drew our attention to some interesting details concerning theoretical aspects of the vast problem of the relations among different cognitive processes.

The Means by Which We Obtain Information About the Physical World

In order to define the topic of the present address, I shall begin by drawing a perfectly straightforward distinction between the three ways in which we obtain information about the physical world including our own bodies. The first means is through concrete, particular, perceptual events occurring at moments in our lives that are not only under the influence of stimulus systems acting on our sensory organs but are directly linked to them. Through these events in their various aspects (sensory, intellectual, affective . . .) we come to know not only objects, processes, or groups of objects or processes, but even complex spatio-temporal situations; and these events are the basis of all the knowledge that we acquire about the physical world. This is the most common sense of the term perception, and though unfortunately it is not exclusive, it is the one we will be adopting in this discussion. The events we are concerned with here are created in a relatively isolated way under artificial laboratory conditions; they are the subject not only of research on "perception" within psychophysics but also of more complicated studies on the influence of past experience, attitudes, motivations, personality, and so on.

In real life, however, perception does not occur in isolation (this idea is just a fiction sustained within the laboratory). Normally, our sense organs are engaged by a flood of stimulation in continual transformation as the result of changes happening in the external world or from our own actions and movements. Such stimulation provides an untold amount of perceptual data. Although when considered in isolation they might seem like a succession of fleeting events, they are in fact the basis of the ceaseless organization of our own activity. As the result of our own personal experience, we continually create and revise the way we conceive of the world and the laws that control it. No matter how we consider the nature of thought itself, it is obvious that the elaboration of such limitless perceptual data—by comparison, relation, analysis, abstraction, generalization, inference etc.—enormously extends the scope of our knowledge; it allows us to go beyond direct perceptual knowledge in so far as understanding and explanation surpass mere evidence.

However, given the social nature of our lives, this process is especially helped by a third source of information, verbal communication among people. This allows us to relate our own knowledge to the experiences and thoughts of others. Verbal communication through the perception of language (either listening to a parent, teacher, or anyone else or reading a magazine or newspaper) provides us with information whose influence undoubtedly varies as a function of its source. Nevertheless, despite the symbolic nature of its transmission, such information is integrated with the acquired knowledge upon which our personal experience is based and indeed enriches it to an incalculable degree.

For much of the time in our lives, the information we obtain directly from perception agrees with that recalled from memory or gained from other people. In certain cases, however, some of this information is contradictory, and these cases can prove very instructive. Obviously, such conflict can occur in every possible way: What different people tell us may conflict, or a current experience may be impossible to reconcile with our past experience or knowledge, and so on.[2] We will restrict our attention here to cases where the conflict involves actual perceptual evidence in some way or another as most of the research we have gathered concerns these cases.

Conflicts Occurring Within the Perceptual Process

The first class of examples we will consider involves a conflict intrinsic to the perceptual process itself. These cases can be produced by combining a group of complex stimuli so that the parts of the system of stimulation give rise to perceptual structures that are more or less incompatible; we will refer to such displays as "discordant stimuli."[3] Such occurrences can have very different effects depending upon the conditions and especially on the perceptual configurations themselves.

In particular, these are the contradictions that most often give rise to the curious situation, which is common enough in the laboratory, where the observers state that they have no idea what they are seeing! By this,

---

[2]The most well known of the many studies on the effects of past experience are by Bruner and Postman. See Vernon (1952) for a general account.

[3]The expression "perceptual process" is used here in a very broad sense and would include the systems of stimulation. We cannot avoid this without excluding some of the examples that have occurred to us. In many cases, opposition and contradictions do not reveal themselves to the subjects as observable facts, and they only become revealed to the experimenter by comparing a variety of stimulation systems.

they do not mean that "what they are seeing" fails to correspond to any kind of clearly defined concept, nor for that matter that they do not possess adequate words to describe it. Rather, the impression itself is confused or chaotic. This can be produced quite easily by presenting several objects moving in a more or less irregular way, or by subjecting a single object to complex modifications, such as change of form as the result of rotation. The observers "know" of course that they are seeing movements, but they seem disordered and the total display completely lacks any organization.

At the opposite extreme are cases where the same object simultaneously appears to have different and contradictory forms. For instance, in our own research on the perception of volume, we presented wooden hemispheres with diameters of about 7 to 10 cm and whose back surfaces were flat. When these were viewed from the front, either binocularly or monocularly, they produced the impression of a complete sphere; there is the curious effect of seeing a "ball" even though the front and the back of the object cannot of course be seen at the same time. Although we are still investigating this interesting phenomenon, it would seem to be related to what we term the "amodal" aspect of experience (cf. Burke, 1952). What is of interest here is a strange effect noted by Prof. Buytendijk on one of his visits to Louvain. He found that if the observer touched the back of the hemisphere while viewing it, it was still perfectly possible to see it as a sphere even though the tactile-kinesthetic information indicated that it was flat! The contradiction did not present the slightest difficulty. We have repeated this experiment many times and have had no problems obtaining the same effect.

In this case, therefore, contradictory configurations exist together, and one may well wonder how this can be. One might suppose, for instance, that the unity of an object only exists at an intellectual level, at a level at which construction would be eliminated by the intervention of the concept of illusion. Obviously, this factor does operate since the subjects are certain of the flatness of the far side of the hemisphere, and they no longer believe that what they "see" is really spherical. They become certain that it is flat once they have manipulated the object. An easy explanation for this would be that the tactile-kinesthetic cues dominate the visual one; yet, this is evidently unsatisfactory since it is easy to find a number of examples where one has "faith" in the visual data and the tactile-kinesthetic impression is taken as illusory. Matters are more complicated, therefore, and in the case of the hemisphere it may be that the "amodal" aspect of the far side of the sphere favors the illusory character attributed to it.

The concept of illusion fails to settle entirely this issue since even at the phenomenal level the object has a single identity: The sphere, which is "seen", is one and the same as the object "felt" as having a flat back! Strangely enough, there is no evidence of suppression (inhibition). The effect, therefore, seems to concern the problem of the relation between impressions of form among different sensory modalities and to suggest that under certain conditions, despite the identity of the perceived object, it is just as though we were concerned with two quite different worlds without any communication. The phenomenon is linked to all the others that indicate the primitive autonomy of the different sensory domains. It would be possible to shed light on this whole question, therefore, by systematic learning experiments on the influence of motor training on visual structures, rather like the studies described later though specially adapted to form perception.

Between the two extreme cases of confusion and coexistence mentioned so far, there are a number of others in which the perceptual configuration is unitary and thoroughly well organized but which is affected in some way by two discordant systems of stimulation that it manages to reconcile. In other words a "compromise" occurs, though this single term covers many different instances, so varied both in nature and the way they appear (immediately, after a series of presentations or systematic training, etc.), that they are quite difficult to classify. We will not even try but will be satisfied with a few points of reference.

Examples of the Resolution of Discordance

Our first example is that of perspective pictures. For a long time, psychologists have drawn attention to the fact that the third dimension can be "seen" in such pictures, though this proves to be rather problematic. Therefore, we have returned to this issue and have conducted some experiments in which subjects were required to match the apparent depth of displays presented under controlled conditions to a parallelepiped made out of metal wire whose depth could be adjusted (its cross-section remaining constant). The models themselves were either real parallelepipeds constructed in the same way but of fixed size or pictures representing a perspective view of these models that was geometrically exact for the viewpoint of the subjects. The "adjustments" were as easy, or nearly so, for the drawings as for the real models. In terms of the objective data, the apparent depth was generally (though not in all conditions) less for the drawings, and the precision of the scores was of the same order. It is clear, therefore, that perspective pictures are not distinguished by any lack of phenomenal depth for the depicted object.

What one sees in a picture is truly three-dimensional, but the volume perceived lacks reality. We believe we have shown that this character of reality should be considered as a particular "dimension" of perceptual experience, one which can be quantitatively varied like any other. It is precisely in this loss of reality linked to the maintenance of three-dimensionality that the compromise between the contradictory demands of the stimulation is revealed (see Michotte 1948a, 1948b).

Indeed, it is easy to demonstrate that a system of discordant stimuli is involved here. It is simply necessary to free the group of lines that form the perspective drawing from the flat surface upon which they are drawn; they then appear as a *real* volume. This can be done by exactly reproducing the shape of the flat perspective drawing with thin metal rods, and the figure then stands out from the distant background yielding a clear impression of real volume when viewed monocularly (or even binocularly if the object is viewed from a sufficient distance so as to avoid detecting its flatness). This impression is even more striking if one views one of these metal figures from even very close with one eye from a fixed viewpoint; the character of reality of the volume then becomes totally convincing and as clear and tangible as a substantial object perceived binocularly.[4]

In contrast, in the case of pictures, the structural factors of perceptual organization lead us to see the lines as "traces" attached to, and belonging to, the supporting surface.

There is, therefore, a contradiction between the tendency for the lines to yield an impression of real volume and the confinement of the lines to the surface. The compromise is satisfactory because once there is no question of real volume as such but only the mere appearance, it can be reconciled with the flatness of the surface.[5]

It may be useful, perhaps, to stress that in a case of this kind we know we are faced with an illusion because we do not *believe* that there is a real object in front of us. However, unlike most illusions where we need to discover that they are misleading through experience, in this case the unreality of the volume is phenomenally present in the perceived configuration itself.

In a way, one could think of the absence of apparent reality here as a parallel, at the phenomenal level, to the concept of illusion in the intellectual domain. Often the two go together, but they are just as often dissociated, as in the case of illusions that are known as such but where

---

[4]See Phemister(1951). The figures were the same as the photographs used in Phemister's study; she presented them at an angle which, as her results show, yielded the most powerful impression of reality.

[5]In our view, Rubin is correct to refer to a *loss of reality* in his experiments (Rubin, 1950). This loss of reality seems to occur very often in cases of incompatibility, especially in the case of the hemisphere we have just cited.

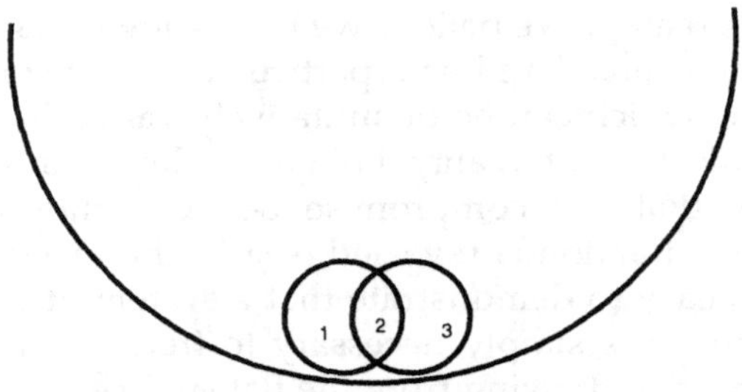

FIGURE 5.1

the content of perception seems perfectly real (as in the Müller-Lyer illusion, etc.).

Everyone is familiar with the ambiguous figures frequently encountered in everyday life, as well as in the laboratory, that give rise to different impressions for different people or change their configuration for the same individual over prolonged or repeated presentations.

The most common example is that of the puzzle pictures found everywhere. In addition, there are perspective reversals, and reversals of movement, "Sinsteden's mill," etc.. These phenomena are linked to differences or changes in the receptive condition of the subjects, though there is little agreement about their actual basis. However, what is of interest here is that such discordant stimulation can produce various impressions and often gives rise to the development of forms of increasing stability.

An excellent demonstration comes from some studies related to an early experiment by Benussi on apparent transparency.[6] The subjects view a disc towards the edge of which are drawn two partly overlapping circles; the disc itself revolves rather slowly around its axis. Objectively, under these conditions, the drawn lines define three adjoining areas: two crescents (1 and 3) enclosing a spindle-shaped region (2) (Figure 5.1). Nevertheless, in accord with the laws of form perception, when the disc is motionless the observers see two complete circles; when the disc is set in motion and the figure is followed visually, the dominant configuration is that of two circles performing eccentric rotational movements by sliding over one another.

If the outlines of the figure are removed and instead the regions are merely colored so that they are different shades—so that, for example, regions 1 and 3 are red and yellow, and region 2 is orange—the system

[6]Quoted in Metzger 1953, p. 130. This book gives further details (pp. 323, 334) of experiments performed by other investigators that seem to be similar to those described in the following pages.

of stimulation at once becomes more discordant. Of course, the continuity of the contours should once again favor the perception of two complete circles, but on the other hand the different colors should serve to segregate the three regions, and the central spindle-shaped area should create a dent in each circle. As Benussi has shown, however, these conditions give rise to a new structure, that of transparency. One usually sees a circle, uniform in color though transparent, revolving partly over another circle, which is also of uniform color, and which can be seen through the first where they overlap. The effect is best, of course, and more easily produced when the colors used are most appropriate to this structure. It is far from the case, however, that this is the only structure that occurs; others happen to precede it, though once it occurs it seems to be very stable. What is remarkable here is that this configuration resolves the discrepancy because, thanks to transparency, there is no longer a contradiction between the form of the circles and the colors: they all seem continuous and uniform.

This kind of experiment is open to limitless variations, but one worth mentioning is simply to enhance the contradiction by means of other colors, such as blue and red for the two crescents and vivid yellow for the central area. Under those conditions and depending on the dimensions, color etc. of the figure, one can obtain extremely different results; here, as an example, are just a few of my own observations. First of all, I saw two discs sliding in relation to one another. The lower disc seemed to be red over its entire surface, whereas the disc that partly covered it was of two colors (a blue crescent and a yellow spindle). After some time, the structure changed in terms of its transparency, the nearer disc seemed transparent; I could see the lower (red) disc through the superimposed blue disc, and as the latter moved, the covered part of the red disc appeared to change color and become yellow. This configuration had the advantage over the earlier one in that the colors of each disc were uniform, though only as a result of the strange color change linked to the movements of the upper disc, and was contrary to both the psychological and physical laws of color.

After further observation, quite a different structure suddenly appeared. I saw a hollow cylinder, which was blue outside with a red interior and a yellow base, rotating and swaying in a complicated way. This effect has been confirmed by a number of subjects, and it is not difficult to create conditions so that the cylinder configuration occurs more quickly. Again, once it is established, the configuration is very stable. As a result of the extension of the object into three dimensions and the effects of perspective and the "screen effect" the anomalous distribution of the colors is reduced to a minimum: Both the inside and outside of the cylinder seemed to have a uniform color, and the yellow base seemed to be a complete circle, its different parts being successively disclosed during rotation.

In this last configuration, we reencounter the presence of discordant stimulation, but the conflict is eliminated in a remarkable way by the effects of the third dimension through perspective form.

Sometimes, however, things become more complicated. In particular, I have been able to see the circular base of the cylinder become completely attached to the disc while the main body of the cylinder engaged in unlikely contortions in relation to the base!

Another very instructive modification of the experiment with the eccentric circles involves the substitution of a square for one of the circles; the tip of one of the corners is set to coincide with the center of the circle (Figure 5.2), and the observer should fixate the center.

When the disc is rotating, it is easy to see the square rotate and make a complete turn around the center, thus covering every part of the circle in succession. This in itself is curious and can be easily shown to occur because the square changes its orientation with the rotation of the disc, but the circle seems to remain unchanged in orientation because it lacks any reference points. The important point here is that when the figures are drawn rather close to the outer edge of the disc so that it would be impossible for the square to physically rotate around the tip of one of its corners without going outside the disc itself, the perception of rotation remains unchanged! The square still seems to execute a complete rotation!

The behavior of the subjects in this experiment is rather remarkable. A certain number simply report the rotation without noticing that there is not enough room for the square to turn. Others do notice the anomaly and try to rationalize what they see by supposing that things would happen like this with the physical rotation of the square because of its combination with the rotation of the disc. Finally, some realize that it is actually impossible for the square to turn in this way, yet this does not

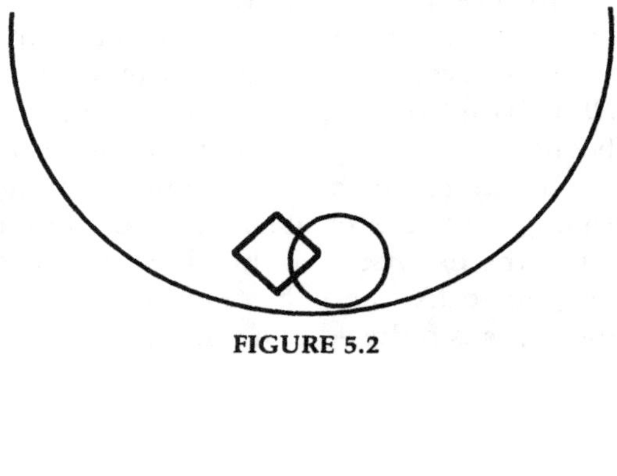

FIGURE 5.2

alter their impression of movement at all: They simply say that it is something strange that they cannot explain, and they are intellectually satisfied to dismiss it is as yet another instance of illusion.

A new example of discordance, in which the role of learning is more prominent, comes from some recent research we have conducted at Louvain with Dr. A. Glynn on apparent transparency and the Rosenbach phenomenon (Glynn, 1954). When an opaque screen, such as a narrow band of paper, is placed over a rectangle or some other figure so that parts of it are visible from either end of the band, one has the impression of course of the band covering a continuous figure that is uninterrupted in the hidden region. This is an example of the screen effect. Obviously, we do not see the figure through the opaque screen (in our terminology it is phenomenally present in "amodal" form). Nevertheless, as Rosenbach demonstrated half a century ago, under certain conditions one has the impression that the screen is really transparent or at least translucent. We have attempted to replicate this effect and systematically investigate its conditions.

Our experimental paradigm was as follows. The subject faces a window of frosted glass in front of which is set a narrow, totally opaque, gray band (the screen). The frosted glass is dimly illuminated from behind, and the apparatus was arranged so that we could back-project a rectangle that appeared to the subject as the same gray color as the screen, though slightly lighter. This figure was moved side to side across the frosted glass along a highly curved trajectory, and it performed a strange sweeping movement as it passed behind the opaque screen.

This display constituted a new discordant stimulus. The rectangle was partly concealed by the opaque screen as it passed so that the usual structure would be that of the screen (or tunnel) effect, and this structure was generally the first to appear to all the observers. However, some factors in the situation favoring the unity of the figure and the continuity of its contours were much more powerful in this case than for static displays: There was the fact of seeing the entire rectangle moving before and after it passed behind the screen, and the fact that while it was screened, the exposed parts of the figure were moving together in a special way (the law of common fate). However, as Glynn has shown, these factors were not sufficient to explain the illusion that occurs.

Under optimal conditions and after a number of repetitions, the tunnel effect progressively (and sometimes even suddenly) gives way to an impression of translucency from the screen; one believes that one is seeing the part of the figure which is in fact concealed by the tunnel. The clarity of this impression and the rapidity with which it develops depends considerably upon the individual subject. Though it is rare, some subjects require powerful suggestion in the form of a screen that is actually transparent; however, the effect is generally very easily observed, even though it does develop gradually.

In this case, perhaps, we should speak of a "compromise" for if the screen looses its opaqueness to a certain degree, the part of the rectangle that is believed to be seen through the screen appears darker than the remainder. Be that as it may, the important point here is the change in structure caused by the discordant stimulation and the fact that the translucent configuration allows contradictory perceptual conditions to have a simultaneous effect.

A final example is of special interest because it reveals even more clearly the influence of experience in the formation of perceptual structures. Most psychologists are familiar with the famous distorted rooms devised and constructed by Adelbert Ames. A small version has been exhibited at this congress; the original, full-sized version is at Princeton University. In these rooms the walls, ceiling, and floor are not square or rectangular, nor are they horizontal or vertical, as in normal rooms, but instead trapezoidal and more or less slanted. They are calculated according to the principles of perspective to project exactly the same retinal image to an observer viewing its interior monocularly and from a fixed viewpoint as would a normal room under everyday conditions. As a result, the room appears to be orthogonal, the windows look rectangular, and so on; it is an almost perfect example of "trompe l'oeil." Nevertheless, Kilpatrick's research has shown that it is possible by training to get observers to "see" the "real" shape of the room (Kilpatrick, 1954).

The training itself occurs in a variety of ways. In the first series of experiments, the subjects tried to throw balls at an illuminated target, which could be projected on various points on the walls of the room, or else they were given long poles with which they could trace the contours of the room, and so on.

In the second group of studies, these activities were performed by the experimenter, and the subject was merely required to watch what was happening in the room. Despite some rather large individual differences, both groups of subjects reported a change in the appearance of the room that occurred in the direction of its "real" shape. On the whole, the results were similar for both groups, though there was perhaps a slight superiority for the active learners.

These experiments can be compared with the earlier examples because once again there is a discordance within the system of stimulation, though here, however, the conflict was revealed to the observers. To the subject, the surfaces, edges and corners of the room appear to occur at distances from the spectator that correspond to the static view; yet once he is required to reach different points in the room, he discovers that the distances are very different. Further, as a mere observer, he must notice that the extent of the movements of the ball and the pole do not agree with the apparent distance. The effect of the modification of the apparent shape of the room through learning is, of course, to eliminate this contradiction.

This experiment is remarkable in a number of ways in comparison to the earlier ones. First, as a matter of interest, it is worth noting that the effect of resolving the discordance here was to make the impression agree with the physical situation, whereas in the other situations the reverse effect occurred. Furthermore, in the former cases, the changes occurred in the direction of everyday perceptual configurations—transparency, hollow container, etc.—whereas the changes that occur here are contrary to our everyday experience of rooms with horizontal ceilings and floors, and right-angled corners, etc.. In addition, it is remarkable that a structure as stable as that of a normal right-angled room can be so easily changed, though, as Kilpatrick himself points out, this may be encouraged by inevitable imperfections in the construction of the room.[7] Finally, these experiments lead us to raise the curious question of why the apparent structure of the room becomes changed rather than the apparent extent of the movements. After all, especially for the tests in which the subjects explored the contours of the room with a pole, it is perfectly conceivable that training should influence our appreciation of the extent of the movements rather than of the framework to which they are referred.

This result, however, may have had something to do with the fact that the subjects had prior knowledge that the rooms were distorted, and it may be that if the experiments were repeated with totally naive subjects, the apparent extent of the movements might then be affected by the training. Nevertheless, this is purely an hypothesis based on the second part of this address.

It is interesting to compare Kilpatrick's findings with those obtained by Ivo Köhler in his recent research on the effects of wearing spectacles, which either totally invert the visual field or modify its local form. In the

[7]Control experiments, however, have shown that the same visual distortion was observed when, after training, subjects looked at an objectively right-angled room or to another distorted room producing the same retinal image. This confirms that we are dealing here with the influence of learning on perceptual structure that corresponds to the same global system of stimulation. This is a good opportunity to thank Professor Kilpatrick for kindly lending me the proofs of his unpublished work and for allowing me to use them in the lecture.

latter case, as you may be aware, training could again produce changes to visual structures. Obviously, an immense field of research is opening up here.

The Perception of Discordant Stimulation Considered as Problem Solving

The examples of discordant stimulation, which we have just considered, can be treated in terms of the experiment as a problem situation for which the subject must find some solution. Actually, one might say the same for all cases of perceptual organization that occur in response to a rather complicated system of stimulation, as well as to more or less ambiguous stimuli (i.e. in practice, all instances of perception in real life, and indeed all phenomena of biological adaptation).

The analogies between the principles that govern the formation of perceptual structures and those governing thought have been noted before as has the intervention of the former in problem solving. However, it does seem that the subject of discordant stimulation is especially relevant in these respects. The problem set by such stimulation certainly is not formulated either verbally or mentally because it arises from conditions of stimulation of which the subject is unaware; what is more, the subject usually fails to realize that any "problem" exists. As far as the experimenter is concerned, there is an attempt to present systematically particular discordances in the system of stimulation and hence elicit the occurrence of a perceptual reaction in the subject. A problem is set, therefore, and the solution is provided by the very nature of the subject's response or series of responses.

Considered in this way, it is interesting to compare situations in which there is discordant stimulation with the international research on problem solving. There is clearly no lack of analogies, either in terms of the actual solutions or the means by which they appear. Thus, in the case of intuition (or insight), it is remarkable how simple and well suited can be the solutions; they are usually unexpected and appear suddenly, resolving the apparently contradictory demands of the task.

There is the enduring question here of the respective contributions of the simple effects of the basic laws of organization, and of acquired experience in the perception of form. Do not the limitless number of forms we see in everyday life provide the subject with a stock of solutions to be unconsciously applied when problems arise? Could not the role of such forms be related to that of the applications in other fields of familiar principles and formulas?

Furthermore, we have found that certain solutions, though satisfactory in some respects, nevertheless reveal obvious limitations and anomalies in others (as in the case of the movement of the cylinder in the study with eccentric circles). The solution only solves one difficulty by creating another! Why should this occur? This is strangely reminiscent of what are known in everyday language as "nested solutions" (*solutions boiteuses*).

Finally, on the topic of such analogies, there are instances where contradictory data coexist that appear to be related to certain fallacies in the intellectual domain; indeed, they seem so closely related that they could properly be referred to as "perceptual fallacies." In both, the proposed solution seems to be clearly compelling, be it a conclusion following from apparently correct and plausible reasoning, or a directly perceived experience; yet a moment's reflection would reveal it as mistaken (as in the example of the square seeming to rotate around the center of the circle).

Conflicts Between Perceptual Evidence and Information Obtained from Other Sources

Often, however, the conflicts that involve perceptual phenomena are different from those we have so far considered. They can arise between the perceptual data and information obtained in other ways, such as personal observation, inference, or verbal communications relating to the situation encountered by the subject.

For instance, students in the laboratory situation usually go on to make their own observations of optical or other kinds of illusion, having already examined the experimental setup and even produced the actual displays. As you know, the contradictory knowledge about the experimental conditions has little influence on what is perceived when, as is often the case, we are concerned with so-called "coercive" systems of stimulation.

Similar cases are encountered in everyday life. I might be allowed to recall an especially vivid experience of my own as an example. Some years ago I attended a magic show; I was seated not more than a meter and a half from the magician who was standing in the center of the room holding a little wooden cage containing a live canary. The magician was talking away in the usual fashion while keeping the cage in view: He then suddenly yelled and rapidly stretched both arms in the air, and both the cage and the bird disappeared. I have seldom experienced so realistic an impression of the sudden annihilation of such a complex object while I was watching it, even though we ourselves have gone on to conduct some research on this topic (Knops, 1947). Nevertheless, I did not for one moment, of course, suppose that the object had really disappeared: My immediate reaction was to wonder what the magician had done with the bird and cage and how this was achieved. There is little point dwelling on this example because nearly all of you must have experienced a similar situation at some time. Indeed, when I was talking about this to a friend recently, he told me that he had been to a magic show with his 10-year-old son where a juggler made a series of balls disappear and then reappear, and so on. The reaction of his child was typical. He asked his father, "but did the juggler really make the balls disappear?" Already, there were doubts in his mind about the value of perceptual evidence.

However, thanks especially to the research by Piaget, we know that younger children do not have the slightest difficulty in accepting the "creation" and "disappearance" of material objects in accord with their sensory impression. It is only gradually, through a long process, that they develop and attain the concept of "the conservation of substance" (Piaget & Inhelder, 1941; see also Piaget, 1947).

Once conservation has been definitely acquired and we then encounter contradictory perceptual evidence, we are convinced that we must be victims of illusion. The knowledge acquired by inference and verbal communication prevails and controls our behavior. The concept of illusion serves to resolve the conflict between the actual evidence and what we "know." It is strange, nonetheless, that an intellectual notion once accepted by the observer is enough to stifle the effect of the vivid impression imposed on the senses.

We must never forget, however, as we said before, that this does depend on a long process of learning that gradually leads us from childhood to the point of no longer necessarily believing in the data provided by our perceptual experiences, or, to be more exact, not blindly believing in certain kinds of experience or those that arise in certain situations, such as magic shows and perceptual demonstrations.

Matters are further complicated by the fact that sometimes the perceptual evidence does indeed prevail and determines the behavior of the subject. I have had the chance of observing such cases in my own laboratory and elsewhere, and I would like to mention a few here.

The first concerns an experience of mine dating from 1937 when one of the public theaters in Paris was beginning to show stereoscopic films using the Lumière process (the anaglyph technique). During one of these shows, which was mainly unremarkable, we were shown a football match, and at a particular moment the ball seemed to leave the screen and shoot into the hall towards the heads of the spectators; many of the audience then ducked to one side as if to avoid the ball. This was a remarkable reaction because they all knew perfectly well that this was an illusion; indeed, the very fact that something like this might happen had made them curious enough to want to see the show. Yet, despite this, a number had reacted as if a real object had been thrust at them. We could try to explain this in a number of ways. A possible reason might be that these individuals were so affected by the apparent reality of the show that the "knowledge" that it was merely an image was suppressed and so was less effective in controlling their behavior. On the other hand, it might be that it was an "instinctive," unlearned reaction that was so strongly linked to the perceptual evidence that it was triggered despite the fact that they knew it was an illusion. This is not unlikely and could be investigated systematically, especially by attempting to inhibit these reactions in simple conditioning experiments.

Let us now turn to some observations from the laboratory. I have previously referred to the objects made of wire set out as flat lines so as to represent a perspective view of a parallelepiped; when these are viewed monocularly from a fixed position, they give the impression of absolutely real volume. More than once, I witnessed some odd behavior by the people taking part in this experiment, even by a well-known scientist. They were all perfectly aware of the conditions of the experiment, for they had been shown the wire model outside of the apparatus and had been offered every possible explanation concerning the illusion. Yet they wanted to repeat the experiment by testing "that there really was no way to place a solid object like a pencil so that it seemed to pass between the two faces enclosing what seemed so real a volume." Their behavior was peculiar because it should have been obvious from just a moment's reflection that their efforts were pointless. From the time they learned that the wires making up the figure were all in the same plane, it should have been obvious that it was impossible to pass a rigid rod behind two of the wires forming the closer of the phenomenal surfaces and in front of two of the wires forming what was phenomenally the back surface. Their test, therefore, was bound to fail, and so one wonders why such intelligent people should have bothered. These are certainly remarkable cases, and one may well ask if perceptual evidence is not sometimes so compelling that it produces a real block or momentary obstruction to thought. In any case, it would be interesting to try to solve this puzzle.

Although somewhat different, a further example also demonstrates the potential power of perceptual evidence. I had once described some experiments to my students on phenomenal permanence set up in the following way. The subject viewed a long slit set in a screen behind which were located two colored rectangles a few centimeters apart. At a given moment, the rectangle on the left moved towards the one on the right and, when it made contact, began to decrease in length until it disappeared entirely. Under the right conditions, all observers reported seeing a rectangle slide behind another while retaining its full size This is the typical "screen effect." (see Sampaio, 1943, Michotte, 1950.)

My students not only knew what was occurring but also the technique employed and the theory of the phenomenon, yet I found one of them go right up to the screen and carefully look at it and touch it in order to check that there were only figures painted on a paper disc but there was no slit in the paper at all! This would have been reasonable if the student had explained that as he was in a psychological laboratory it might have been that I had been trying to make him believe that actual sliding of one rectangle behind another was only apparent when it was in fact real; but his reply was quite different, and rather odd. He said, "I wanted to check what was happening because the sliding was so vivid that I could not believe it could be an illusion." Of course, this reply was beside the point since what defines an illusion is the very fact that the impression seems so "evident" despite its lack of correspondence to the physical situation.

I would like to conclude with a final example where I reacted in a way rather similar to this student. It is related to the work on apparent transparency I mentioned before (Glynn, 1954). Although I was already familiar with this work, on a new trial I once insisted that there must be a fault in the apparatus because I saw the rectangle so clearly through the screen that the screen must actually be translucent. I knew full well that Dr. Glynn was a careful experimenter, but then, of course, we all make mistakes sometimes. We therefore examined the apparatus only to find that the screen was totally opaque after all.

The Role of Perceptual Evidence in the Control of Behavior

In all of the three examples I have referred to, the perceptual evidence proved dominant and controlled the behavior of the observers, but the last two seem to be especially instructive. First, they emphasize that although we gradually learn to mistrust our sensory impressions and acquire a concept of illusion, our scepticism is not universal because the effects of such learning are very selective. Generally, the concept of illusion only comes to be applied to those instances or areas in which we have learned that a conflict may well occur between our impressions and the corresponding physical situation. Everyday experience teaches us that our impressions of distance, size, and even shape, as well as our impressions of color are often misleading; and we are prepared to admit that illusions can occur in this domain once we are told. Things are different, however, when we are dealing with new cases that have not been experienced before; then we behave as if we were children; we "cannot believe that it is an illusion."

In my own case, I was almost convinced that there must be a fault in the experiment. Yet the scepticism I have talked about is more general than one might suppose because despite the evidence of my senses there must have been an element of doubt, as evidenced by my checking the apparatus. It seems likely that a sophisticated adult never has absolute faith in perceptual data alone; at most, this faith leads us to question contradictory information arising from other sources.

In any case, in all such instances of discordance we are faced with a dilemma. Is it an illusion of our senses, an error in our reasoning or in our measurements, or are other people mistaken in what they tell us about the situation? The problem is to know how to chose among them.

If asked for my opinion on the relative weight of perceptual evidence and acquired experience in the control of our behavior, I must reply that the question is inappropriate since it all depends upon additional considerations.

As we have seen, it is reasonable to suppose that instinctive, unlearned behavior can be directly triggered by perception, even when we know there is an illusion. Sometimes, however, in the case of patterns of behavior acquired over a lifetime, it would seem that our behavior is determined to some degree by our belief that one source of information is more reliable than another. The degree of belief or certainty is then crucial, and thus, ultimately the motives that justify them. We should note, however, that when perceptual evidence is challenged by logical evidence based on a proper test it is always overridden by the latter, and thus reinforces the superiority of thought over perceptual evidence as such.

All this goes to show that for individuals above a certain level of development, the perceptual event, in all its complexity, involves a personal aspect of acceptance, denial, faith or doubt, which must be considered in the study of behavior. This point reminds me of the title of an article by Klein and Schlesinger (1949), which sounded a bit like a slogan: "Where is the perceiver in perceptual theory?". I think that what I have been discussing in this address highlights at least one aspect of the role of the perceiver in perception.

References

Burke, L. (1952). The tunnel effect. *Quarterly Journal of Experimental Psychology, 4,* 121–138.

Glynn, A. (1954). Apparent transparency and the tunnel effect. *Quarterly Journal of Experimental Psychology, 6,* 125–139.

Kilpatrick, F. P. (1954). Two processes in perceptual learning. *Journal of Experimental Psychology, 47,* 362–370.

Klein, G. S., & Schlesinger, H. (1949). Where is the perceiver in perceptual theory? *Journal of Personality, 18,* 32–47.

Knops, L. (1947). Contribution à l'étude de la "naissance" et de la "permanence" phénoménales dans le champ visuel [Contribution to the study of phenomenal "coming into being" and "permanence" in the visual field]. *Miscellanea Psychologica Albert Michotte* (pp. 562–610). Louvain: Éditions de l'Institut Supérieur de Philosophie de Louvain.

Metzger, W. (1953). Gesetze des Sehens [The lawfulness of vision]. Frankfurt: Kramer.

Michotte, A. (1948a). L'énigme psychologique de la perspective dans le dessin linéaire [The psychological enigma of perspective in line drawings]. *Bulletin de la Classe de Lettres de l'Academie Royale Belgique, 5ième serie, 34,* 268–288.

Michotte, A. (1948b). Le caractère de 'realité' des projections cinématographiques [The character of reality of cinematic projections]. *Revue Internationale de Filmologie, 1,* 249–261.

Michotte, A. (1950). A propos de la permanence phénoménale: Faits et théories [Phenomenal permanence: facts and theories]. *Acta Psychologica, 7,* 298–322.

Phemister, M. R. (1951). An experimental contribution to the problem of apparent reality. *Quarterly Journal of Experimental Psychology, 3,* 1–18.

Piaget, J., & Inhelder, B. (1941). Le developpement des quantités chez l'enfant [The development of the concept of quantity in the child]. Neuchâtel: Delachaux.

Piaget, J. (1947). La soustraction des surfaces partielles congruentes à deux surfaces totales égales [On the conservation of shape]. *Miscellanea Psychologica Albert Michotte* (pp. 167–180). Louvain: Éditions de l'Institut Supérieur de Philosophie de Louvain.

Rubin, E. (1950). Visual figures apparently incompatible with geometry. *Acta Psychologica, 7,* 269.

Sampaio, A. C. (1943). *La translation des objets comme facteur de leur permanence phenomenale* [The translation of objects as a factor in their phenomenal permanence]. Louvain: Publications Université de Louvain.

Vernon, M. D. (1952). *A further study of visual perception.* Cambridge: Cambridge University Press.

Albert Michotte 1881–1965: Bibliography

Compiled by Alan Costall

Three earlier bibliographies exist: one in *Miscellanea Psychologica Albert Michotte* (Louvain: Éditions de l'Institut Supérieur de Philosophie, 1947); another, specifically on phenomenal causality, in A. Michotte et Collaborateurs, *Casualité, Permanence, et Réalité Phénoménales.* (Louvain: Publications Universitaires, 1962. Pp. 88–90); and a third prepared by Eileen Gavin, published in *The Journal of the History of the Behavioral Sciences,* 1972, *8,* 302–320. *Casualité, Permanence, et Réalité Phénoménales,* published to celebrate Michotte's 80th birthday, is a useful compilation of many of Michotte's later papers and those of his students. Papers included in this collection are indicated by the abbreviation, *CPRP.*

Michotte, A. (1901). Deux faits intéressants à signaler [On two cases of precocious child development]. *Revue Néo-Scolastique, 8,* 66–74.

Michotte, A. (1904a). La fibre nerveuse et sa bifurcation dans les ganglions [The nerve fibre and its bifurcation into ganglia]. *Le Névraxe, 6,* 201–215.

Michotte, A. (1904b) Contribution à l'étude de l'histologie fine de la cellule nerveuse [On the detailed histology of the nerve cell]. *Bulletin de l'Académie Royale de Médecine de Belgique, 63,* 515–556.

Michotte, A. (1905). *Les signes régionaux. Nouvelles recherches expérimentales sur la répartition de la sensibilité tactile dans les états d'attention et d'inattention* ["Local signs": New experimental studies on the distribution of tactile sensitivity in states of attention and inattention]. Paris: Alcan.

Michotte, A. (1906a). Contribution à l'étude de la répartition de la sensibilité tactile dans les états d'attention et d'inattention ["Local signs": New experimental studies on the distribution of tactile sensitivity in states of attention and inattention]. *Atti del V Congresso Internazionale di Psicologia, Rome,* pp. 247–250.

Michotte, A. (1906b). Sur l'application de la méthode esthésiométrique à l'étude de l'attention et de la fatigue mentale [On a new method for the study of attention and mental fatigue]. *Atti del V Congresso Internazionale di Psicologia, Rome,* p. 250.

Michotte, A. (1907) À propos de la "méthode d'introspection" dans la psychologie expérimentale [Concerning "the method of introspection" in experimental psychology]. *Revue Néo-Scolastique, 14,* 507–532.

Michotte, A. (1909) Gedächtnisversuche mit mehrfachen Assoziationsrichtungen [On remembering and multiple assocations]. *Bericht über den III. Kongress für experimentel Psychologie,* pp. 259–263.

Michotte, A., & Prüm. E. (1910). Étude expérimentale sur le choix volontaire et ses antécédents immédiats [Experimental study of voluntary choice and its immediate antecedents]. *Archives de Psychologie, 10,* 113–320.

Michotte, A. (1912a). Description et fonctionnement d'un nouveau tachistoscope de comparaison [An account of a new tachistoscope]. *Archives de Psychologie, 12,* 1–13.

Michotte, A., & Ransy, C. (1912b). Contribution à l'étude de la mémoire logique [A contribution to the study of logical memory]. *Études de Psychologie* (Louvain) *1,* 1–96.

Michotte, A. (1912c). Nouvelles recherches sur la simultanéité apparente d'impressions disparates périodiques; Expérience de "Complication" [New researches on the apparent simultaneity of differing, periodic impressions]. *Études de Psychologie* (Louvain) Institut Supérieur de Philosophie, 97–192.

Michotte, A. (1912d). Note à propos de contributions récentes à la psychologie de la volonté [Concerning recent contributions to the psychology of will]. *Études de Psychologie* (Louvain), *1,* 193–233.

Michotte, A. & Portych, T. (1912e). Deuxième étude sur la mémoire logique. La reproduction après des intervalles temporels de différentes longueurs [Second study of logical memory: Reproduction over different time delays]. *Études de Psychologie* (Louvain), *1,* 237–364.

Michotte, A., & Fransen, F. (1912f). Note sur l'analyse des facteurs de la mémorisation et sur l'inhibition associative [On the analysis of factors influencing remembering and an associative inhibition]. *Études de Psychologie* (Louvain), *1,* 365–413.

Michotte, A. (1922). Note sur la mesure de l'énergie acoustique au moyen du miroir de Rayleigh [On the measurement of acoustic energy by means of Rayleigh's mirror]. *Archives Néerlandaises de Physiologie, 7,* 579–587.

Michotte, A. (1924). Over Psycho-analyse [On psychoanalysis]. *Vlaamsch Opvoedk Tijdschrift, 2,* 3–7.

Michotte, A., & Galli, A. (1925). *Recherches sur les synthèses sensorielles dans le domain de la sensibilité kinésthetique* [Research on sensory integration within kinaesthesis]. Travaux du Laboratoire de Psychologie Expérimentale de l'Université de Louvain.

Michotte, A. (1927). Rapport sur la perception des formes [Report on the perception of forms]. *VIIIth International Congress of Psychology. Proceedings and Papers* (pp. 167–174). Groningen: Noordhoff.

Michotte, A. (1929). Quelques aspects de la psychologie de la perception négligés dans les recherches expérimentales [Some aspects of the psychology of perception which have been neglected in experimental research]. In *IXth International Congress of Psychology, held at Yale University, New Haven, Connecticut, 1929: Proceedings and Papers* (pp. 307–308). Princeton, NJ: Psychological Review Company.

Michotte, A. (1930). La perception, el pensamiento y la acción [Perception, thought, and action]. *Annales de la Seccion de Orientacion professional de la Escuela del Trabajo. Barcelona, 3,* 41–56.

Michotte, A. (1936). Psychologie et philosophie [Psychology and philosophy]. *Revue Néo-Scolastique de Philosophie, 39,* 208–228.

Michotte, A. (1938a). Discours prononcé à la séance inaugurale du XI Congrès International de Psychologie [Address presented to the opening session of the 11th International Congress of Psychology]. *Onzième Congrès International de Psychologie, Paris* (pp. 516–521).

Michotte, A. (1938b). L'étude morphologique des réactions motrices [The morphological study of motor reactions]. *Onzième Congrès International de Psychologie, Paris,* (pp. 29–41).

Michotte, A. (1939a). De Pontificale Akademie der Wetenschappen. *St. Luc Médical (Bruxelles), 3,* 1–10.

Michotte, A. (1939b). Discours prononcé à l'occasion du Jubilé de la psychologie scientifique française [Address presented on Jubilee of French scientific psychology]. *Centenaire de Th.Ribot.* Agen: Imprimerie moderne (pp. 47–59).

Michotte, A. (1939c). La psychologie expérimentale et la problème des aptitudes [Experimental psychology and the problem of aptitude]. In *Mélanges Pierre Janet.* Paris: Editions d'Artrey, (pp. 155–167). (*Psychological Abstracts,* 1941, *15,* Abstract No. 2074).

Michotte, A. (1941). La causalité physique est-elle une donnée phénoménale? [Is physical causality a phenomenal given?]. *Tijdschrift voor Philosophie, 3,* 290–328. (In *CPRP,* pp. 91–127.)

Michotte, A. (1946a). La causalidad física, es un dato fenoménico? [Is physical causality a phenomenal given?]. *Revista de Psicología general y aplicada, 1*(1), 11–58. (*Psychological Abstracts,* 1948, *22,* No. 108.)

Michotte, A. (1946b). *La perception de la causalité* [The perception of causality]. Louvain: Études de Psychologie, Vol.8,. (Second edition, 1954; available in English as The perception of causality, London: Methuen, 1963. T. R. Miles & E. Miles, Trans.)

Michotte, A. (1947). *Jubilé Albert Michotte.* Louvain: Éditions de l'Institut de Philosophie.

Michotte, A. (1948a). Le caractère de "réalité" des projections cinématographiques [The character of "reality" in cinematic projections]. *Revue Internationale de Filmologie, 1,* 249–261. (In *CPRP,* pp. 435–453.)

Michotte, A. (1948b). L'énigme psychologique de la perspective dans le dessin linéaire [The psychological enigma of perspective in line drawings]. *Bulletin des Lettres de l'Académie Royale de Belgique* (5e Série), *34,* 268–288. (In *CPRP,* pp.

454–471.)
Michotte, A. (1949). À propos de l'article de P. Francastel, "Espace et illusion" [In reply to P. Francastel's article, "Space and illusion"]. *Revue Internationale de Filmologie, 2,* 139–140.
Michotte, A. (1950a). The emotions regarded as functional connections. In M. L. Reymert (Ed.), *Feelings and emotions: The Mooseheart Symposium* (pp. 114–126). New York: McGraw-Hill. (In *CPRP,* pp. 128–144.)
Michotte, A. (1950b). La préfiguration dans les données sensorielles de notre conception spontanée du monde physique [The prefiguration within sensory data of our spontaneous conception of the physical world]. *Proceedings and papers of the XIIth International Congress of Psychology* (pp. 20–22). Edinburgh: Oliver & Boyd. (In *CPRP,* pp. 541–544.)
Michotte, A. (1950c). À propos de la permanence phénoménale: Faits et théories [Concerning phenomenal permanence: Facts and theores]. *Acta Psychologica, 7,* 298–322. (In *CPRP,* pp. 347–371.)
Michotte, A. (1951a). La perception de la fonction "outil" [The perception of the "tool" effect]. In *Essays in Psychology, Dedicated to David Katz* (pp. 193–213). Uppsala: Almqvist & Wiksells. (In *CPRP,* pp. 145–167.)
Michotte, A., & Burke, L. (1951b). Une nouvelle énigme de la psychologie de la perception: Le "donné amodal" dans l'expérience sensorielle [A new enigma in the psychology of perception": "Amodal data" in sensory experience]. In *Proceedings and papers, 13ème Congrès International de Psychologie, Stockholm* (pp. 179–180). (In *CPRP,* pp. 372–373.)
Michotte, A., & Clerck, J. de. (1951c). Structures perceptives circulaires correspondant à des formes géométriques angulaires [Circular perceptual structures corresponding to angular geometric forms]. *Année Psychologique* (50ème année), 305–326.
Michotte, A. (1951d). La psychologie néothomiste: Échange de vues [Neothomist psychology: An exchange of views]. *Revue Philosophique de Louvain, 49,* 713–718.
Michotte, A. (1952). Albert Michotte van den Berck (Autobiography). In E. G. Boring, H. S. Langfeld, H. Werner, & R. M. Yerkes (Eds.), *A history of psychology in autobiography* (Vol. 4, pp. 213–236). Worcester, MA: Clark University Press.
Michotte, A. (1953). La participation émotionelle du spectateur à l'action representée à l'écran: Essai d'une théorie [The emotional involvement of the spectator in the action represented on the screen: An attempt towards a theory]. *Revue Internationale de Filmologie, 4,* 87–96. (In *CPRP,* pp. 501–511.)
Michotte, A. (1954). Autobiographie. *Psychologica Belgica, 1,* 190–217. (French version of Michotte 1952)
Michotte, A. (1955a). Perception et cognition [Perception and cognition]. *Acta Psychologica, 11,* 70–91. (In *CPRP,* pp. 561–587.)
Michotte, A. (1955b). L'influence de l'expérience sur la structuration des données sensorielles dans la perception [The influence of experience on the organization of sensory data in perception]. In A. Michotte, H. Piéron, & J. Piaget (Eds.), *La perception: Deuxième symposium de l'association de Psychologie de Langue Française* (Louvain 1953) (pp. 31–45). Paris: Presses Universitaires de

France. (In *CPRP*, pp. 545–560.)

Michotte, A., Piéron, H., & Piaget, J. (1955c). Discussion entre les trois rapporteurs [Discussion among the three contributors]. In A. Michotte, M. Piéron, & J. Piaget (Eds.), *La perception: Deuxième symposium de l'association de Psychologie de Langue Française* (Louvain 1953) (pp. 47–61). Paris: Presses Universitaires de France.

Michotte, A. (1956). Introduction au symposium (Extrait) [Introduction to the symposium on the question of stages in the psychology of the child]. *Lè probleme de stades en psychologie de l'enfant: Symposium de l'association de Psychologie Scientifique de Langue Française (Genève 1955).* Paris: Presses Universiaires de France.

Michotte, A. (1957a). La causalité phénoménale [Phenomenal causality]. *Studium Generale, 10,* 383–390. (In *CPRP*, pp. 214–230; parts translated in Vernon, M. D. (1966). *Experiments in visual perception* (pp. 253–263). Harmondsworth: Penguin.)

Michotte, A. (1957b). Les variations de réalité apparent de la troisième dimension dans les perceptions visuelles [Variations in the apparent reality of the third dimension in visual perception]. *Archivio di Psicología Neurologia e Psychiatría, 18,* 200–213. (In *CPRP*, pp. 512–522.)

Michotte, A., Knops, L., & Coen-Gelders, A. (1957c). Étude comparative de diverses situations expérimentales donnant lieu à des impressions causales d'entraînement [A comparative study of the various experimental conditions which give rise to causal impressions of "entrainment"]. In *Rencontre-Encounter-Begegnung: Contributions à une psychologie humaine, dédiées au professeur F. J. J. Buytendijk* (pp. 284–294). Utrecht-Anvers: Het Spectrum. (In *CPRP*, 231–243.)

Michotte, A. (1959). Réflexions sur le rôle du language dans l'analyse des organisations perceptives [Reflections on the role of language in the analysis of perceptual organization]. *Acta Psychologica, 15,* 70–91. (In *CPRP*, pp. 588–609.)

Michotte, A. (1960). Le réel et l'irréel dans l'image [The 'real' and the 'unreal' in the image]. *Bulletin de la Classe des Lettres de l'Académie Royale de Belgique* (5e Série), *46,* 330–344. (In *CPRP*, pp. 523–540.)

Michotte, A., et collaborateurs. (1962). *Causalité, permanence, et réalité phénoménales* [Phenomenal causality, permanence, and reality]. (Studia Psychologica.) Louvain: Publications Universitaires.

Michotte, A. (1962a). Théorie de la causalité phénoménale: Nouvelles perspectives 1961 [The theory of phenomenal causality: New perspectives 1961]. In A. Michotte et collaborateurs, *Causalité, permanence, et réalité phénoménales.* (Studia Psychologica.) Louvain: Publications Universitaires. Pp. 9–90. (Available in English as Appendix II in Michotte, A. (1963). *The perception of causality.* London: Methuen.)

Michotte, A. (1962b). Centres de rotation, et perceptions visuelles de mouvements circulaires [Centres of rotation, and the visual perception of circular movements]. *Psychologische Beiträge, 6,* 531–543.

Michotte, A. (1963). *The perception of causality.* (T. R. Miles & E. Miles, Trans.) London: Methuen. (English translation of Michotte, 1946.)

Michotte, A., & Thinès, G. (1963). La causalité perceptive [Perceptual causality]. *Journal de Psychologie Normale et Pathologique, 60,* 9–36.

Michotte, A., Thinès, G., & Crabbé, G. (1964). *Les compléments amodaux des structures perceptives* [Amodal completions of perceptual structures]. (Studia Psychologica.) Louvain: Publications Universitaires.

Michotte, A. (1966). Phenomenal causality. In M.D. Vernon (Ed.), *Experiments in visual perception* (pp. 253–260). Harmondsworth: Penguin Books. (Translated excerpts from A. Michotte, 1957a.)

Michotte, A., & Thinès, G.L. (1966). Die Kausalitätswahrnehmung [Perceived causality]. In W. Metzger & H. Erke (Eds.), *Handbuch der Psychologie,* Vol. 1(1). Göttingen: Verlag für Psychologie Dr. C. J. Hogrefe, 954–977. (German translation of Michotte & Thinès, 1963.)

Michotte, A., Thinès, G. L., & Crabbé, G. (1966). Die amodale Ergänzung von Wahrehmungsstrukturen [Amodal completions of perceptual structures] In W. Metzger & H. Erke (Eds.), *Handbuch der Psychologie,* Vol. 1(1). Göttingen: Verlag für Psychologie Dr. C. J. Hogrefe, pp. 978–1002. (German translation of Michotte, Thinès & Crabbé, 1964.)

Michotte, A. (1972). *La percezione della causalità* [The perception of causality]. Firenze: Giunti-Barbera, 1972. (Italian edition of Michotte, 1946.)

Michotte, A. (1982a). *Albert Michotte Gesammelte Werke, Band 1 Die phänomenale Kausalität* [The collected work of Albert Michotte: Phenomenal causality]. (Edited by O. Heller & W. Lohr.) Bern: Verlag Hans Huber.

Michotte, A. (1983). *Albert Michotte Gesammelte Werke, Band 2 Die phänomenale Beständigkeit* [The collected work of Albert Michotte: Phenomenal permanence]. (Edited by O. Heller & W. Lohr.) Bern: Verlag Hans Huber.

Author Index

Subject Index

For Product Safety Concerns and Information please contact our EU representative GPSR@taylorandfrancis.com
Taylor & Francis Verlag GmbH, Kaufingerstraße 24, 80331 München, Germany

www.ingramcontent.com/pod-product-compliance
Lightning Source LLC
LaVergne TN
LVHW011121300926
849160LV00008B/464

* 9 7 8 1 1 3 8 9 9 5 8 2 6 *